Return to Lovecraft Country

Fifteen Frightening Forays into the Lovecraftian Landscape

Conducted By

Donald R. Burleson
Don D'Ammassa
Peter Cannon
Fred Behrendt
Richard A. Lupoff
Mollie L. Burleson
Benjamin Adams
James Robert Smith
C. J. Henderson
Gary Sumpter
Robert M. Price
J. Todd Kingrea
T.E.D. Kline
Thomas Ligotti
Lin Carter

Selected and edited by Scott David Aniolowski
Published by Triad Entertainments
1997

Return to Lovecraft Country

is published by Triad Entertainments

ISBN: 1-57502-535-3

Library of Congress Catalog Card Number: 97-90723

Cover art by Harry Fassl. Cover layout by Michael Szymanski. Editor-in-chief Scott David Aniolowski. Proofreading by Michael Szymanski and Scott David Aniolowski.

Address any questions or comments concerning this publication to:
Triad Entertainments, PO Box 90, Lockport, NY 14095, USA.

Triad Publication 0006. Published in 1997

FIRST EDITION

1 2 3 4 5 6 7 8 9 10

Printed in the U.S.A. by Morris Publishing
3212 East Highway 30, Kearney, NE 68847

A Whisper in Darkness, A Shadow out of Time

"I find the lore & colour of my native soil a very powerful & fascinating influence, hence tend to give my tales an emphatic geographical background. I am by nature an antiquarian of lifelong enthusiasm, with a curious sense of kinship with the 18th century. My chief hobby is colonial architecture, & my chief pastime is visiting various ancient towns where strong traces of the past linger in the houses & streets."

-- H.P. Lovecraft in a letter to Robert Bloch, April 27, 1933

Next to his squishy, nasty space-blobs, Howard Phillips Lovecraft is probably best known for the haunted New England settings he used in his stories. Arkham, Dunwich, Innsmouth, Kingsport, Foxfield[1] -- these are the legend-shrouded, witch-haunted Massachusetts towns Lovecraft used as the backdrop for much of his work. Like Castle Rock or Oxrun Station, though, you won't find Arkham on any ordinary map[2]. No, Lovecraft created these ancient New England towns, based on or inspired by some of his favorite local haunts[3], and populated them with dark legends, weird beings, forbidden tomes, and colorful characters. Over the years, of course, Lovecraft's many disciples have laboriously expanded upon and added to his creations. And now it is this that we call "Lovecraft Country", just as the ancient Severn Valley towns in England created by Ramsey Campbell for his fiction might be referred to as "Campbell Country".

Since Lovecraft did not confine his stories just to the region of Arkham, but also used Boston, Providence, Salem, and parts of New York and Vermont as settings, I interpret "Lovecraft Country"to mean that general area of New England and up into New York. With that in mind, I present *Return to Lovecraft Country*, a collection of short stories set in Lovecraft Country and environs. The premise of this collection is not the Cthulhu Mythos, but is instead meant to focus on the towns and area (although Cthulhu's brethren do peek out from behind a few of the tales). What other secrets does Arkham keep? What about Dunwich? Whatever became of that horror at Red Hook?

Here is a diversity of authors and styles: some pro, some small press -- some old, some new. Something for everyone and every taste. I am delighted to have had the

---

[1] Foxfield is a "new" Lovecraftian town, recently discovered

[2] Unless, perhaps, it was drawn by the talented Jason Eckhardt!

[3] "In a way, "Arkham" may be considered as a sort of modified version of *Salem*, while "Kingsport" roughly corresponds to *Marblehead...*" HPL in a letter to Bob Bloch, April 27, 1933

opportunity to work with so many talented people again (I had the great fortune to work with a number of these folks on *Made in Goatswood*). It was equally thrilling to work with other authors for the first time, and to see what they might create for me. I am especially excited to be able to present two of my favorite Lovecraftian stories: T.E.D. Klein's "The Events at Poroth Farm" and Thomas Ligotti's "The Last Feast of Harlequin"[4]. Readers may have seen either or both of these fine works before, however, I thought them worth presenting again, and those who have not yet read these tales are in for a treat.

The tale by Lin Carter has also been published once before, but almost a decade ago[5].

So come with me now on a tour of Lovecraft Country, and discover for yourself what secrets lurk in the shadows, and what ancestral evils await. Stop by the home of a Miskatonic University professor, or keep Festival with a strangely-familiar gentleman, or look up Dr. Armitage at the Dunwich Institute. What about strange old books? If books is your game then you'll want to visit the Arkham Collector. Then drive out to the old Poroth farm, and maybe later a trip out to Mirocaw just in time for the Last Feast of Harlequin winter festival. This is Lovecraft Country, my friends, and anything is possible. Anything. Unpleasant dreams....

And finally, I have a number of people to thank. First of all thanks to all of the talented authors who took the time to create for me; thanks to Michael Szymanski at Triad Entertainments for producing the book (and asking me to do it in the first place); to Kevin A. Ross for the help, support, and advice (well, bitching, actually!); to Cliff and Paula Ganyard for "technical support"; and Marc Michaud at Necronomicon Press for providing me with a disk of T.E.D. Klein's excellent contribution, and allowing me to reproduce the Necronomicon Press edition of the story here; to Thomas Ligotti and T.E.D. Klein for the use of their stories; to Robert M. Price for the Lin Carter piece; and thanks to Keith Herber, whom I'm pretty sure coined the phrase "Lovecraft Country", and who has done more for my interest in writing than he probably knows.

-- Scott David Aniolowski
Lockport, NY
June 2, 1996

"*West of Arkham the hills rise wild, and there are valleys with deep woods that no axe has ever cut. There are dark narrow glens where the trees slope fantastically, and where thin brooklets trickle without ever having caught the glint of sunlight. On the gentler slopes there are farms, ancient and rocky, with squat, moss-coated cottages brooding eternally over old New England secrets in the lee of great ledges....*"

-- H.P. Lovecraft, "The Colour Out of Space"

---

[4] Although set in the mid-west town of Mirocaw, this tale has ties to Lovecraftian New England

[5] In Bob Price's infamous *Crypt of Cthulhu* magazine, issue #54; the special Lin Carter issue.

TABLE OF CONTENTS

Dedication

This book is dedicated with the utmost respect and admiration to Marc Michaud, whose own Necronomicon Press just celebrated its 20th anniversary this year. Marc, through Necronomicon Press, has consistently published quality material by and about H.P. Lovecraft, and has kept the fires burning and the faith alive.

Connect The Dots

By Donald R. Burleson

Scott Linton was married to a woman he didn't know.

He *had* known Sheila Linton once, but now he had to open dusty old photograph albums and peer at brittle pictures to retrieve that waning familiarity, that old comfortable feeling. The Sheila whose girlish face sprang up in a rosy glow from beneath the plastic sheets that covered the old photographs like strange clear shrouds allowing one to view the dead--*that* Sheila was no more. It wasn't just that she had grown thirty years older; she had grown away from him, had become someone else.

It was a kind of betrayal when you thought about it. *He* was still the same person, essentially. Well then, she should still be too, he reflected, taking the cup of coffee she was handing him across the breakfast table. She looked at him with one of those quiet, cryptic expressions that he could never quite fathom.

"Don't you have a nine-o'clock class, Scott?"

"Yes."

"You're going to be late."

Sheila Linton. And Sheila Linton. The name of the exuberant girl in the yellowing photos; the name of the bland-faced woman who sat across from him now in her houserobe. They couldn't both be Sheila Linton. What did it mean when an older person usurped a younger person's name? Perhaps he had done that himself, but he didn't think so. He saw his life as a logical, natural progression of gradual changes, a shading-off into middle age and beyond. But Sheila--well, that process of change had been gradual too, but the results were startling now that he really thought about things, juxtaposing his memories with his perceptions.

Sheila had become someone strange.

And for him that meant rethinking a number of things. Like how he felt about her, when he scarcely knew her any more. How did she feel about him? Heaven only knew. He wasn't sure he wanted to know. Maybe that old trouble between them, years ago, wasn't really over, wasn't really forgotten. Maybe she'd never entirely forgiven him after all, deep down, and was thinking altogether different sorts of things than he imagined.

It might be silly, but sometimes he was almost afraid of her.

* * *

Between classes, he sat in his office at Miskatonic University and thought about Sheila. Not the one he had married, but the one he was married to. He wondered what it was about her that bothered him.

A student came in, breaking the train of thought. He was from the English 100 class, and was wearing a baseball cap screwed around backwards on his head, and was wondering if he could pick up his paper. "Hi, Doctor Linton. Didn't make it to class Friday. Did you do anything?"

"We spent the time lamenting your absence," Scott said, putting on his best sardonic smile. It felt tired on his face. The boy took his paper (a generous C-minus) and left.

Never mind student absences; it was Sheila's absence that Scott really lamented. The old Sheila. Rather, the young Sheila who should have *grown* older, instead of disappearing.

And what was it about this strange woman who had come to replace her? In part, he thought, it was the aura of uncertainty she generated, uncertainty about where he stood in her scheme of things. She was never really unpleasant toward him; there was just--what? Something too reserved; something wrong.

At times, he found himself wondering if she might not altogether prefer to be by herself.

But then she had her friends. That too was part of what bothered Scott: not that she had friends, but that she had such *odd* friends. They were over to see her from time to time, in peculiar little groups of two or three. Somehow he tended to find them repellent, and he avoided their company. Something in their demeanor made him think of darker days here in the old town of Arkham, Massachusetts, with its extravagant traditions and its rumors of unsavory characters and unwholesome alliances. Surely this was nonsense; witches and their demonic conclaves were no more. But these associates of Sheila's worried him.

Once he had asked her where she'd met them, and she had looked at him as if the question were misguided, and had only said, "Oh, heavens, I've known them for ages. You're always so busy, but I must have you meet them." But he didn't want to.

* * *

Then again, he thought, glancing across the living room at her over the top of his evening paper, part of her strangeness was her ever-advancing procession of hobbies. Years ago it had been ceramics and other crafts, and back then he had understood, had loved her all the more for these things. Over the years she had shifted from one craft or hobby to another to another, and he'd thought little about it. Then a few years ago it had been astrology, and she had seemed to begin to change, slowly, subtly. Darkly. A kind of disquieting quietness--there was a fine term, he thought--a kind of mystery had crept into her manner. He would catch her looking at him in peculiar ways; she would smile and pass it off as nothing important, but it would always leave him feeling as if their relationship were growing more distant. After a while, this past year anyway, she no longer talked about astrology, and he saw that the books and charts had been put away; but he could never tell if her interest in the subject had faded, or if she had absorbed so much that she simply no longer needed to bother studying it.

Then most recently it was her astonishing obsession with these puzzles.

Not the *Arkham Advertiser* crossword, not magazine puzzles in logic or cryptography, not anything so engaging, not anything one would think a woman of her age and intelligence would find appealing.

No--it was 'connect-the-dots' puzzles, those puerile-looking things from elementary school, where you drew lines from numbered dots to numbered dots, ultimately making a picture of some sort. She was working on one even now. Looking at her again over the top of his newspaper, he ventured a remark.

"You--ah--really like those things."

She spared a second to glance up at him wide-eyed before her eyelids fluttered back down with her gaze, settling like butterflies. "Oh, yes. Why do you ask?"

"Well," he said, clearing his throat, "it's just that I always thought they were--what I mean is, I've seen them mostly in children's magazines. . . ." He regretted this the moment it was out, but she didn't seem to take offense.

"Oh no, Scott, some of these are very difficult. Look." She brought her puzzle over for him to see. It was a complex welter of closely-packed dots, hundreds of them numbered in tiny print on a large sheet, and she had only begun to draw pencil lines connecting them. "I trace over the lines later in ink. But this one's only for practice. I'm going to be working on one that's much harder. It's a challenge."

He shrugged, folding his newspaper. "Mm. I see what you mean, I guess. I'm glad you enjoy them, anyway. But I've never seen a puzzle quite like that. Where do you get them?"

"Some of my friends get them for me," she said.

* * *

He saw some of those friends a few evenings later, a curious little knot of them, three people huddled about her in the living room when he came down from his study to get a cup of tea. They were all bent over some papers spread out on the coffeetable, and for a moment he could have sworn that Sheila and her companions were singing or chanting or something until they sensed that he was there, and fell silent. Sheila gestured to him over their heads, but he waved her off and withdrew. In the glance that he had had, the visitors appeared swarthy and unpleasant somehow, the two women's faces pinched under voluminous and tightly drawn scarves, the man's shadowy face beetling and scowling over a dirty-looking overcoat too heavy for the season. Or maybe it was all just the effects of the dim, grainy light. He didn't care to ponder the matter right now, and tried to put it out of his mind.

* * *

But this was about the time he started seeing things that were rather difficult to ignore.

The first time was one evening when he had thrown a jacket on and stepped outside to put a bag of trash in the bin. On his way back to the porch steps he caught a glimpse of something in the shadows beneath the steps, something small, rather like some furry little animal, a squirrel perhaps, but something that seemed to scurry almost insect-like. In the bare moment that he saw it before it shrank out of sight, it filled him with loathing, for reasons he couldn't entirely understand. He thought it was the way the thing moved; something in its manner of moving put him in mind of a sort of rubbery-mucoid quality that made the thing more like a snail or a slug than anything with fur. Altogether, his impressions were confused, contradictory, and he would have needed a longer look to clarify them. But the thing had vanished in an instant.

He wasn't sure he would actually have wanted a longer look.

In any case, he decided not to say anything about it to Sheila.

* * *

He kept busy with his classes in freshman composition and American literature at Miskatonic, lecturing, giving exams, talking with students in his office, keeping his mind on normal things. Keeping his mind *off* the thing he had seen.

But a week later he saw another one.

He was coming home after an evening class, walking from his car to the back door. This time he was already up on the porch when he sensed a little suggestion of movement in the shadows in the corner behind the porch swing. It was as if his coming up the steps at this hour had been unexpected--had disturbed something. There was a faint little hiss, and the thing slipped between the wooden rails and was off the porch and gone, a vague blot of dark against dark.

Again, the impression was unpleasant, but he tried not to let it bother him. This neighborhood was in the wooded outskirts of Arkham, after all, and there had always been a certain number of small wild animals around--raccoons, squirrels, rabbits, cats. Nothing to worry about, really.

* * *

Nothing to worry about until the night he saw them in the house, and more than one at a time.

Sheila was sound asleep, having stayed up late talking quietly downstairs with some of her friends, who finally left. Scott had been up late himself grading papers upstairs in his study and had come down for a glass of milk around midnight. As always, he was cutting through the dining room without turning on the light in there, because the faint light from behind him, from up the stairwell, was enough to guide his steps, though leaving the room mostly in darkness. Now, before he reached the door to the kitchen, he had the impression of a furtive, multiple movement near him in the shadows.

Near him in more than one spot.

He froze in his tracks. The light switch was just a little out of reach, and he felt reluctant to move toward it. Before he could make up his mind, the sense of something near him focused into four or five places around the room, nervous little pockets of movement, of something not quite clear to the eye. A noxious little chorus of hissing rose like steam in the air, and the things scuttered out of sight. Where they went, exactly, he didn't know. It was quite some time before he realized that he was still standing there in the near-dark, cold with perspiration.

He went to bed without his glass of milk.

* * *

For a while he saw nothing else out of the ordinary, and he still said nothing to Sheila. Then one night he found himself, in his pajamas in the dining room, found himself immersed in a nest of the things, strange trundling little creatures beginning, even as he realized his position, to gnaw on his legs with wormlike mouths, filling the darkness with repulsive slurping sounds. Gasping, he awoke to find that there really was some unaccountable suggestion of sound, in the house, downstairs in the dark somewhere.

He lay perfectly still, listening. Sheila, beside him, was breathing heavily in sleep, but she turned over and became quiet, and then he could hear it again, something like soft, pulpy objects stirring, bumping, moving around.

He was out of bed and down the stairs, a dawning of anger in him by the time he got down to the dining room. Wild animals finding their way into the house? It was outrageous, even if they were only squirrels or chipmunks.

But by now he really knew better than that, in all honesty, and the only thing that surprised him when he ran across to the kitchen door and switched on the dining room light was that the things seemed to be in clusters now, like wet chunks of raw meat connected by strands of sinew, a cluster in the corner beside the china cabinet, another across the room, another just inside the kitchen, all low down near the floor, all quivering as if his presence disturbed them. Or excited them.

Screaming, he turned to run, not knowing which way to go. He was halfway up the stairs before he realized that he had left the dining room light on, and that he could see most of the room from here, and there was nothing there.

Cautiously, he eased himself back down the stairs and looked into the lighted room, and crossed that space and went into the kitchen turning the light on in there ahead of him, and inspected the whole downstairs and found nothing at all.

Back up in the bedroom, he saw Sheila half sitting up on her elbows in the bed. "Scott? Did you call out, when you were downstairs?"

He swallowed. "Uh, no. No. Just--ah, no, nothing. Go back to sleep."

How could he tell her what he thought he'd seen? She might think he was losing his mind. And she might be right.

* * *

Some few days later, on a Saturday, Sheila was out of the house for a few hours, gone on a shopping trip, she said, to Kingsport, and on some impulse Scott went into her sewing room upstairs. Ordinarily he never came in here; he scarcely knew what the little room looked like.

Right now, it looked rather unlike a sewing room.

On the hobby table in the middle of the room a big piece of paper or parchment was spread open, rather like one of those large terrain maps used in military operations. What was on this paper was no display of topographic swirls or map coordinates, though, but rather an immensely compact, dense, complicated system of faintly numbered dots, many of them connected in thick lines that Sheila evidently had drawn, but not with a pencil or an ordinary pen. The instrument itself lay in the middle of the paper and somewhat resembled a grease-pencil, but when Scott picked it up and made an exploratory mark with it in the margin, the mark came out thick and nasty-looking, greenish-black like some foul sludge, or like the semiliquid ooze on the underside of a head of putrid lettuce. The markings that Sheila so far had made on the puzzle itself gave the impression of something feverishly complex, though he couldn't have said exactly what they suggested. Scott saw now that all Sheila's lines had been made with the same dubious ink, and he was only too glad to drop the grease-pencil and leave the room.

Later when Sheila came home he wanted to ask her about what he had seen, but he felt ashamed that he had invaded her little domain. She had never asked him not to go in there, but still he felt now that the room was not supposed to be for him to see.

* * *

The rest happened two nights later.

He had felt uneasy all day, even while teaching his classes, but especially when sitting in silence in his office, looking out his window, thinking, then trying not to think. Across the way, storm clouds gathered over the huddled University spires and ancient gambrel roofs of Arkham like the drifting and unwelcome burden of his thoughts.

What was happening to him?

What was happening, when he saw things in the night that no sane mind could conceive, when he felt he no longer knew his wife, when he found things in her sewing room that made no sense, or made no sense of any kind that he cared to acknowledge--what was becoming of him?

At home that evening things scarcely improved. A grumble of thunder started up outside, far away but coming closer, and even inside the house the air felt charged, tense, whether because of the impending storm or for other reasons. But Sheila, reading for once, was quiet, pensive-looking, and seemed to have the attitude that everything was fine tonight, was all she could have wanted it to be. She went up to her sewing room early, and on walking past the door to the room later Scott could hear her in there humming (or talking?) to herself--at work once more, no doubt, on her bizarre puzzle. It began to infuriate him that she was so pleased with her life when he was so displeased with his. But he gave up thinking about it and went to bed early, and must have fallen asleep almost on the instant out of sheer emotional exhaustion. Later he awoke in the dark, or half awoke, to notice that Sheila had come to bed too, and he rolled over and went back to sleep.

And awoke once more, this time to an eerie sensation of sounds in the house again, downstairs.

When he went to the top of the stairs, with only the night-light on at the end of the upstairs hall, the stairwell was a hollow throat of darkness yawning below him. Outside, the thunder grew louder, more insistent, and the wind was coming up, moaning under the eaves now and sending cold washes of rain whispering at the windowpanes. Carefully, slowly, trying to make no sound, and trying not to ask himself *why* he was trying to make no sound, he felt his way down into the blackness of the lower house, and stood in the dining room.

And held his breath, and listened between mutterings of thunder.

Nothing.

Or--was there some faint, faint rustle, some nearly unnoticeable trace of undefined sound in the dead air? A furtive movement?

No, no, he had unwittingly dragged his slippered foot against the carpet, in nervousness.

Nothing to worry about.

Except that now the low, low susurration in the black air was there again, somewhere near, and he wasn't moving his foot this time. He wasn't moving at all.

Somewhere near, and somewhere else near, and--*there*, and there, and there, and there. In the dark. Moving. Scuttling, hissing.

Real.

No doubt about that whatever.

Real.

He lunged for the light switch, not knowing what else to do. Maybe the light would still dispel it, dispel *them*, whatever they were.

But the moment the light flooded the room, he regretted it. It would have been better not to see. Almost immediately, with a roar of thunder, the lights went out, but the rapid flashes of lightning still showed him far more than he wanted to know anything about. In convulsions of light and dark and light, things shifted and twitched around him like a lantern show, things that couldn't be there, but were.

It wasn't just that they were everywhere around him, it wasn't just that there were more of them this time, far more--jittering, writhing, dangling on threads of purulent sinew connecting them to each other in frenetic seeping clusters that danced like mad ropy puppets to a chorus of thunder and howling wind.

That was bad enough, but when the lightning-illumined clusters began to swing their clotted masses into each other and reach with frothy fingers to each other and connect to each other one by one until they formed a single throbbing network of nightmare tissue around him, a single shiny-wet web of raw menace leaning to him with a great many eager mouths--then in concert with a last deranged crash of thunder, the last he would hear, his mind collapsed, though not without the one final clear realization that Sheila, up there somewhere, up and out of bed after he was, must just now have connected the final dots to complete her creation. But then maybe *he* was the final dot.

His consciousness faded like a dying picture screen with the ember of this simple thought glowing pale within it, even as the carrion thing that surrounded him, hissing and gibbering and squeaking in triumph, moved in to fasten itself upon him.

Dark Providence

By Don D'Ammassa

It all started when they moved the river. Moved it again, actually, back to its original course. The Providence River had been diverted to allow the development of the land at the foot of College Hill, but by the early 1990's, there was already growing interest in ripping up the Canal Street area and restoring the original watercourse.

No one could have realized the consequences, of course. The only man who might have warned them was long dead, buried in Swan Point Cemetery. His name was Howard Phillips Lovecraft.

Personally, I'm indifferent to the man's work, but Kerri was an addict. It was her only vice other than cigarettes, and she was trying to give those up. Kerri had read every word that Lovecraft had written, could quote long passages from memory. She collected alternate and foreign editions, many of which she would never be able to read. She'd spent thousands of dollars to acquire the original Arkham House collections and a complete run of *Weird Tales*. The walls of her bedroom were lined with Lovecraftiana, which had spilled over into the living room, den, even the bathroom. There were two long shelves of critical works, and two more with Mythos stories by other authors. She'd even spent several weekends in the John Hay Library, painstakingly copying the notes HPL had written in the margins of his own collection of magazines.

"Feel like doing something this weekend?"

We were standing in the parking lot at Eblis Manufacturing, the end of a long and frustrating week of inventory. Kerri looked blank for a moment, then smiled, a transformation that made me want to kiss her right on the spot.

"Sure, Danny. How about a picnic?"

"Sounds great. Roger Williams Park or Lincoln Woods?"

Her eyes shifted to one side and she bit her lip. "I was thinking about Swan Point."

I should have figured. I liked Kerri a lot, maybe a bit too much considering her abstraction from the real world. God knows I'd tried to lure her away from her obsession, but nothing seemed to work. At the art show, she remarked on similarities to scenes from Lovecraft stories, she interpreted concert music as possible soundtracks, and when I took her to a Pawsox baseball game, she carried a paperback collection in her purse and ignored what was happening on the field.

I knew better than to argue. "Sure, down on the river bank. Sounds great."

* * *

Actually, once we got past the obligatory visit to Lovecraft's grave, it really was pretty great. Kerri wore cut off jeans and a white halter top that drew my eyes like a magnet. The Brown University rowing team was practicing just offshore, but otherwise there was no one in sight. We found a shady spot under an oak tree and spread out the blanket, emptied our basket of tuna fish sandwiches, apple juice, and miscellaneous finger food. After we'd eaten, Kerri lay back against the swell of a hill and stared out across the water, and I wanted her so badly I had to turn away.

"Feel like an adventure?"

"I feel like a turkey stuffed for Thanksgiving." I rolled over onto an elbow. "What did you have in mind?"

"They've been digging at the foot of College Hill, near the bus tunnel."

"Pedestrians aren't allowed down there."

She slapped the side of her thigh irritably. "That's part of what makes it an adventure. Besides, college kids go in all the time to party."

"Late at night, maybe. After the buses stop running."

"Yeah, that's when I thought we should go, around midnight."

I'd have gone just about anywhere alone in the dark with Kerri, but the bus tunnel through College Hill struck me as considerably less than romantic. I hesitated, not crazy about the idea, but not wanting to miss whatever chance might offer itself. "I thought it was all fenced off, to keep people away from the construction."

"Not all of it. They broke into an older section this afternoon and only had time to put up a barricade."

So I agreed.

"This isn't such a great idea." I moved the flashlight around, illuminating the yawning chasm in front of us. "There could be rats in here."

"Rats in the walls," she whispered. "They just cut away this part of the bank today. I was sitting up there watching," she gestured vaguely behind us. "When they broke through, there was a big cave-in. It was high tide and the water came rushing through, so they just plowed a berm up to contain it and shut down the site."

I felt a mild tremor of anxiety. "Doesn't sound particularly safe."

"Tide's out now." That was supposed to satisfy me, I guess. It didn't. I glanced around, searching for a way to back out of this expedition. When

I looked back, Kerri was gone.

"Wait up!" The thin thread of her flashlight was already receding.

The footing was uncertain, a steep slope of crumbling shale and loose soil, plenty of clearance to either side but the ceiling was low enough that I had to duck from time to time. The gloomy darkness seemed to be fraying the edges of our flashlight beams. The air was heavy with moisture, chilly, clammy, and it smelled and tasted of mold, dust, corruption.

Kerri stopped suddenly, only a few meters ahead of me, and I breathed a sigh of relief, assuming she'd come to the far end of the cavity.

"Danny, come look at this!" There was a husky undertone in her voice, excitement, almost sexual. I tried to hurry, but the footing was so uncertain, it made little difference to my progress. I was so intent on avoiding a misstep that I bumped into Kerri without realizing how close I'd come.

"Easy. What do you make of this?"

"This" was a metal door anchored between two columns of rock. There was no clearance on either side.

"An old maintenance access, I'd guess. Or something left over from the original construction."

"Let's try to get it open."

"I don't think..." But it was too late. Kerri put the flashlight down, wrapped both hands around the handle, spread her feet and tugged. Loose earth shifted and fell but the door didn't move.

"Probably rusted in place. Let's get out of here; there's nothing more to see."

"Don't give up so easy. I think it moved a little bit. Maybe the two of us can shift it." There was a smear of dirt across the front of her halter top, exactly where I wanted to put my hands.

"All right."

Just before I decided to abandon the effort, the door shifted. Not much, only about an inch, but that was enough to dislodge a small avalanche of damp earth that rained down on us. I started to swear as I brushed away the worst of it.

"Don't be so anal. Let's get this open."

It was the first time I'd actually come close to losing my temper with Kerri, but I bit my tongue and joined her. A few minutes later, at the cost of more fallen dirt and a great deal of sweat, we had shifted it enough to let us pass through.

I didn't think that was such a great idea, but Kerri was not to be denied. "This is the first chance at a real adventure I've ever had and I'm not going to miss it. Who knows what we might find? There could be treasure...or dead bodies." She seemed to find both alternatives appealing.

"Or rats and spiders and centipedes," I countered.

"Are you coming or not?" She stepped forward into my flashlight beam. Her long blonde hair was matted with dirt, and there were broad streaks across her face. I'd have followed her into the mouth of hell.

Maybe that's what I did.

The chamber beyond the door wasn't very large. The two of us made a crowd inside. Kerri was so close, I fancied I could feel the heat of her body even through the mugginess. We played our flashlights around the chamber, but it seemed bare stone and earth, without content or meaning. Kerri shrugged and had half turned to go when I, to my eternal regret, looked more closely at the opposite wall.

"Wait a minute. There's something here." The texture of the soil was different and I reached out to touch it, jumped back in astonishment when my hand disappeared into what seemed to be solid earth.

"I don't see anything." Disappointed, Kerri had lost interest; her voice was impatient, irritable.

"Put your hand on the wall here. Tell me what you feel."

She hesitated, then took three quick steps across the chamber and stretched out her arm. It disappeared up to her wrist. "Cool! How deep do you think it goes?"

"I don't know. It's some kind of optical illusion, I guess." I reached out again, this time lost sight of my arm up to the elbow. There was a faint tingling that might have been imagination. "Can't feel anything."

"Let me." And before I could say or do anything, Kerri stepped through the barrier. I was suddenly alone in the chamber.

"Kerri!" No answer. I was summoning the courage to follow when she reappeared.

"Oh, there you are! Where the hell did you go?"

"Where did *I* go? You're the one who vanished."

"Well, you weren't here a minute ago. Or at least..." She glanced back over her shoulder. "Hold my hand a minute."

I didn't need much prompting. Her fingers were cool but they were surprisingly strong. Strong enough to pull me off balance and through the barrier.

At least, that's what I thought happened. But the flashlight revealed that we were back where we'd started. "I don't get it."

"Wait." Kerri crouched, still holding my hand, and placed her flashlight on the floor. "Okay, here we go again." And for the second time she dragged me into the illusory wall.

And once again we were back where we'd started. Except that there was no flashlight on the ground.

"What's going on?"

"I thought I'd gotten turned around in the dark, but there really are two sides. They just look an awful lot alike."

But I distinctly remembered seeing a passage leading up toward the surface, and said so.

"So let's find out where it goes." She released my hand and vanished again before I could argue the point. What choice did I have? I followed her.

She'd already recovered the flashlight and was on her way up. It was a lot more difficult than coming down; the mud was slippery and there was nothing solid to hold onto for leverage. Both of us fell a couple of times and by the time we reached the top, we looked pretty awful.

Canal Street was a line of ravaged pavement. I knew they'd been planning to demolish the roadway but hadn't realized how far they'd progressed. The city was quiet. It was well after midnight and I couldn't even hear traffic sounds from the interstate.

We sat on a mound of asphalt and caught our breaths. Kerri admitted being disappointed, but her normal good humor prevailed and we were making fun of each other before long. Even in the darkness, we were pretty sorry looking, dripping filth, soaked with perspiration.

"I don't know how I let you talk me into this, Kerri. If anyone sees us like this, we'll never live it down."

She laughed at me. "You could have said 'no'. I didn't exactly hold a gun to your head."

"Yeah, well I've always wanted to do something dirty with you." It came out unbidden, and an uneasy silence interrupted our playful mood. The seconds stretched before Kerri broke the tension.

"My apartment's not far. You could take a shower."

I glanced down at my shirt. "I really need some clean clothes."

"There's a washing machine."

I chose my words carefully, hopefully. "That might take a while."

"I think we could find a way to pass the time."

I was so preoccupied with the possibility of finally realizing my favorite fantasy that it took a while to realize that something was wrong with the city. It was too dark for one thing. Hospital Trust Plaza and Fleet National were both completely dark. The streetlights were out. In fact, none of the skyscrapers showed lights; the only illumination seemed to originate closer to street level, out of our line of sight. It flickered, like fire. And it was quiet. A faint rumbling in the distance was probably highway traffic, though it sounded different, wrong.

We made our way across the construction site, which seemed far more extensive than I remembered. Surely they hadn't reached South Main Street already. And the Providence & Washington Insurance building was partially demolished; rubble covered the sidewalk and adjacent street.

"Something's wrong here."

"Yeah." Kerri's voice was tense. "What happened while we were down there? Power failure?"

At the next corner, we surprised someone. He appeared to be a street person, almost as dirty as we were, clothes tattered, hair long and unkempt. Cadaverously thin, his clawed hands sorted through a pile of trash. It looked as though he meant to challenge us at first, but then he broke and ran off before we had time to react.

Vaguely disturbed, we reached the foot of College Hill and started to climb. About halfway up, Kerri touched my arm and whispered a warning. "We have company." I started to turn my head but she tightened her grip. "Don't look. There's a half dozen of them following us."

"A half dozen of who?" I whispered back.

"I don't know." Her voice caught and I realized she was frightened. So was I.

"Let's move a little faster."

Three dark shrouded figures stepped out of an alley into our path. Their clothes were shabby and filthy and they moved with an odd gait that seemed furtive, uncertain, but menacing.

"This way!" Kerri hissed the words as she tugged at my arm, drawing me through the gates into the Brown University Quadrangle.

We ran through the darkness, crossed the open space and exited on the opposite side. An oak tree had fallen across the wall and we had to brush its branches aside before getting clear.

We hurried along for two blocks, then cut through a parking lot and back onto Angell Street. There were no signs of pursuit.

Which is why we were so surprised when two more tattered figures stepped out from behind a garbage dumpster. Kelly and I froze, then tried to retreat. Someone grabbed me from behind, wrapped wiry arms around my upper body. I heard Kerri shouting as I twisted free, and saw her struggling with two of our assailants. I knocked down the man who'd grabbed me and shrugged off his companion, whose back was twisted into an unusual shape. They attacked silently and with determination, but there was an odd insubstantiality about them, as though they were all half starved. Kerri had already shaken off one of her attackers by the time I reached them, and the other fell silently when I clipped him behind the ear.

We started running, almost directly into the arms of three more, one of whom was carrying a torch. By its flickering light, I saw his face quite clearly, though it was smeared with dirt and sweat. It was Phil Martin, who lived in Kerri's apartment building, two doors down. At least, it looked like Phil Martin. But the man I'd made small talk with a week earlier didn't have an enormous wen bulging from the side of his neck, and this one did.

We hopped over a low, wrought iron fence and crossed a small, badly maintained lawn. A gate opened onto the opposite side of the block and we emerged cautiously, then turned left. We could hear our pursuers' footsteps but they remained eerily silent, not calling out to one another, not speaking.

At the next corner, we spotted another group, half a dozen this time, led by a woman who held a flaming torch in a withered arm that ended with three clawed fingers.

"What's going on?" Kerri's whisper was frantic, near panic.

"Quiet! In here!" We climbed through the shattered window of a gutted store, a copy shop, and crouched behind the counter while they passed. We were both shivering despite the humidity, and shaking with tension.

"What's happened, Danny? What are we going to do?"

I didn't answer until the torch was no longer in sight. then I sat with my back against the counter and searched for calm. "We'll wait here until morning. Once the sun comes up, we'll have a better chance of figuring this thing out."

And that's what we did, dozing fitfully, waking occasionally when some noise penetrated the gloom. Twice I heard what sounded very much like a human scream, but in both cases it was a brief, staccato sound, ended almost as soon as it began. Eventually I fell into a deeper sleep, and when I next stirred, my wristwatch told me it was almost ten o'clock.

But it was still pitch black outside. The sun hadn't risen.

Kerri stirred a few minutes later. "I'm thirsty." Her voice sounded like that of a petulant child.

"I think we should move. Are you ready?"

"I guess so."

We made another effort to reach her apartment, and almost ran into a crowd two blocks short of it. There were at least twenty people sitting in the street, gathered in small groups around a bonfire. Occasionally someone would throw in fresh fuel, pieces of furniture, cardboard boxes, stacks of books. There was enough light to see their faces, and Kerri identified two of her neighbors. One was a hunchback and the other had a club foot.

Neither had been disfigured before now.

Watching from concealment, we noticed that most of them bore some deformity. There was a woman with an oversized head, a man whose spine was twisted into a corkscrew, and another of indeterminate sex was completely bald, skin covered with what appeared to be a dark tattoo. On the far side of the intersection, yet another sat stroking his thighs with something that didn't look at all like an ordinary arm.

We were about to turn away when something changed. Several of the figures stood and began looking around in something close to panic. Kerri's fingers tightened on my arm as the sudden tension reached us, but before I could respond, an enormous black shape erupted from within one of the adjacent buildings.

The bonfire was scattered in the first few seconds, so I didn't see much of what happened clearly, but I would swear that it was an oversized tentacle that attacked those people, people who remained silent even as they died, except for one man who gave a prolonged hopeless scream that was abruptly, and terrifyingly truncated. There was a sudden fetid smell in the air so powerful it was palpable. I don't know how many of them escaped, because we turned and ran ourselves, ran back the way we had come. Something deadly had come to Providence.

We kept on until we were short of breath, then ducked into a private residence, fell to the ground in the shelter of some lilac bushes.

Kerri recovered her breath before I did. "What's going on, Danny? What happened to the world while we were underground?" She sounded close to tears.

"I'm not sure that anything happened, Kerri." I sat up. My head spun a few times, then settled down. "I don't think this *is* the world. Not ours anyway."

"I don't understand."

"Neither do I, but we have to go back."

"Back?"

"Back to the excavation. It's our only chance." But it was a long time before either of us summoned the strength to move. When we started back toward the downtown, my wristwatch indicated it was early afternoon, but the sky said it was midnight.

The darkness was unrelenting. The moon was the most obvious light source, but when I looked closely, I couldn't find the familiar features I expected. I wondered if this might be the dark side, if the moon's rotation had changed to expose its hidden face. Even the stars seemed changed; I couldn't find any familiar constellations.

Providence was similarly altered now that I was looking for differences. Some of the buildings were missing, and there was at least one misshapen tower that I'd never seen before.

"If this isn't Providence, then what *is* it?" Kerri didn't sound like she wanted an adventure any more.

"Another dimension, a parallel universe, a different timeline? Who knows? Something happened here, some incredible catastrophe has altered the rotation of the Earth and moon, maybe changed their orbits. And creatures have arrived on Earth and are hunting down whoever survived the catastrophe."

Kerri stopped in her tracks. "The Old Ones," she said softly.

"What're you talking about?" But I realized what she was implying. "You think Lovecraft came here? That he visited this world and wrote about it?"

"No, not really. But maybe, somehow, he knew about it. I don't know, psychic dreams, clairvoyance maybe. Something like that must have happened."

Maybe.

We made our way down College Hill without seeing another living being. There were fires in the distance, columns of black smoke obscured the stars. The distant hum I'd heard earlier was louder now, and no longer resembled traffic sounds. It sounded organic. We reached the edge of the construction site without incident, although it now seemed evident that there was no construction underway here. The city of Providence was being destroyed in this world, not rebuilt.

I glanced up at the skyline just before it moved.

The unusual building whose shape had been dimly visible before was closer now, and I was staring right at it when the change began. The thin gap of night sky visible between it and the Hospital Trust Tower vanished first, then the upper floors changed shape. And the low rumbling we'd been hearing all night was suddenly louder.

It wasn't a building; it was some kind of gigantic creature.

This time we heard the residents of this dark Providence before we saw them. They were screaming with despair as they poured out of the city, scores, hundreds of them, all desperately leaving their hiding places to flee ahead of this incredible menace. Kerri and I continued forward, desperate to reach the excavation site, but the flood of humanity engulfed us within seconds, clawing their way over torn pavement, shattered buildings, and fallen debris. I was knocked to the ground twice, and Kerri's hand was torn from mine. When I regained my feet, she was gone, and a fresh wave of refugees overwhelmed me as well. Like it or not, I was running back toward College Hill, calling Kerri's name whenever I could draw breath.

Within seconds I was disoriented, but there was a momentary ebb in the stream and I ducked into a doorway, waited breathlessly while the city disgorged more and more of its residents. There must have been thousands of them. Then the darkness grew momentarily more intense, as though something blocked even the pale light of the night sky from the street outside. A final few stragglers raced by and the screaming receded, became more distant.

An hour later, I emerged from my hiding place. There was no other sign of life, and the gigantic shape was nowhere to be seen. I spent the next several hours searching for Kerri, checking each of several dozen dead bodies I encountered, but never calling her name. Even if I'd wanted to, I'm not sure I could have summoned a voice.

Against all the odds, I found her. Stumbled across her, in fact. She was lying behind one of the barricades, so covered with filth I barely recognized her. Blood stained the side of her head and she was unconscious, but her breathing and heartbeat were strong.

I carried her to the tunnel.

The descent was an absolute horror, but nothing compared to what I'd already experienced. I dropped Kerri once and twice we both fell. The second time we slid down the last few meters completely out of control. At the bottom of the slope, I waited long enough to catch my breath, then lifted Kerri over my shoulder and crossed the barrier.

I could never have made it up the other side if Kerri hadn't regained consciousness, partially at least. She moved in a daze, answered my questions in monosyllables, and seemed to have trouble concentrating. I was worried about a concussion, but desperate to confirm that we were back in our own world. By the time we reached the surface, I'd forgotten all my romantic intentions towards Kerri and was swearing at her to keep moving.

Downtown was speckled with electric lights, and a steady stream of traffic moved along the interstate. It was night in this Providence too, but not the same night we'd left. And this one would have an ending.

I brought Kerri to my apartment and left her sleeping on the couch, then flopped onto my bed after shedding most of my filthy garments. As much as I wanted a shower, it would have to wait until morning.

* * *

Kerri was still asleep, her breathing easy and regular. I left her undisturbed and took a long, refreshing shower. My head was spinning - I hadn't eaten in almost thirty-six hours - but I had to wash off the residue of our misadventure first. With fresh clothing on my body and a stale donut in it, I touched Kerri's shoulder.

"C'mon, Kerri. Wake up. You need to eat something."

She mumbled something unintelligible and her eyes opened, but they were unfocused.

"Are you okay?" The swelling on her head had subsided and the bleeding had stopped, but I was still concerned about a concussion.

"Dirty." She was staring down at her body, completely covered in dried blood.

"Why don't you take a shower while I fix something to eat?"

She seemed to understand, began unbuttoning her blouse. I felt as though I should turn away, give her some privacy, but the previous day's events were already receding and I felt a fresh awakening of my sexual interest.

I had a moment to realize something was wrong before it happened. Kerri hadn't been wearing a blouse the night before; she'd worn a halter top.

And then the last button was undone and she peeled back the filthy material to release two coiled tentacles from her chest and I fell back in horror, realizing the Kerri I'd rescued from that other Providence was not the one with whom I'd entered it.

The Arkham Collector

By Peter Cannon

Of all my friends Sam Lowell takes the prize as the most considerate. Two acts of generosity in particular put me forever in his debt. The first was his adulatory advance review of my novel *The Golden Doom* for Books Weekly. All BW reviews are of course unsigned, so it wasn't until after I'd written to the anonymous reviewer in care of the journal to thank him or her and he's responded that I learned his identity. His second great gift came as an even more welcome surprise quite recently, almost a decade after we first got in touch, indeed during our first face-to-face meeting.

I know such a delay may seem odd, but let me explain. If not for his mother's health we might've met sooner. Sam had been living in Manhattan, only blocks away from my own West End Avenue address, in fact - so he'd informed me in one of his early letters. Then his mother, who'd always been something of an invalid, took a sudden turn for the worse - about the same time his notice of my book appeared, as it happened - and since he was her only family he packed up his place in New York and within a month was settled back in Arkham.

Yes, that's right, Arkham - the venerable Massachusetts seaport that H.P. Lovecraft fixed on the literary map, so to speak, just as firmly as Nathaniel Hawthorne did his native town of Salem. Like any horror fan, and back then freshly minted horror author, I was tickled to find his response to my initial note postmarked Arkham, Mass. I'd visited there a couple of times myself, during the most intense of my Lovecraft infatuation. Miskatonic had been my backup for college, but once Brown accepted me I'd opted for the more prestigious institution. In truth, as my literary horizons have broadened, HPL and the New England territory he immortalized have lost some of their glamour. As Sam pointed out in his review, *The Golden Doom* chiefly reflects a Dunsanian influence. Perhaps on account of my Celtic heritage, too, I find on balance the gentle mysticism of the Irish fantaisiste more to my taste than the eldritch horrors of the Providence Gentleman.

Like Lovecraft, I enjoy writing letters, and Sam Lowell soon became one of my most active and stimulating correspondents. At first we mainly discussed horror fiction, debating the relative stature of the greats in the field, but later I learned a fair amount of personal data as well. Thanks to computer technology, Sam was able from his mother's place in Arkham to continue to do freelance work for publishing clients in New York, including BW. Though he never more than hinted at it, I guessed he also had another source on income (family money?) to help support himself and to indulge in what I gathered was his principal passion - collecting books.

While I don't consider myself a book collector per se, I do like thumbing through dealers' catalogues and checking out the offerings at used-book shops and library sales. If I own any valuable items it's usually because I chanced to purchase them while they were still in print, like Lovecraft's *Dark Brotherhood* and *Selected Letters III*. Frankly, I'm a lot more interested in reading a book, turning down page corners, and making marginal notes if so moved than enshrining it on a shelf like some goddamn virgin. For others, such as Sam apparently, the pleasure lies less in the text itself than in the physical package of paper and print.

Which is not to say Sam's communications suggested he was anything less than highly literate. Besides the standard authors in the genre, he was clearly well versed in the mainstream tradition of English letters, ranging from Jane Austen and the Bronte sisters to contemporary Americans like John Updike and Nicholson Baker. He disdained the commercial and popular, unless it had literary merit, swearing he collected only those works that would survive the test of time. He possessed nearly a complete run of Arkham House books of the Derleth era, spurning the later science fiction titles favored by Derleth's editorial successor. While he must've engaged in buying and selling with other diehard collectors, I had the impression that, with few exceptions, he was loathe to part with a single volume. Every acquisition was a treasure. Making money scarcely entered the equation.

Though I was an English major at Brown, I confess I have some big gaps in my knowledge of literature, gaps I don't expect ever to fill. You'd have to put a gun to my head before you'd get me even to consider reading another one of those long and pious nineteenth-century novels, with their mawkish heroines. When Sam inquired if I was familiar with the works of Maria and Elizabeth Bronte, for example, I wrote back to say I wasn't and maybe it was my loss but I doubted if I'd ever get around to them. Unless you're Harold Bloom, who has time for all the classics? One has to be selective, and I'd rather reread an old favorite than plod dutifully through some so-called masterpiece just because some smartass citric tells me I should.

One book much on my mind was, of course, my own. During the first year or so of our correspondence I was full of news of the efforts to publicize and promote my novel. Sam's led the parade in a series of largely friendly reviews, while the hardcover advanced enough copies for my agent to make a lucrative paperback sale. As a rule I don't like to toot my own horn, but with Sam it was different. I sensed early on that, with virtually no personal life of his own, he got a vicarious kick out of the tales of my success, which I always took care to leaven with a healthy dose of self-depreciating humor. (Among my friends I'm reputed to be a bit of a raconteur.) Then again, though he never confirmed or denied it, I imagine Sam to belong to the old New England aristocracy, as rich in blue-blooded ancestors as Lovecraft himself. I, with my humble Irish roots, couldn't help being envious, and therefore was perhaps more intent on impressing him than certain other members of my epistolary circle, who in all honesty I kept up with merely to be polite. (For an egotist, I'm very attentive to others, who in gratitude often try to please me in return.)

The only family Sam did mention from time to time, as to be expected, was his mother. She was a sensitive and refined woman who suffered from some degenerative hereditary disease that kept her confined to the house. Shades of Lovecraft again! When in response to this revelation I jokingly asked if his mother originally came from Innsmouth, he didn't reply for two months. (At times, I admit, in my attempts to be funny I go too far.) Sam hardly left the house himself, other than to shop for necessities or to attend the rare auction in Boston. If his life was limited, however, he never complained. Books were his world, and in provincial Arkham he could house his ever-growing collection under one roof as he could never have afforded to in cosmopolitan Manhattan.

It was I for the moment who was basking in the limelight of the New York literary set, or at any rate that segment of it that didn't automatically look down its nose at horror fiction. (Incredible what literary snobs people can be.) I reached my peak with the signing of the contract for my second novel, provisionally titled *The Laughter of the Gods*, based on a three page outline. (My agent, alas, was only too efficient a deal-maker.) With the proceeds I bought a weekend place in the Poconos, where I anticipated settling down with my new Macintosh to a regular writing schedule, free of the big city's distractions. All this I recounted to Sam in great and, judging from his appreciative comments, entertaining detail.

Well, things didn't work out quite as planned. Yes, there wasn't much to do of an evening, or of a day for that matter, in Greentown, but then the new house required lots of attention and I found myself filling my house in meetings with contractors and electricians and plumbers. In addition to fan mail, I had stacks of magazines and catalogues to go through, not to mention an assortment of girlfriends whom I brought along to keep me company. In the end, I realized I was doing everything I could think of to procrastinate on writing. A major part of the problem was I'd set myself an impossible task. In my gut I knew that to deliver on the epic I'd so grandly and glibly outlined I'd need to be a genius on the order of Lord Dunsany.

And I was no Dunsany - though I will say I am rather a perfectionist, the sort of compulsive type who can spend hours over proper word choice, preferring to polish existing text than to plunge ahead with a rough draft. I can't let a sentence alone for long without tinkering. The Golden Doom had taken me five years of blood, sweat, and tears to produce, but then I hadn't been under any deadline pressure. Now was different. As time went on, I said less and less about progress on the new novel in my letters, instead dwelling on the ups and downs of home ownership. In response Sam sent me a copy of humorist S.J. Perelman's classic work on the subject, *Acres and Pains* - which I'd already read but whose delightful novelty I was careful to relish in my reply.

So the years rolled on. I invited Sam to come visit me, either in the city or in the country, but his mother's condition precluded any overnight travel, as well as his receiving any visitors at the house in Arkham. I cut down on all my correspondents, even at the risk of hurt feelings, except for Sam, whose undiminished enthusiasm for this or that new author helped to alleviate my gloom. I might've dropped letter-writing altogether if it hadn't provided a further excuse for avoiding the novel. Sam in his turn continued to insist on how much he valued my letters, which he claimed gave him a unique and precious perspective on the larger world - even though, I countered, it was ever more that of a jaded and disillusioned hermit.

As the whole business with the second novel dragged on, about the only person I could bear to see was my agent. After the third extension of the delivery deadline for the manuscript passed, he arranged an incentive plan with my editor. When that didn't work, the publisher started making legal threats. Ultimately, though, neither carrot nor stick could induce me to do much more than fiddle on my Mac with the design for the chapter heads (a grinning Buddha). To boost my income I was forced to go back to substitute teaching in the New York City public schools, with the dreaded prospect of a full-time career in the classroom looming unless I finished the frigging novel.

Then, after an uncharacteristically lengthy delay between letters, word came from Sam that his mother had "made the transition," as he euphemistically put it. For weeks he'd been grief-stricken, but now life was starting to return to normal. He was lonely, he hinted. Was there a chance I might be persuaded to swing by Arkham next time I was in the area? On impulse I wrote back proposing a weekend in August, almost a month away, which just so happened to include my birthday - not that I told him than. I'd been dating a cute but not very exciting girl who I knew wanted to celebrate my (shudder) fortieth birthday in a way which would only bring home to me how little I had to celebrate. That I had to go console a friend whose mother had recently died was exactly the sort of excuse I was looking for.

By the time that August weekend was at hand, however, I can't say that I was feeling all that eager. After years of envisioning Sam as this ideal gentleman, I feared that in person he might be a disappointment, rather like a certain female fan who'd written in admiration of my author photo on *The Golden Doom*. Foolishly I'd called the phone number she'd supplied in her perfume-scented note and scheduled a rendezvous without first asking for her picture. Come to think of it, maybe this isn't a fair analogy. Still, I was anxious about our meeting, and wrote Sam to expect me late Friday night, with departure set for Sunday morning. I had to be back in New York, I fibbed, in time for an important dinner with my agent that evening. One full day with Sam should be plenty, I figured.

Deciding in emulation of Lovecraft to use public transportation, I rode Amtrak up the Connecticut coast, through Providence and ending in Boston, once again left to wonder why HPL had chosen in his fiction to disguise these two capital cities under made up names and not other, less prominent places like Arkham and Kingsport. From Boston's North Station I took the B & M out to Arkham, where Sam did not meet me at the depot. As advertised, his house was an easy three-block walk from the railroad, even in the dark. I had no sense, by the way, of passing from the mundane into the magical, such as Wilmarth describes in his journey from New Hampshire to Vermont in *The Whisperer in Darkness*.

The real Arkham, in contrast to Lovecraft's romanticized version, is not terribly scenic. Yes, you can find Federal-style mansions in the tiny "old town," but today Arkham, like Salem, is a small industrial city of mostly undistinguished commercial streets and nondescript residential buildings inhabited by ethnic types such as myself or my relatives. Since I already knew Sam lived in an untouristed part of Arkham, I wasn't surprised to discover at his address a clapboard "triple-decker" of late Victorian vintage.

The guy who met me at the door was slight, pale, of indeterminate age though older than myself - in sum, utterly unmemorable in appearance. His smile and effusive greeting, however, made him immediately likeable. Since I was exhausted from traveling most of the day, we talked books for only five minutes or so before he showed me upstairs to the "guest room," which judging by the old-fashioned furniture, the floral curtains and carpet, and the antiseptic odor - not to mention the dearth of reading materials - must've been his late mother's bedroom. Sam confirmed that he'd preserved it just as it was when she was alive. Truly I felt honored having the most sacred room in the house!

In the morning, after a sound sleep, I met my host downstairs in the kitchen, where he prepared a sumptuous breakfast - eggs, bacon, and fried potatoes. Sam himself only had coffee and a bagel. When I protested at this inequity, he said he was one of those people who eat to live rather than live to eat. He survived on purely cerebral nourishment.

At any rate, as good as Sam's cooking was, it wasn't the main attraction. We shortly moved into the study, although we could've started the tour almost anywhere, seeing how nearly every inch of wall space was given over to bookshelves. From the study's packed floor-to-ceiling cases there was an overflow, on desks and tables, but Sam was both tidy and systematic, not at all in the mold of the stereotypical eccentric who carelessly heaps volumes any old place and never bothers to dust. The study had a pleasantly musty smell, an air reminiscent of the Strand Bookstore, if without the crowds of pushy customers and rude salespersons. Through the bay window one could tell it was going to be a hot summer day, but an air-conditioner and dehumidifier ensured we would remain in comfort as long as we stayed indoors.

We never did get outside, so enchanted was I to dwell in this secondhand book dealer's paradise. Sam evidently had his own peculiar organization within categories, which ranged from genre literature, mainly horror and fantasy with a smattering of s.f. and mystery - his tastes in this respect were similar to mine - to mainstream fiction, some of it quite obscure.

The first odd volume to attract my attention was J.R. Ackerley's *My Sister and Myself*. Not counting his one play, I knew this minor mid-century author had written only four books. What was this?

"I'm a big fan of Ackerley's *My Dog Tulip*..." I began.

"Greatest dog book ever written..." my host interjected.

"After Dunsany's *My Talks With Dean Spanley*..."

"Then there's Virginia Woolf's *Flush*..."

"...but I don't know this one, though it does sound kind of familiar."

"You must be thinking of his autobiographical memoir, *My Father and Myself*."

"Oh, right."

"*My Sister and Myself* was compiled from his diaries several years after his death. It made more of a splash in England. The American edition is quite scarce."

From Ackerley we somehow got onto the subject of mainstream authors who've dabbled in the horror genre. By way of illustration Sam pulled out a recent acquisition, Brad Leithauser's *Norton Book of Ghost Stories*, with the comment, "Mostly mediocre tales by Henry James and other highbrows."

"Yes, how idiotic to exclude writers like Dunsany and Lovecraft."

"I'm not saying there hasn't been some wonderful work done by writers outside the field. Take *The Green Man* by Kingsley Amis, for instance. It deserves to be far better known."

"Agreed."

"I'm afraid, though, old Kingsley has of late been overshadowed by son Martin."

"At least John Updike doesn't have that problem."

"Another example is Evelyn Waugh's *The Temple at Thatch*, written while he was at Oxford. Do you know it?"

"Uh, maybe. It was a long time ago..." I hate admitting my ignorance, especially when it comes to literary matters.

"Harold Acton was right - most if it's dull - but the parts where the hero practices black magic are superb. I have a first edition. Let me show you." Sam guided me to his Waugh section, which was so extensive it took him a minute to find *The Temple at Thatch*. "Ah, here it is, in between *A Little Learning* and *A Little Hope*."

I glanced at the text of the slim, elegantly bound volume Sam handed me, my eye drawn mainly to the satirist's decadent line drawings.

"Speaking of first novels, have you read Barbara Pym's future fantasy, *Some Tame Gazelle*?"

"Sure." Luckily, *Some Tame Gazelle* was the one Pym novel I had read. Though I wasn't about to tell Sam, it hadn't inspired me to read more of her.

"Too bad she didn't cut out the Nazis."

"Nazis? In Barbara Pym?"

"In her defense, she did write it in the thirties, after a trip to Germany. Later, of course, Nazis weren't so funny any more."

"Yes, their presence does give it a dated quality." Again, though I had no memory of Nazis in the novel, I wasn't going to admit I had forgotten.

As I've indicated, Sam had his collection pretty well organized, but it wasn't always obvious to me why he grouped certain things as he did. In a Mission-style bookcase in the front hall, for instance, I noticed such standard titles as Poe's *Narrative of Arthur Gordon Pym*, Hawthorne's *Dr. Grimshawe's Secret*, Twain's *Mysterious Stranger*, Fitzgerald's *Last Tycoon*, and Capote's *Answered Prayers*. But what was humorist P.G. Wodenhouse's *Sunset at Blandings* or a three-volume set of German master Thomas Mann's *Confessions of Felix Krull* doing on the same shelf with these American classics? And why weren't August Derleth's *The Watchers Out of Time* and Frank Belknap Long's *Cottage Tenant* back with the rest of these authors' works in their respective sections in the study?

Into this Mission-style bookcase Sam put a copy of what he said was his latest acquisition - *Emma*.

"Jane Austen?"

"No, Charlotte Bronte," Sam replied. "A far more outspokenly feminist work that Austen's novel of the same name."

"To each his own, I guess. Or should I say *her* own?"

Sam chuckled. He knew my tastes well enough from my letters not to be surprised by my lack of enthusiasm for certain writers. On the other hand, this didn't stop him from trying to convert me to his own pet authors - like the British novelist Anthony Powell, whose works occupied a large nook in the dining room.

"I remember Anthony Powell was one of your first recommendations to me," I said.

"You mean Anthony Powell?"

"Did you say *Pole*?"

Yes, *Powell* - rhymes with *Lowell.*"

"Gee, I didn't know that."

"Did you ever read *A Dance to the Music of Time*?"

Over the years Sam had urged me to read the man's twelve-volume masterpiece, supposedly a fascinating portrait of English society from the 1920-s to the 1970's, but I'd never gotten beyond the first book in the cycle - too slow, too understated for someone of my Celtic temperament.

"I'll get to it one of these days, I promise."

"Like Lovecraft's, Powell's style can be offputting. But believe me, he's worth the effort. Another English writer of roughly the same generation worth the effort, incidentally, is X. Trapnel."

"Never heard of him."

"Like you a bit of a rogue with the ladies. *Camel Ride to the Tomb* is brilliant, but I'm more partial to *Profiles in String*. First printings are hard to come by, especially of the latter novel." These and other Trapnel titles were on the shelf in the Powell nook, but a glance at their spines was examination enough for me. If I was probably never going to read Anthony Powell (excuse me, *Pole*), then almost certainly I wasn't going to get around to X. Trapnel.

With relief I followed Sam to the other end of the dining room, where in a wooden chest he kept his bound galleys and page proofs. These were all of modern vintage, both mainstream and genre.

"Say, what should I do with my Stephen King bound galleys?" For a number of years I'd dated the book reviewer of a women's magazine who'd given me her King galley's for free, even after our relationship had turned platonic. It was only after she admitted throwing out the bound galleys of Ian Hamilton's suppressed biography of J.D. Salinger that I dropped her. I have my principles.

"I'd sell them and invest the money in Frank Long paperbacks."

"Like *Cottage Tenant*?"

"Yeah, that's one of the more desirable ones."

In truth I'm not much of a Long fan, but I could see since his death how his paperback novels might increase in value. I assumed Cottage Tenant was yet another forgettable piece of hack work ground out in his last years by this pathetic pulp-era survivor.

From the dining room we moved into the parlor, where in a glass-fronted cabinet were displayed the collected works of a no less industrious but infinitely finer author, John Updike. Sam appeared to possess not only a complete set of the Knopf editions, from *The Poorhouse Fair* to *The Afterlife*, but a lot of Updike's small press stuff as well, including his poetic homage to female pudenda.

"You know," I said, "looking at all these books, I can understand why Nicholsen Baker has such a thing for Updike. It's not just the exquisite prose, it's his obsession with sex. Not a point Baker makes clear in *U and I*, as I recall."

"What do you think of *U and I*?" asked Sam.

"Rather impudent of Baker, I thought, to write a book like that about a living author."

"A case of a lesser talent trading on the name of a greater."

"Yeah, but to be fair, Baker's almost as amazing a stylist as Updike. I bet you it won't be long, now that Baker's arrived, before someone writes a book about his, or possibly even her, obsession with him."

"That's an idea," said Sam, a dreamy look on his face. "I'd love to add it to my collection."

On the wall past Updike was a series of open shelves devoted to post-war American Jewish writers: Bellow, Roth, Malamud, Beck, among others. Again, not an area of literature in which I've done much delving. I listened patiently as Sam held forth on the place of Jewish fiction in our culture.

"Bellow, Roth, and Malamud are giants, admittedly," he said, "but Beck's in a class by himself. *After Travel Light* and *Brother Pig*, I can't wait to read *Think Big*."

"*Think Big*?"

"His work in progress."

"How long has he been working on it?"

"I believe he first announced it in 1966 or '67."

"Jesus."

"Oh, sorry, I didn't mean..." Sam must've sensed he'd touched on a delicate topic.

"It's okay. With any luck it'll take me only another ten years to come up with *The Laughter of the Gods*." As with many such things in my life, I tried to turn this painful reminder into a joke, albeit a feeble one. Sam mumbled some encouraging words, then changed the subject.

So through the morning, the afternoon, and the evening, from attic to basement and all floors between, with the occasional food or bathroom break, we indulged our book lust. During this orgy we engaged in a sort of friendly one-upmanship, each trying to outdo the other in knowledge of literature - old and new, major and minor, mainstream and genre, American, British, and Continental. For all the vast extent of his collection, Sam owned he could never approach anything like completeness. Such rare Americana as Cotton Mather's *Biblical Commentaries* and Margaret Fuller's *History of the Roman Republic* he feared would elude him forever. In debating the issue of Lovecraft versus Dunsany, I argued the superiority of the Irish lord, despite my innate pessimism, because he had the courage in his fiction to resist despair and hold out the hope of a happy ending.

Finally, near exhaustion, I said, "Tell me, what's your single most prized volume?"

"Funny you should ask," he said. "I've been saving the best for last."

By this time it was close to midnight and we were in the kitchen, nodding over the remains of some Cantonese delivery and an empty bottle of Chardonnay, my house present, all of which I'd imbibed since it had turned out my host, like HPL, never touched alcohol. With no little effort we got up and staggered into the study. There Sam lifted the cushions off the seat of the bay window, ignoring my facetious guesses as to the title of this most awesome of tomes.

"I keep the really esoteric stuff hidden," he said as he raised the hinged seat. I was suddenly aware of a strong musty odor.

"Esoteric? How Lovecraftian."

"You're getting warm."

"You don't mean you have...?"

"Yes..."

"No, it'd be too much of a cliche!"

But yes, there it was, in a compartment below the window seat - the *Necronomicon*. Or was it? Maybe it was a fake, like the Neville Spearman edition of the one that merely repeats a sixteen page signature of Arabic script. The oversized copy that Sam now held in his hands, however, looked authentic - dark, worn, centuries old.

"Personally I prefer Edward Casabon's *Key to All the Mythologies*," Sam said with a smile, "but by any objective standard, this is the all-time winner. Care to take a peak?"

With trembling hands I took Abdul Alhazred's fabled volume, which felt strangely light.

"Go ahead, open it," my friend urged.

I undid the clasp. A moment later I'd dropped it and let out a scream - at the thing that had leapt at me from the book as soon as I'd lifted the cover. Sam laughed. On the floor was a crude octopoid creature on a spring. The *Necronomicon* was hollow. It had been a joke. Cthulhu-in-the-box.

"On that note," I said, doing my best not to show my irritation, "let's go to bed."

Later, under the sheets, I felt less annoyed. I had to give Sam credit for a sly sense of humor. Something else, though, vaguely troubled me as I teetered on the verge of sleep. from earlier in the day. I realized there was a link between Updike and Bech, the Jewish writer. I've by no means read all of Updike's massive oeuvre, but it struck me that our most respected living novelist had written a book about Bech - and while it approached its subject with a certain mock reverence, somewhat akin to Baker's *U and I*, there was one extremely crucial difference...

In the morning I was all set to ask my host some pointed questions about Updike and Bech, along with a few other anomalous authors who had stalked my dreams. I was distracted, however, by what I found at my place at the breakfast table - a bulky, gift-wrapped package.

"Happy birthday, Sean!" exclaimed Sam, who was smiling by the stove.

"How the heck did you know it was my birthday?"

"No problem. I have Contemporary Authors on-line, as well as the Necro Press 1995 Dunsany calendar. Most of the standard references still list you."

"Gosh, after last night I'm not sure I dare open it."

"Go ahead. I don't think you'll be disappointed."

"Okay, but I warn you, if this is another trick..."

A few days after my visit to Arkham, I sat down to write Sam a quick note:

Dear Sam,

Many thanks for your hospitality over the weekend. It was truly a thrill for me to share in your fantastic collection. As for your birthday present, what more could an author ask for? I've just finished the manuscript, and it's perfect, right down to the grinning Buddha heads. The ending's more upbeat, a trifle more Dunsanian than is my usual style - but who says the protagonist always has to get his comeuppance? I'll be sending my agent a chapter a week starting tomorrow. He'll be ecstatic. Again, you WASPS are too kind.

As ever,
Sean

In the Times After

By Fred Behrendt

"*The face of the spider-idol was lit by that fatal gem; there was no other light.*" -- Lord Dunsany

I set out from the temple, where I know, eventually, my journey must end. In my left hand I grasp the withered stick carved with the 1000 faces of my multi-eyed god; in my right is a gray flask containing a draught for inducing dreams -- and all about me is the perpetual dusk of my accursed homeland. I seek the wisdom to understand what I have seen, but know it can never steal upon me within the cold walls of our temple. Instead, I mount into the desolate mist-wreathed foothills. The mist's clammy tendrils seem determined to confound my journey. But, in time, I rise above the hills and mist, and find the cold, naked crags I seek.

It is time to drink and sleep. It is time to lie staring into the gulf of waking dreams. It is time to learn the meaning of what I have seen on the idol's face.

* * *

The dog's fur prickles expectantly at the stink of rotting food, and his ears stand forward. The dog's mouth opens and his tongue is pink in the semi-darkness. The stench of garbage draws out his saliva.

He pads out of the briar passage, into a wide area lit by pale sunlight, and stops abruptly. An unexpected smell burns into his sensitive nose. Sour and bright, it drives the garbage stink from his mind. Sour like a man, the new smell is otherwise totally new to the dog. A muffled sound above causes him to look upward. A shadow moves over the dog, and something faster than an in drawn breath catches the animal by the neck, snatching it lightly from the ground. The dog utters a single sound, not a bark nor a yelp nor whine -- the sound is too brief to take any form -- and then it is over. The dog falls, limp and bloated; and when it strikes the ground it splits wide, like a wet paper sack.

* * *

Only one knew the dog was dead.

* * *

Someone else looked for the dog, nonetheless, and although she did not know where to find him, she did know her feet had grown weary during her search.

Her sense of smell was not so sharp as the dog's. As a result, she smelled garbage alone, and was only partially distracted when she came upon the house.

A faded window curtain, sagging from its rod, was the first thing that caught her eye. Her eye strayed from the sagging curtain toward the side of the house. There she saw two metal drums brimming with garbage. A third drum lay on its side, spilling its contents in a cluttered fan of stinking waste.

She had to admit to herself, the spilled drum looked like it could be the dog's work.

She turned from regarding the mess, to look at the house again. Aside from the obvious clue of the full garbage cans, she detected no signs of life in or around the house. Shaggy, wet grass clung around her shins and ankles as she stepped forward. Her feet were soaked.

The doorbell collapsed silently under her finger. She waited a few moments, then knocked. The door bounced inward, away from her knuckles, then floated open a few inches. The interior of the house was visible through the gap.

The place was neater inside than she would have judged from the exterior condition of the house. A bundle of folded *Providence Bulletins* and *Providence Journals* tied with brown string rested just within the door. A blue and white windbreaker hung alone on the central of three brass hooks. Blond-colored, hardwood flooring looked recently swept. Further along the hallway she saw shelves stuffed with paperback books.

The door swept inward, sucking at her with its draft. Her head snapped and she looked up into a pair of eyes. "Can I help you?"

Thin brown hair receded from his forehead. His round glasses had shiny iron frames. His face was impassive. A clean blue shirt and tan cotton trousers hung on him loosely. His feet were bare.

"Uh . . . Hi. I was looking for my dog."

His eyebrows raised and he smiled. "No dogs in here, I'm afraid." He looked around behind himself. "At least, I don't think so."

She studied his smile briefly, and found it appealing.

"But you almost got in here without my noticing, so maybe something smaller could have gotten by me. Come in for a moment. I'll take a look around."

She hesitated.

He shrugged, and smiled again. "OK. Wait here."

He came back after a few minutes. "Most of the house is closed off. But no dog in the part I use. Want to look around in the back yard?"

She nodded. His friendliness had put her off-balance and she felt mute and stupid. She had expected a very different person to live in this house. Her mind had been filled with pictures of swollen little people with dirty children . . . or somebody too weakened by age to push a lawnmower.

"Here, let me show you around."

He padded barefoot across the narrow porch and into the tall grass. Internally, she winced at the thought of what could lay hidden in the dark grass. What kind of insects or sharp-pointed bits of trash might lurk beneath each of his steps? Daunted again, she silently followed.

He seemed observant enough, stopping here and there to look into the base of this or that overhanging bushy shrub. As they rounded the house, he stepped over the jumble of stinking trash, hardly seeming to notice the gleaming crescents of knife-sharp can lids as his naked feet brushed over them.

He looked down briefly at the trash, then looked up at her. "Still wonder how that got spilled. Been meaning to clean it up for the last few days. But you know how hard it is to get around to some things."

He let his voice trail off, good naturedly. He probably realized she found the mess disgusting, though there was no indication he did -- but otherwise, he didn't seem concerned about how she felt. She suddenly felt at ease, and began thinking she might like him.

She now saw that bordering the lawn on this side of the house was a tangled wall of briars. Later in the year they would be heavy with blackberries, now the briars formed a thick curtain of arching red whips. Budding leaves bristled dark green both on the surface, and in the depths. She heard the muted hum of what sounded like bees deep within. Occasional strands of spiders' web, glinting in the morning sunlight, stretched between the briars. The webbing appeared to grow thicker the deeper into the briars she looked. Well, she thought, if he's in there, he'll have to get himself out. I'm not going in there with the bees and spiders.

He led her around the back of the house. Here, the lawn was higher and thicker. Her jeans were now soaked to the knees from dew. At one end of the yard a rounded boulder's top was visible poking above the grass. At the other end was a rough mortared stone well. A skeleton of weathered gray boards, once a peaked cover, collapsed over the well's dark opening.

He scanned the yard. "One advantage to this tall grass is that you can see if anything of any size has passed through. You know -- where it's been pushed aside." He gestured toward trails of bruised grass behind them.

"Is your dog very big?"

She nodded.

"I don't see any trails today other than ours." He said.

She had to admit he seemed to be right. Their own trails through the grass were apparent enough, and Titus *was* a big dog. He certainly ate enough to qualify as a third person in their house. She shrugged, again inwardly. Titus was probably all right, anyway. The big lug was just about indestructible.

She turned to the tall man.

"Thanks for the look around," she said.

He smiled again. Perhaps a bit too warmly. Then dropped his eyes, "No problem. You're free to look around here. Anytime."

He turned then, dragging his eyes over her one last time, then strode away through the high grass.

Strange guy, she thought. He didn't even tell me his name. She turned and watched him walk away. An unfamiliar, tingling sensation grew between her eyebrows and at the base of her skull as she watched the easy movement of his shoulders and hips. She rubbed at the back of her neck. Was she feeling excitement, or disquiet? She was not sure.

A tiny half-heard voice said, let it be excitement.

She shivered, shaking off the feeling. Then she waited, looking down at the unkempt grass at her feet. The sun rose over the line of trees surrounding the yard. It warmed her shoulders and burned off the dew. She found herself becoming too warm. That, in turn, reminded her of her aching feet and the long walk back to her car. She sighed, her shoulders slumped, she pushed back through the clinging strands of wild grass and made for the front of the house.

As she walked along the side of the house the web strands appeared to have grown thicker within the briars, expanding like a mist rising in morning thermals. The sunlight must be striking the strands at a different angle, she thought, I can see more of them now. Glad I didn't go pushing my way in there -- I hate the feeling of all those strands clinging across my face.

When she reached the front of the house, he was gone inside and the door was closed -- all the way this time, she noticed.

She made a note of the name on the mailbox as she passed by on her way out. "Phillips, 454 Angell Street," it read, nothing more.

She was relieved. He did not emerge from the house to say goodbye. She had nothing against the guy, in fact she liked him; but she needed a moment with herself to consider her new, emerging feelings. She realized she wanted to know his name. She wanted to know his name without his knowledge, without his consent. An indefinable quality in this guy was drawing her . . . or, perhaps, it was a quality in him she was compelled to draw to herself.

And perhaps this time her plan, though still half-formed, would work.

* * *

His dream is always the same.

He is in a room and the door before him is always open. They come before him, meek faces lit by the cold light of something he holds before him. It is the only light in the room and it is hardly enough to see by. And sometimes in the dim light he knows they cannot determine if he is moving or not moving. And then he sees fear in their eyes and he is tingling with excitement as they study him in a yawning paralysis of fear, trying to decide whether he is about to pounce. Or it is only a trick of the cold light?

If only they would take that cold light away, for it is his prison. This cold imprisoning glow. This prison of their fear. If the cold glow was gone he would be among them. They would feel him among them but they would not see him. Quietly resting his strength, waiting for the moment when their fears begin to wane -- but are not vanished completely -- in that moment that last quiet moment when their fears are gone to rest, they will turn and see their slack features reflected in each of his cold black eyes.

And always, in that moment of abrupt fulfillment, he awakens.

* * *

I cannot, she thought, believe I am doing this.

Condensation from the cool wine bottle settled along the back of her thumb, a wet line of cold, reminding her of the pinpoint of icy regret threatening to grow in her stomach.

The path through the budding trees was quiet and very creepy in the dusk. The closeness of the untrimmed bushes had seemed cozy during the daylight, but made her feel uneasy and hemmed in now. A white haze she did not remember hung in the trees. The white haze reminded her of the web strands in the briar patch this morning. Pausing a moment, she could swear the haze grew thicker as she watched. Then she shrugged dismissively. Must be . . . must only be the evening fog closing in, she thought.

The sudden welling up of garbage odor did not ease her mind. She had almost forgotten the cluttered spill of stinking trash.

What did she know about this guy, anyway? He seemed nice in his loner kind of way. But maybe he was not as he seemed. Maybe he was unemployed and lazing around while his wife brought home the bread and butter. And here she came with her romantic bottle of moderately priced wine barging in on their meager supper without an invitation. What would she say to them? What, for that matter, was she going to say to him if he were in the house *alone*?

Face it, Sonia. This is totally stupid.

She stopped on the foot-worn path, feeling irregularities in the packed earth through her thin rubber soles. Now the odor grew unaccountably stronger -- though she was no longer moving closer to the house. A wave of nausea swept at her up the pathway, and an odor of rotting, sun putrefied flesh stabbed up into her sinuses. A whiff of total corruption blocked all other perceptions. Sonia had a sudden thought of Titus. His lank dogs' body stretched out in her mind as she had seen him just yesterday. Where was he now?

The smell of rot choking Sonia's mouth and nose bloomed and enfolded her mind, the wine bottle slipped to the ground with a gurgling thud, and she crumpled forward.

* * *

One of her eyelids felt sticky, and she had difficulty opening it. The other eye opened easily enough, but the sight revealed was so blurry she still could not decide where she was. There was no clear memory of bedtime, or of pressing her dry lips to Mom's puffy cheek. Memories of more nights like that than she could count since the divorce ticked off silently in her head -- like a relentless metering of lost time. She seemed to have misplaced the most recent of her bedtime rituals. Then she remembered the plan, the wine bottle and the walk through the dark.

Both her eyes snapped open.

She focused on a plastered ceiling, then rolled her eyes to take in blond-colored wall paneling. Looking straight up again, she noticed something swung pendulously above her, but she could not see it clearly.

"Good. You're awake. I was beginning to get worried about you. Would you like some water?"

She turned her head, and there he was . . . holding out a squat tumbler of clear water. He smiled tentatively, his face held a conflicting mixture of expressions: concern, relief, pleasure. She took the offered water gratefully and took a sip. She felt a dampened cloth on her forehead. She grasped the cloth and used it to wipe her eyes. Then her gaze returned curiously upward.

Most everything else was clearing up, but the object swinging back and forth above remained out of focus. It'll clear in a moment. I must be coming down with a bit of flu. Whey else would I pass out like that just because of a bad smell?

She turned her eyes back toward him, then looked beyond him to the opposite wall. A number of small aquariums, stacked up like laboratory specimen cases, covered the entire opposite wall. She could not see what any of the cages contained, and for some reason, was reluctant to find out.

She turned suddenly and awkwardly, one hand still holding the water glass, she extended the other.

"Hi. My name is Sonia Greene. I guess I should have introduced myself this morning. I came back to do just that."

He took her hand, tentatively, barely squeezing it and said, "Howard. Howard Phillips. I am pleased to meet you."

He released her hand, but looked like he wished he had not. Then he smiled unsurely and said he would be right back.

She looked above her again. It was a small thing, and seemed to be floating unsupported in the air. But the way it swung back and forth made her think it was hanging from an effectively invisible thread.

She was just getting ready to stand and look at the thing -- it must have been right at eye level -- but then he returned. In one hand he carried her silly wine. In his other hand he held two wine glasses. One of these was a long-stemmed white wine glass, the other a bulbous red wine glass.

She noted that a few condensate slicked blades of grass still clung to the bottle from her fall on the pathway.

Thinking of her fall suddenly made her think of that odor and she sniffed suddenly, her emotions a strange mixture of anticipation and disgust. She was relieved to smell nothing.

"You apparently went through quite a bit to get this here. Would you like some?"

What did he mean by that? She wondered.

He held out the two glasses, stems protruding from between whitened knuckles. "Red? Or White?" He then emitted a nervous little laugh that she decided to ignore.

She assured herself that both glasses were clean, then touched the rim of the white wine glass with a fingertip. He immediately sat, cross-legged on the floor and silently and methodically peeled away the bottle's lead foil to the last fragment. He produced one of those knives with all the blades and tools, flipped out a corkscrew and used it to extract the cork. It took him about a minute and half, maybe two.

She had watched him intently. She leaned out and touched his wrist as he prepared to pour the wine. "Let the bottle breathe for a bit."

She wanted to say more, to open him up the way he had the bottle, but the task was not so easily begun. She could see this guy as a case come into the office downtown seeking help -- complaining they were holding back his food stamps, or something -- and maybe he needed help, but she was not here to do social work on her off hours. If she were going to retrieve Howard from some quiet, dark place, it would be the same place she would emerge from and she needed to make the journey with him.

He suddenly looked right at her from the corner of an eye.

"I had not expected you to come back," he said. "But I have to admit that I'm glad to see you."

"Laying on your front path, unconscious?" She tried to smile and give it a humorous twist, but the phrase came out of her mouth with too much force. She looked into his face and realized she had almost silenced him.

He looked away, and spoke into a corner of the room.

"No. No. Nothing like that. I had just realized that I could have done a better job of helping you find your dog. You know, I regretted I hadn't done more to help you."

. . . Like I had a regret of not making more effort of getting to know you, she thought. But here I am, making just about all the effort I can.

She realized the water glass was still in her hand, but could see no place in the uncluttered room to put it down. She held it out to him. He exchanged it for the wine glass and took it away into another room.

Holding onto the empty glass, she unsteadily levered herself off the sofa and walked over to the wall of glass cages. She peered inside one.

Within was the biggest spider she had ever seen in her life.

She leaned closer. Conflicting sensations of fascination and disgust warred within her again. The spider leapt forward as her face neared the glass, its legs palping the transparent barrier. She straightened and recoiled, brushing into Howard as he re-entered the room.

Her heart raced in her breast.

"One . . . one of your pets . . . just tried to jump me."

Her breath was rasping in labored gulps.

Howard glanced mildly at the hand-sized black shape spread out against the glass. Others began to appear, assaulting the glass barriers in the same way. Most of these were smaller, a few, however, were larger.

He touched the cage. His fingers touching the glass mirrored the spider's position against the opposite side of the barrier.

"It's around feeding time. Even spiders can fall into a routine. Sorry if he gave you a fright," he said, bemused.

Most of his nervousness had disappeared.

"He does not know yet how you fit into my dreams."

Her scalp prickled. Did he really say that?

He turned to her, and said, "They'll keep for a bit though. You want to have some of that wine, or are you out of the mood?"

His face bore a tight smile.

Despite her misgivings, she had some wine, and it helped make her calm. They each drank two glasses while discussing the countryside surrounding Providence. She realized that he must get out more than she had earlier surmised. He spoke as if intimate with most of the surrounding area. Since returning from New York City she had not really taken the chance to get out into some of her favorite places in the countryside. Maybe this is something they could do together, she thought, a way to get acquainted without allowing drinking wine in the presence of his spider zoo to become a habit.

She had a sudden insight.

"What's over in the briars beside your house?"

His eyebrow raised and he said, "The briars?"

After a moment he continued with obvious reluctance.

"The dogs have beaten a run though the briars and made a mud path under the thorns."

"What dogs?" She asked. "You didn't mention it when we were looking for Titus this morning."

"Titus?" He looked at her with renewed interest. "Was that his name? I didn't know. It's easier when you know their names. . ." His voice trailed off, and she noticed he had assumed his inward look again. But she did not know what he was talking about. Easier?

"Easier?" She blurted.

Almost imperceptibly, his eyes widened, and he shot her a quick, worried looked.

"I mean. . ." He took a breath. "I meant easier to *look* for them. If you know their name you can call to them and they'll come to you." His voice grew quiet. "They'll come to you easier." He mumbled on, but by then she had ceased listening.

Easier than what? she thought. He acted like he had done this before. Dogs disappeared around here all the time?

Yes.

Dogs disappeared around here all the time.

It was like a voice in her head, identical to the one that had advised her to be excited earlier that morning.

She had almost forgotten the thing swinging above her head. The thing she had seen upon awakening. Like on the end of a long, invisible strand of spiders' web. But now she remembered.

Look up, said the voice.

She looked up, but saw nothing.

Keep looking.

The thing faded into view again.

Legs palping the air, it hung about six inches above the bridge of her nose. Perhaps ready to drop. That tingling sensation came alive between her eyebrows and she sat back involuntarily. The vision receded but remained solid. Her eyes dropped to Howard's face. He was apparently looking up at the same point. His mouth partially open, and the rest of his features completely relaxed. His lids dropped, almost completely closing his eyes.

Placing her eyes again on the sight above, she edged from beneath the brown, translucent, succulent, throbbing body.

Wine from the glass she still gripped slopped onto her thigh, wetting her jeans. Then she was standing. The room stretched to the distant hallway, and the hall stretched away to an even more distant door.

One step. Two. Three. Four. The hallway door frame was beneath her sweating palm.

This was the moment. She did not know what made her think that.

"Howard," she whispered.

He turned his head slowly. His eyes were now fully closed as if he slept, his mouth was slitted and unsmiling.

His voice vibrated through the room, like a breathy buzz.

I'm glad you came for a visit, he said.

Howard's lips did not move but his voice rose from the walls and floor. The window panes hummed and rattled with his voice. To Sonia it seemed the entire house was an extension of Howard, speaking with his voice.

But maybe. Maybe it's time for you to go.

His eyes remained closed in sleep, but his lips broke into a broad smile, showing his long white teeth.

She stepped backward into the dark hallway so she could not see his smile, then turned and ran back to her car.

* * *

Home again, home again, jiggedy jig. Home from the market without so much as a fat pig. And later, in her bed, Sonia's lips feel dry from the touch of her mother's wrinkled cheek. Eventually, she sleeps uneasily.

In her dreams she sees a wall of balled fists looming before her. The wall bulges nearer, until the knuckles of the fists brush her skin. It is then she notices that she wears no clothes. And each balled fist nudges at her like the sleek head of a cat seeking love. Touching her everywhere touching her face and lips, the tips of her breasts, her thighs and their touch is hot and somehow promising.

And when, as she knew they would, each of the hands eventually opens to continue their caresses with greater attention to detail the fingers are jointed, covered with stiff dark fur, each ending in a brief, spatulate pad. They stroke her.

She does not understand why she feels no horror.

No horror, only a growing wave of passion she can neither comprehend or resist in this silent, dislocated scene of dreaming. Sonia's knees weaken and buckle and she presses her body full against the wall of waving legs, pressing her flesh against their soft yielding touch and instead of remembering the unfolding fingers that have become waving arachnid legs, she recalls her third drive to the rundown neighborhood on Angell street.

Why did she come here again? Is her disgust with her empty life with mother and her dreary job in the welfare office making her nuts? This Howard Phillips guy has at least one screw loose -- maybe more -- but here she is outside his door once again. What time was it? It must be the middle of the night.

She is surrounded by cobalt darkness. Only dim light from a window reveals the paint flecked surface of Howard Phillips' front door.

God damn it, she thinks, I should just get out of here. But then she can not remember exactly where she has parked the car, and this growing pillar of hot willingness and the stirring memory of something touching her skin. 1,000 delicate brushings awake in her memories and her skin tingles alive.

She reaches up and knocks on the door thinking maybe this is just a dream. The door opens lightly before her touch, swinging inward.

Howard's house is dark and she walks silently through his front hallway. Entering the living room, everything is as she remembers it. As Sonia hoped, he is sleeping -- dimly visible on the sofa in the wan light from the spider cages. This is the first time she has seen him without a shirt. Even in the dim light, she can see that he is too thin. His ribs stand out against his pale flesh like the arched bands.

Everything she has planned to say drains from her mind. She cannot believe she has come here again, sneaking into his house. But she has to talk with him. That dream. That dream . . . it is like he had been truly there offering . . . offering something unspeakable. Something unspeakable blurred into a smeared image of insane delight. Her throat tightens. Her cheeks flush with the memory of his dream offering.

And in that moment he stirs.

Her flesh tingles again in a surging moment of strange apprehension. She opens her mouth to say something, anything to fully awaken him. But nothing comes out except a gasp.

He twists, his head whipping around. A single eye snaps open to look on her. His mouth slowly opens, as if in a long, irresistible yawn. That one eye still looking right at her. His jaws stretch and stretch, as if his mouth will never stop opening.

And then, when he speaks, it is an explosion of hoarse screaming.

"No! You cannot be here! It is too soon. My dream is not done. I cannot wake up now! N-o-o-o-o-o-o-o-o!"

His ribs heave in unison, wetly tearing free of the white flesh, extending, unfolding until their eight precise horny tips each find purchase on the floor. His torso rises upward and his legs dangle, then fall away like sodden, rotting logs, striking the floor with a muffled thud. Both misshapen cylinders burst, and ten thousand black spiders pour forth, tumbling, biting and crawling over Sonia's feet and ankles.

Despite the stinging pain, she is paralyzed by another moment of awful insight -- Sonia realizes that all Howard's dreams are coming true . . . that all his dreams *are* true.

For a moment Howard's face, distorted with unimaginable pain, hovers before her eyes, then blade-like mandibles thrust through the sagging tissue of skin. An acrid, sweaty odor washes over her and her eyes burn and she falls back as the mandibles begin their feverish work of cleaning the useless flesh and lips and limp brown hair from the round flat head and its eight flat staring eyes. Eyes shiny as eight glimmering black stones.

She spins on her toe then, and runs.

She can feel her legs and arms stiffening from spider venom, and prays this is only a dream. Please, God. This is only a dream!

But at the pathway she turns back -- for just one last look -- and something like a spider; but tall, tall as a man, emerges from the house then turns aside into the webbed-over briars. Briars now almost completely obscured in a dreamy haze of white strands.

* * *

Dreams within dreams within dreams. Where am I? Who am I? How did I come to be this dreamer in this dream? Or am I, after all, the waking one? I do not know.

I lay awake, cold and dreamless, thinking on what I have seen in my sleep. Eventually, however, I realize I cannot put off the rest of my journey, no matter how much I want to lay forever on this windswept crag of jagged rock. So, I rise, lean upon my gnarled cane and walk slowly down from the mountains, and down through the misty hills.

And when my long journey comes to its end, I enter the temple and look again upon the spider-idol. Upon that once inscrutable face I see what I know I must -- the cold glow of the gem still plays upon its features; but glowering tears rim each hard, black eye.

The Doom that Came to Dunwich

By Richard A. Lupoff

We are told that humans -- or creatures that could reasonably be defined as humans -- have walked the earth for 2,000,000 years at the least, and perhaps for as long as 5,000,000 years. And yet civilization, in any form that we would recognize and acknowledge, has existed for a mere 10,000 to 15,000 years. We are thus asked to believe that Gug and her mate Ug led a primitive existence, hunting and gathering or perhaps scratching a few crude holes in the ground and dropping seeds into them each spring, and made little more progress than that for a minimum of 1,985,000 years. Following this there sprang into being virtually simultaneously the miracles of Angkor Wat, Babylon, Thebes, Kukulcan, Yucatan, and Cuzco.

We are also told that life has existed on the earth for at least 2,000,000,000 years, and perhaps as long as 6,000,000,000. Uncounted millions of species have evolved and disappeared. Whole orders of life have emerged and departed. Creatures as tiny as a virus and so huge as to dwarf the mammoth or the whale, creatures of infinite variety and endless complexity, have lived and died on this world. And yet we are told that of all these species, only one, our own, and at that, only in a relative flicker of an eyelash, has developed true consciousness and intelligence.

What nonsense! What arrogance! What blind, ignorant balderdash!

-- from the preface to *Paleontology and Paleoanthropology: the Failure and the Fraud*,
by Lindsey and Plum,
Canyon Press,
San Carlos, California, 1981

* * *

When a traveler in north central Massachusetts takes the wrong fork at the junction of Aylesbury Pike just beyond Dean's Corners he may feel that he has fallen through a crack in time and emerged into an earlier era in New England. The countryside is marked by rolling hills and meadows, spotted here and there with stands of woodland that, at first glance, appear lush and healthy, but that, upon closer examination, seem to emit an almost palpable miasma of *wrongness*. The grasses are oddly yellow. The tree trunks seem to be writhing in pain, while their leaves appear oddly *fat* and to give off an unpleasantly oily exudation.

If one arrives in what has become known as Dunwich Country at night, the sense of temporal alienation is especially strong. The few advertising billboards that were erected along the Pike in earlier decades have fallen into wrack and ruin, but no one has bothered either to rehabilitate or to remove them. The few tatters of once-colorful posters that remain attached to their frameworks, flapping in every errant gust of wind, remind the traveler of products long removed from the market: Graham-Paige automobiles, Atwater-Kent superheterodyne radio sets, Junius Brutus Cigars.

Even tuning the radio to stations in Boston, Providence or Worcester does little good, for the particular conformation of the terrain, or perhaps the presence of deposits of as yet undetected ores beneath the ground or of unexplained atmospheric conditions, makes it impossible to receive more than an unpleasant melange of sound, interspersed with indecipherable whisperings and gurglings.

Rounding the base of Sentinel Hill on the outskirts of Dunwich, the site of the infamous "horror" of 1928, the traveler beholds an incongruous sight: a modern laboratory and office building of mirrored glass construction. Activity in the building proceeds uninterrupted, day and night. A wire-mesh fence surrounds the facility, and a single rolling gateway is guarded at all times by stern-faced young men and women. These individuals are clad in dark uniforms of unfamiliar cut and tint, identifiable neither as military nor police in nature. Each uniform jacket carries a shoulder patch and each uniform cap a metal device, but the spiraling helix into which these insignia are formed is also unique to the Dunwich facility. This ensign, it may be noted, is laminated as well on the stock of the dull-black, frightening sidearm which each uniformed guard carries.

A small wooden plaque is mounted beside the rolling gate, in sparse letters identifying the facility as the property of the Dunwich Research Project. No newspaper files or directories of government organizations make mention of the Dunwich Research Project, and neither the directory issued by the Dunwich Telephone Company, nor that company's Directory Assistance operators are able to furnish a number by means of which the facility may be contacted.

However, careful study of federal appropriations documents of past years may reveal "black" items in the budgets of major agencies which, a selected few Washington insiders are willing to concede, may indeed have been directed through back channels to the Project. Further study of federal records will show that these covert appropriations for the Dunwich Research Project began in 1929.

The initial appropriation was extremely small, but in later years the funding for the Dunwich Research Project increased despite crisis, Depression, or war. The names of every President from Herbert Hoover to the present time will be found attached to these "black" items.

It was to this region that young Cordelia Whateley, a graduate student of anthropology at McGill University in Montreal, Quebec, drove her conservative gray four-door sedan in the late spring of the year. Her examinations over for the semester, she had determined to spend the next several months researching her master's dissertation on the events of 1928. It was Miss Whateley's belief that an encounter with one or more alien beings had provided the basis for those horrific happenings. Because she was herself a member of a distant (and undecayed) branch of the Whateley family, she had been inculcated from infancy with a revulsion for her (decayed) kith and kin. This she wished to resolve once and for all: to prove that her distant cousin Wilbur Whateley had been not so much a menace to be feared and loathed as he was a sport of nature deserving of the sympathy and aid which he failed to receive from those around him.

Miss Whateley brought her automobile to a stop outside the rolling gate of the Dunwich Research Project. The guard on duty, a young man with a square jaw and muscular build, approached her and courteously asked her business at the Project. She showed him a letter from her faculty adviser at McGill, addressed to the Director of the Dunwich Institute, and a response, on Institute letterhead, welcoming her inquiry and authorizing all concerned to offer the bearer every possible courtesy and assistance.

The merest suggestion of a smile played around the lips of the guard as he handed the documents back to Miss Whateley. "You'll want the Dunwich Institute, miss," the guard explained. "This is the Dunwich Research Project. The Institute is in Dunwich Town. On South Water Street. Dr. Armitage is the Director. That's his signature on the bottom of your letter. You want the Institute, miss. The Research Project is off limits."

He gestured courteously, suggesting but not exactly duplicating, a military salute. Then, with a series of clear and vigorous hand gestures (he was wearing white gloves) he directed Miss Whateley to depart and return to town.

Cordelia Whateley complied, swinging her automobile around and pointing its nose back toward Dunwich proper. As she circled Sentinel Hill she could not help noticing that an array of radar dishes dotted the top of the hill. To her, they looked like a recrudescence of white, puffy toadstools.

The town of Dunwich had neither grown nor changed noticeably from the illustrations and descriptions Cordelia Whateley had studied in preparation for her visit to the region. Authorities in the United States had been reluctant to send materials dealing with Dunwich out of the country, even to so friendly a neighbor as that to the north, but a friend of Miss Whateley's at the University of Massachusetts had managed to borrow many such documents and share them with the researcher by means of electronic transmission.

As Cordelia Whateley motored down Winthrop Street toward South Water, she noticed that Osborne's Store still stood at the corner of Winthrop and Blindford. Beside it, a grimy-windowed establishment advertised EATS and ALE. No other name identified the establishment, but after a lifetime in which her world had become increasingly dominated by malls and franchise enterprises, Cordelia Whateley found the survival of Osborne's Store and of an establishment identified solely as EATS and ALE oddly comforting.

Opposite Osborne's Store stood a steepled, greystone building. Cordelia tried to make out the device that topped the steeple. In the darkness she could not be certain, but she thought it was the same ensign she had seen on the uniforms of the guards at the Dunwich Research Project. Lights flickered inside the building, and the sound of chanting could be heard.

She located the Dunwich Institute and stood before its Spartan exterior, searching for a means of admittance. The Institute was located in a building of Colonial architecture, but rather than serving as a source of elegance and charm, the frame construction with its chipped and faded whitewash and its black front door surmounted by a dust-shrouded fanlight, caused a shudder to pass through her body.

Beside the door a rectangular brass plate, once gleaming but now covered with a patina of dullness, still bore the legend, *Dunwich Institute -- founded 1928 -- Henry Armitage, Ph.D. President.* Cordelia Whateley searched for a doorbell, and, failing to locate one, instead reached for the brass knocker bolted to the wooden door. The knocker, covered with the same dull patina as the plate, was shaped like a creature differing from any Cordelia Whateley had ever before seen. It bore many tentacles, and great staring eyes, and from it there seemed to seep a miasma of pure evil such as she had never in her life encountered.

Cordelia Whateley had taken her large, well-filled purse with her when she left her automobile. Now, having retrieved the purse and clutching it with one hand, she drew a breath, grasped the brass creature, raised it and let it fall. It struck with a loud, metallic sound of unpleasant nature. Cordelia Whateley found herself staring from her hand to the knocker, and then to her hand once again. Surely the knocker was of brass: of old, tarnished brass. Why, then, did her hand feel as if her fingers had grasped the rubbery, slimy, moist tentacles of a living creature? And why, when she released the door-knocker, had it seemed to cling stubbornly to her fingers so that she had to pull them away to gain her release?

She had not long to ponder the problem, for the door drew back noisily on rusted hinges and she stood face to face with an aged individual who blinked at her with faded, rheumy eyes. He stood well over six feet in height. His sparse hair was pure white and his face bore an expression of despair overlaid with chronic fear.

"I am Henry Armitage," the old man said. "Who are you, young woman, and what do you want of me?"

Cordelia Whateley was taken aback by the old man's appearance but she had rehearsed for this moment and she delivered the lines she had prepared. "I -- I am Cordelia Whateley. From McGill University. I -- I wrote to you about my work, and you sent me this reply." She held Armitage's own letter so he could see it in the yellow light filtering from behind him. Was it possible? Yes, the Institute building was illuminated by oil-lamp and candle. With a chilling shock she realized that she had not seen an electric appliance or even a gaslight in Dunwich.

Although Cordelia Whateley had arrived in Dunwich Country at an hour when the afternoon sunlight was still fairly bright, here in the narrow streets of the town itself a darkness had descended that was not the comforting, pleasant darkness of a New England evening. Involuntarily, Cordelia Whateley looked behind her. The streets of Dunwich seemed abnormally empty of pedestrian traffic, and the few canvas-covered vehicles that moved on the old streets seemed almost to huddle within themselves as they passed.

Armitage extended a thin hand covered with pale, wrinkled skin. "Come in. You are late. Almost too late. I receive very few visitors. I expected you earlier in the day."

Cordelia Whateley followed Armitage into the ancient building. An almost palpable miasma of age and decay seemed to arise from the heavy furnishings and threadbare carpet. Armitage indicated an overstuffed chair covered in faded velvet. Cordelia Whateley lowered herself carefully into it.

"I would have been here earlier," she tried to explain, "but -- "

"But you went to Sentinel Hill, didn't you?" Armitage cut her off.

"Yes, I -- "

"You tried to get into the Project. The Dunwich Research Project. I was afraid of that. You're very lucky indeed."

"Lucky? I don't understand. I -- " Cordelia Whateley put her hand to her forehead. "I'm so sorry. Could I have a glass of water? I'm afraid I'm feeling faint."

While Armitage was out of the room, Cordelia Whateley studied its contents as best she could without leaving her chair. The walls were covered with glass-fronted bookcases, all of them filled to their limits. Many were locked. The books themselves, for the most part, looked ancient. The bindings were tattered; such lettering as Cordelia Whateley could make out was faded. In size, the volumes ranged from huge tomes that would cover a desktop if opened, to tiny items little larger than a common postage stamp.

Her eye was caught in particular by a small book, little more than a pamphlet, in fact, with an illustration on its cover. The illustration, barely visible in the yellow light of the dark, musty room, seemed a crude representation of the door-knocker that Cordelia Whateley had handled at this very building. The slim book was bound in black leather, and its title, embossed in gold lettering in an obsolete typeface, read simply, *De Obéissance à les Maîtres Vieux*.

Henry Armitage's hand on her shoulder startled Cordelia Whateley. She gasped and turned. He extended a glass toward her. It might once have been part of a set of fine crystal but its rim now showed a jagged chip, its sides were streaked and the water it contained was of a vaguely unpleasant color and odor. Cordelia Whateley accepted the vessel and took one reluctant sip of its contents before placing it on a dust-coated table.

"You asked why I thought you lucky," Armitage said. "Visitors to the Project sometimes disappear. Young Selena Bishop went up there last spring and hasn't been heard of since. In Dunwich Town, people don't like to receive an invitation to visit the Project."

"But then," Cordelia Whateley frowned, "why do they go? Why don't they just refuse to go?"

"When you're summoned to the Project, you go. That's the way it is in Dunwich Town."

"But people could just move away, couldn't they? Don't the buses run? And the Aylesbury Pike is nearby. It's only an hour or two to Boston by automobile."

"You don't leave Dunwich Country as easily as you might think, young miss. No, not if *they* want you to stay here. Rice and Morgan thought they could leave. They learned better. I'm the only one left now, of the three of us. I was the oldest, and you'd think I'd be long gone by now. But Rice was buried at sea and Morgan was cremated. They'd both left instructions that, whatever happened, *they were not to be interred in Dunwich Country.*"

He clapped his hands, and the sound was like an exclamation mark at the end of his sentence. Then he resumed. "The undertaker, Hopkins, respected their wishes. I made him do that. He wanted to bury 'em, he wanted to bury 'em in the town graveyard out near Jacob's Pond, but I wouldn't let him. We had a terrible battle, believe me, young miss. But if I ever see Rice and Morgan again -- I don't expect to, I don't think we get to go on once our flesh is finished, but I could be wrong, and if I am, and if I ever see Rice and Morgan again, I'm sure they'll thank me for making that fool Hopkins do what they wanted him to do."

He stopped, short of breath after his long statement. But before Cordelia

Whateley could speak, he put a question to her. "How old do you think I am, young miss?"

She looked at him appraisingly. Her own great-grandfather, Cain Whateley, had lived to 109, and Armitage looked every bit as old as Cain had in his last days. "I've read what I can find about the horror, and it says that you had a white beard in 1928. If you are the same Dr. Armitage..."

He gave her a sly grin. "You've done your homework. I'd expect as much of an undecayed Whateley. I think I see a tinge of the Wizard himself in your face. Yes, I'm the same Henry Armitage. Shaved off my beard in '42. Hoped to get into the army then, and get out of Dunwich Country. *They* were onto me, though. Said I was too old, but I'd shaved it off by then so I kept it off."

"But if you're the same Henry Armitage -- " Cordelia Whateley looked longingly at the chipped goblet of water but could not bring herself to take another sip. "You were an old man in 1928, and that was nearly seventy years ago. That's impossible. You'd have to be -- "

"Yes," he nodded, "I was almost eighty in 1928. I'm afraid I've given up on ever leaving Dunwich, but if the town is still here in a few years, I hope you'll come to my 150th birthday party."

He stood over her, reached down and patted her on the knee. Could this incredibly old man be -- Cordelia Whateley shook her head. She must have misread the look in his eye. What she thought for a moment she had seen there was impossible.

She said, "I don't mean to keep you up. I could come back in the morning. I mean," she made a show of looking at the battery-powered watch on her wrist. She frowned and held it closer to the nearest oil-lamp. "I just put a new battery in," she muttered.

Armitage smiled. "Electrical implements don't always work well in Dunwich. You did drive here, did you not, young miss?"

Cordelia Whateley nodded.

"You may have trouble starting your car in the morning."

"But -- "

"Never mind. We can dine at the inn. Then we can return here and I will assist you with your work as best I can. I have always felt a certain sense of -- well, obligation is not exactly the word, but it will do -- toward the Whateleys."

Cordelia Whateley was flustered. "You're very kind, Professor. But you need your sleep. A man your age -- "

"I do not sleep," Armitage replied. "Come, let us go to the inn. We can walk from here."

They walked from the Dunwich Institute back past Osborne's Store. The inn to which Armitage referred was not the restaurant Cordelia Whateley had seen, but another, located in a building that must have existed since the days of King George III and Governor Winthrop. They were waited on by a young woman -- she could hardly have been into her teens, Cordelia Whateley realized -- who seemed terrified of Henry Armitage. Armitage whispered a few words to the waitress, who nodded and disappeared into the kitchen, her long skirts brushing the floor behind her. Apparently Armitage had ordered for both of them, a custom that had gone out of fashion in Cordelia Whateley's world long ago.

Cordelia Whateley looked around the room. Dour New Englanders of past centuries frowned down from framed canvases that lined the old wood-paneled walls. A small fire struggled fitfully to survive on a gray stone hearth. The only other illumination was furnished by oil-lamps. Beside the hearth a musician sat upon a high stool, picking out a tune on a stringed instrument that Cordelia Whateley did not recognize. The tune, however, seemed vaguely familiar: it was a transcription of a piano composition by the mad Russian composer Alexander Nikolayevich Scriabin.

The musician was a woman. At first glance she appeared to be aged, perhaps as much so as Henry Armitage himself, but as Cordelia Whateley studied the woman she realized that her hair was that of the albino rather than the crone. In her features, Cordelia Whateley suspected that she could detect a hint of the legendary Lavinia Whateley or -- perhaps -- of herself.

Without ceasing to play, the woman raised her eyes from the fingerboard of her instrument and focused them upon Cordelia Whateley. Even in the faint light of wood flame and oil-lamp, it was clear that those eyes were hopelessly clouded by milk-white cataracts, cataracts the color of the woman's wild albino hair.

The only customers aside from Cordelia Whateley and Henry Armitage were a group of dark-clad persons wearing the uniform and insignia of the Dunwich Research Project.

After a few minutes one of them, a gray-haired, severe-visaged woman, approached their table. "Professor Armitage," she said sharply, "I didn't know that you had invited a guest to visit you."

Armitage said, "I didn't invite her. She wrote and said she was coming from Canada. I couldn't prevent."

I couldn't prevent, Cordelia mused. What an odd expression.

The uniformed woman nodded angrily and returned to her own table. Henry Armitage had not introduced Cordelia Whateley to her.

The waitress reappeared with a tray of dishes and glasses. A dust-coated bottle stood on the tray as well. The waitress set the dishes and bottle on the table. Cordelia Whateley's dish held a slab of very rare meat -- she assumed that it was beef. It was set off by a portion of broccoli and several very small roasted potatoes. Henry Armitage's dish was empty save for a sprig of parsley.

"Is that all you're going to eat?" Cordelia Whateley asked.

Armitage shook his head. "I have had my nourishment."

"But - - - - I could have come here alone for dinner. You didn't need to -- "

"It is not good to be alone on the streets of Dunwich after dark, young miss." Armitage reached across the table and took Cordelia Whateley by the wrist. He held her briefly, then dropped his own hand to his lap. He wore a threadbare black suit, a white shirt with a frayed collar, and a bow tie in an abstract print that Cordelia Whateley found almost hypnotic in the flickering yellow light of the oil-lamp on their table.

"Why not? Is Dunwich unsafe? We have muggers in Montreal, too, you know. I think I can protect myself."

"Muggers?" A tiny laugh escaped Armitage's lips, but even so Cordelia Whateley noticed a reaction among the uniformed men and women at the other table. "There are no muggers in Dunwich," Armitage said. "No, young miss. There are no muggers."

After a long day's journey from her home in Montreal, Cordelia Whateley experienced a combination of hunger and fatigue. She lifted her knife and fork and prepared to slice the rare meat on her plate. Her usual preference was for meat more thoroughly roasted than this, but appetite and reluctance to provoke any disagreement in the inn caused her to plunge the tines of her fork into the roast, and then the sharp point of her knife.

Perhaps it was the dim and unsteady illumination in the inn coupled with the effects of fatigue and several sips of wine that created an illusion, but the meat appeared to *writhe* away from Cordelia Whateley's implements. An involuntary gasp escaped her. The uniformed diners and even the blind musician turned their eyes toward her. She whispered, "Doctor Armitage, I'm -- I'm afraid I've lost my appetite. If we could leave now, and we'll start our work in the morning...."

The ancient man shook his head negatingly. "You must not put off. We will return to the Institute."

Half fainting from fatigue and wine, yet equally eager to be at her work, Cordelia Whateley agreed. Upon returning to the Institute, Professor Armitage produced a ring of keys from the pocket of his shabby black suit and unlocked the glass-fronted bookcase containing the largest of the volumes Cordelia Whateley had previously seen.

He selected one and carried it to a heavy deal table beside which a wooden reading-chair had already been placed, and laid it carefully upon the table. "You will find useful information here, young miss." Having said this he retired to a far corner and folded himself into a chair. To Cordelia Whateley he seemed to disappear.

She examined the volume Armitage had laid out. It was a bound collection of large news pages, the paper yellowing and flaking away at the edges. "I thought everybody was transferring newspaper files to microfilm," Cordelia Whateley said.

From his darkened corner, Henry Armitage replied, "Many in Dunwich Town like things as they were."

Cordelia Whateley, examining the masthead of the bound newspaper, read aloud, "The Dunwich Daily Dispatch."

"Only called it a daily," Armitage commented. "You could never tell when there'd be an issue. The editor, Ephraim Clay, used to say it was a daily, came out once a day, just not every day. I think that was some kind of joke. Never understood Ephraim very well. A strange man. But look at those issues for 1928. You'll learn all you need to know."

Cordelia Whateley fumbled in her large purse and brought out a small tape recorder. She pressed a switch and began dictating segments from various 1928 issues of the *Dunwich Daily Dispatch*.

One of them, reprinted from a Boston newspaper, reported the death of Cordelia's distant cousin, Wilbur Whateley. The article bore no byline, but it described the youthful, dying giant in shuddersome detail. Cordelia's voice quavered and shook as she spoke, but she managed to continue to the end of the article.

Above the waist it was semi-anthropomorphic (the dispatch ran) *though its chest, where the dog's rending paws still rested watchfully, had the leathery, reticulated hide of a crocodile or alligator. The back was piebald with yellow and black, and dimly suggested the squamous covering of certain snakes. Below the waist, though, it was the worst; for here all human resemblance left off and sheer phantasy began. The skin was thickly covered with coarse black fur, and from the abdomen a score of long greenish-grey tentacles with red sucking mouths protruded limply. Their arrangement was odd, and seemed to follow the symmetries of some cosmic geometry unknown to earth or the solar system. On each of the hips, deep set in a kind of pinkish, ciliated orbit, was what seemed to be a rudimentary eye; whilst in lieu of a tail there depended a kind of trunk or feeler with purple annular markings, and with many evidences of being an undeveloped mouth or throat. The limbs, save for their black fur, roughly resembled the hind legs of prehistoric earth's giant saurians; and terminated in ridgy-veined pads that were neither hooves nor claws. When the thing breathed, its tail and tentacles rhythmically changed colour, as if from some circulatory cause normal to the non-human side of its ancestry. In the tentacles this was observable as a deepening of the greenish tinge, whilst in the tail it was manifest as a yellowish appearance which alternated with a sickly greyish-white in the spaces between the purple rings. Of genuine blood there was none; only the foetid greenish-yellow ichor which trickled along the painted floor beyond the radius of the stickiness, and left a curious discolouration behind it.*

* * *

Cordelia Whateley collapsed into the wooden reading-chair. She pressed her hands to her chest, trying to steady her breathing. After a while she managed to raise her face and peer into the darkened corner where Armitage sat, patiently waiting for her to speak.

Finally she managed to mumble, "It's impossible. Impossible. I know my Cousin Wilbur was -- not normal. Not like other men, even other Whateleys. But this -- how could such a being exist?"

Armitage did not respond directly. Instead, he asked, "Did you know that Wilbur was a twin?"

"No. My parents and grandparents would never speak of the Dunwich branch of the family. Only my great-grandfather, Cain Whateley, told me stories. I remember my parents were furious with him. I used to ask them about the Whateleys, but they would never tell me anything, and when I asked about things that Great-grandfather Cain told me, they said it was all nonsense. They said he'd seen too many horror movies when he was a boy, and read too many cheap magazines, that he was so old he couldn't distinguish what he'd read about or seen in the movies from what was real."

Armitage made a soft sound but spoke no words.

"Even Great-grandfather Cain never mentioned Wilbur's being a twin."

"But still he was," Armitage told her. "Read on."

Cordelia Whateley felt a painful thirst, the wine she had sipped at the inn had left a dry aftertaste in her mouth and throat. But recollection of the malodoriferous water Armitage had offered her earlier militated against her renewing the request. Instead, she continued leafing through old *Dunwich Daily Dispatches*, pausing frequently to dictate excerpts into her miniature tape recorder.

A gasp of horror and revulsion escaped her when she came to the description of another creature, but she read the words aloud from the yellowing page, first attributing them accurately to still another cousin, Curtis Whateley. The reporter, once more anonymous, seemingly had seen fit to record Curtis Whateley's degenerate Miskatonic Valley speech in its full phonetic peculiarity:

Bigger'n a barn...all made o' squirmin' ropes...hull thing sort o' shaped like a hen's egg bigger'n anything with dozens o' legs like hogsheads that haff shut up when they step...nothin' solid abaout it -- all like jelly, an' made o' sep'rit wrigglin' ropes pushed close together...great bulgin' eyes all over it... ten or twenty maouths or trunks a-stickin' aout all along the sides, big as *stove-pipes, an' all a-tossin' an' openin' an' shuttin'...all grey, with kinder blue or purple rings...**an' Gawd in Heaven --that haff face on top!***

And another quotation, from another news page, attributed to the same Curtis Whateley.

Oh, oh, my Gawd, that haff face -- that haff face on top of it...that face with the red eyes an' crinkly albino hair, an' no chin, like the Whateleys....It was a octopus, centipede, spider kind o' thing, but they was a haff-shaped man's face on top of it, and it looked like Wizard Whateley's, only it was yards and yards acrost....

* * *

Cordelia Whateley collapsed, sobbing.

"That was Wilbur's brother." Henry Armitage spoke in an ancient, papery voice. "He never had a name, or if he did, no one in all the Valley ever knew it. Save, perhaps, Wilbur, or his mother, Lavinia." Armitage's breath rasped. "Or mebbe his step-father, old Wizard Whateley."

Cordelia Whateley managed to raise her eyes. She ran her fingers through her hair. She had heard superstitious tales of men or women whose hair had turned white in a single night, from sheer terror. She wondered if that was happening to her. She wondered if she was going mad.

"What do you mean, step-father?" she croaked. "Wasn't Lavinia's husband the real father? Who was, then?"

"Not old Wizard Whateley, you can be sartin.'" Armitage was lapsing into the local argot.

"Who was the father?" Cordelia Whateley demanded.

Armitage uttered a frightening chuckle. He rose, an elongated, shadowy figure still obscured by darkness. To Cordelia Whateley he seemed unnaturally tall, perhaps as tall as her Cousin Wilbur's legendary stature. But maybe all was illusion, maybe all was the effect of the dim, flickering illumination of fireplace and oil-lamp.

"Wizard Whateley was not the father of the twins. Not any more than Joseph the Carpenter was the father of Jesus of Nazareth." He paused. "That is, ef you b'lieve that Christian balderdash, o' course. Ef you do, then the father was God, wa'nt he? An' Joseph merely the foster-father of the infant Jesus? Ef you believe that Christian balderdash, o' course."

"Well, I -- I've never thought about it very much, Professor."

"Wilbur Whateley and his giant brother, his daemon brother, were star-spawn, young miss. Their father was a bein' from the vaults of space, a member of a civilization old beyawnd human comprehension an' distant beawond human imagination. An' he come here to earth -- Gawd alone knows why -- an' he fathered two sons awn the blessed Lavinia Whateley. An' the good people o' Dunwich Town kilt 'em. Yes, the good people o' Dunwich

Town refused t' understand, refused t' care, refused t' give the slightest sympathy or assistance to them two innocent children of an alien father and an earthly mother. We kilt 'em. The Romans had nothin' on us. They kilt themselves one Son o' Gawd. We kilt us two. An' our punishment will be terrible, young miss. The stars are right, know it, young miss, the stars are right and our punishment will be terrible."

A low moan escaped Cordelia Whateley. She had come to Professor Armitage in hopes of learning the truth about her cursed relatives, and instead had been subjected to the ravings of this madman. "It's impossible," she managed, "an alien and a human could never interbreed. It's a biological impossibility."

"You think so?" Armitage challenged. He was growing calmer, and reverting from his Dunwich dialect into the cultured academic pronunciation he had used at first. "A mere few years ago it might have seemed impossible, but we are learning better. Most of the people of Dunwich know little of such things, and such things have been wisely kept from them. But a few of us -- those ones at the Project and I alone here at the Institute -- we keep abreast of modern science. And we know that genetic material from one creature can be implanted within the ovum of another, even a creature of another species. Did you know that DNA extracted from a laboratory mouse and injected into the cells of a common fruit fly has produced eyes on the legs of that fly? Eyes, young miss, eyes. Think of what you've just read."

"But -- but its horrid. It's blasphemous! How can you countenance such wickedness in the name of science?"

"Ah." Armitage seemed pleased. He advanced toward Cordelia Whateley and stood with his back to the fireplace. His dark suit now longer seemed threadbare, his white hair appeared to stand out from his scalp like a hydra's snakes. He seemed to tower nearly to the high, echoing ceiling. He seemed simultaneously as young as an infant and as old as the continents. "Ah," he repeated, "I suspect that you do believe in that religious nonsense. You use words like wickedness. Like blasphemy. Next you'll accuse us of sinning."

"Yes," she almost shouted. "Yes. It is sinful!"

She thought she caught the flash of firelight glinting off Henry Armitage's teeth as he grinned down at her. "He's coming, you know."

"Nobody is coming." She felt a growing desperation in the pit of her belly.

"But he is. He is. He's on his way now. You'll see."

Cordelia Whateley pushed herself to her feet. "I have to leave now." She scrambled toward the door, clutching her purse in one hand and her small tape recorder in the other. "Don't -- don't help me -- don't see me out -- I'll find my own way."

Armitage seemed to loom even taller. She couldn't understand how he managed to stay in the building without his head colliding with the rafters and beams overhead. But he did not pursue her. He merely stood with his back to the fireplace, hands balled in fists, resting on his hips.

And he laughed. He laughed, and he roared in a voice like the voice of a blaspheming godlet, "The father is coming. He's coming to Sentinel Hill, young miss. And he's mad. You know what the students like to say? The few students we have left in this demon-damned town? He's coming back, young miss, and he's mad as hell!"

Cordelia Whateley plunged through the door and stood panting on the portico of the Dunwich Institute.

Behind her, through the open door, the voice of Henry Armitage boomed out, "He'll come to Sentinel Hill. Trust me. See if you can get in. He's coming to Sentinel Hill."

Cordelia Whateley managed to fumble the keys to her conservative sedan from her oversized purse. She unlocked the automobile's door, plunged inside, started the engine after several tantalizing false attempts and switched on the lights and tore madly through deserted Dunwich streets, heading finally for the outskirts of town and the installation at Sentinel Hill.

The grounds of the Dunwich Research Project were illuminated as glaringly as if it had been noontime on a brilliant day. Vaguely military-looking vehicles crowded the roads inside the gates and were parked helter-skelter around the buildings. The rolling gate itself had been left wide open and utterly untended, and Cordelia had no trouble driving her car onto the grounds and finding an opening near a cluster of military vehicles. They were parked halfway up Sentinel Hill, and Cordelia had to swing her sedan around the end of a row and leave it pointing downhill.

The giant radar dishes atop Sentinel Hill swung slowly in unison as if following a single object that approached from far overhead, invisible to the naked eye. Great searchlights like props from a monochromatic motion picture about a long-concluded war sped beams of vivid white light into the black night sky.

Men and women in the distinctive garb of the Dunwich Research Project raced past Cordelia Whateley, ignoring her utterly in their concentration on their assigned tasks.

Now a tiny speck appeared fleetingly in a searchlight beam. A woman near Cordelia Whateley pointed at it and shouted, "He's coming, he's almost here!"

Cordelia Whateley watched until the black dot was picked up by another searchlight, and another. Near her a corpulent man in dark uniform fell to his knees on the oddly-colored New England grass. He held a book in his hands, and on its cover Cordelia Whateley recognized the illustration and the title as those she had seen in a locked bookcase at the Dunwich Institute.

Strangely, as the man knelt and opened the leather-bound volume, his costume seemed less to reflect a military origin than an ecclesiastical one. He began to read aloud, but in a language utterly unlike any that Cordelia Whateley had ever heard.

The speck in the sky was growing perceptibly larger. Cordelia Whateley had half-expected the Dunwich Research Project to be a branch of the American military establishment, most likely a refined version of the controversial Strategic Defense Initiative of former years. She half-expected to see missile-launchers rising from Sentinel Hill, and deadly rockets rising from them to destroy the thing that was growing larger with each passing moment.

But to her shock she realized that the open meadow beside Sentinel Hill was spread as a gigantic altar. It was covered with tapestries into which were woven depictions of blasphemous beings performing unspeakable acts upon writhing humans, their mouths open in silent screams of anguish and terror. And standing in the middle of the huge altar, naked, motionless, seemingly drugged, were men and women, boys and girls, clearly every missing person whose disappearance from the Miskatonic Valley and all of Dunwich Country for years past had gone unexplained.

And all around Cordelia Whateley dark-clad men and women were kneeling in adoration, singing and gesturing to that which drew closer and closer to them.

The thing was unbelievably huge. Cordelia Whateley revised her estimate of its size again and again, expecting it to land at any moment, but instead it grew, and it grew, filling the sky, blotting out the stars.

And in the illumination of the searchlights Cordelia Whateley could make out the shape of the thing. It was like a gargantuan jellyfish, literally miles in breadth. Thousands -- no, millions -- of tentacles dangled from its underside, writhing and squirming, stretching eagerly toward the hapless, naked victims who awaited them below.

The tentacles were greenish at their base, and white along their expanse, and deep crimson at their tips. And as they approached the altar those tips opened to reveal rows of glittering, triangular teeth that snapped and gnashed in anticipation of their coming feast.

And among the tentacles, on thicker, longer stalks, were large, round, rolling eyeballs that flashed and shifted from victim to victim, from altar to sycophant. And around the edges of the being rows upon rows of ciliated, translucent, gelatinous extensions rippled in repulsive rhythmic sequence.

Cordelia Whateley snapped to awareness as if awakening from a hypnotic trance. She raced across the meadow to her automobile and turned the key in the ignition. Nothing happened. But the car stood at the end of a row of vehicles halfway up Sentinel Hill, and she set the gear lever in neutral and released the parking brake, struggling with sheer will power to make the sedan roll downhill.

It did!

Just before the ground leveled out she shoved the gear lever into low, whispering a prayer. The engine caught and she sped through the open gate of the Dunwich Research Project. She kept the accelerator pressed to the floor, ignoring laws and obstacles equally, tears streaming down her cheeks and screams emerging from her mouth, until she reached the Aylesbury Pike.

Here she drew up and climbed from the car. She clambered onto its hood and from there onto its roof and turned her gaze back toward Dunwich. The distinctive shape of Sentinel Hill was silhouetted against distant clouds and stars.

The giant, jellyfish-thing was still settling. Cordelia Whateley realized now that even her greatest estimate of its size was grossly insufficient. It was larger than the altar, larger than Sentinel Hill, larger than the entire Dunwich Research Project compound.

It was easily as large as all of Dunwich Town.

And coming from it was a horrible, wet sound. A sucking, slithering, *hungry* sound. And from the ground beneath Dunwich, even as far away as the Aylesbury Pike, could be felt a terrible, trembling, rumbling.

It could only have been a matter of minutes, perhaps even seconds, until the great creature struck the earth. All of the equipment on Sentinel Hill must have shorted in that moment, and for all that Cordelia Whateley was ever able to determine, it was the immense electrical field created by that equipment that caused all the other problems with electrical devices in Dunwich.

There was flash brighter than the noonday sun, and a coruscation of pulsing colors, and a strange display of chromatics that Cordelia Whateley could only describe, in the days and years that followed, as *the very sky and earth screaming in terror and in pain.*

Then all was silence and all was darkness, and Cordelia Whateley knew nothing until she opened her eyes and looked into the face of a brawny individual wearing the garb of a Massachusetts State Trooper. He was shining a flashlight into her eyes, and when she blinked and moaned he said, "Are you all right, ma'am?"

She lifted a hand to her face and said, "Yes. Yes. I just -- I managed to escape from Dunwich Town."

The trooper frowned. "There's been a terrible disaster there, ma'am. Looks as if some kind of giant meteor crashed on Dunwich. Wiped out the town, the hull entire town." He shook his head. "Every man, woman and child. And there's some kind of horrid goop all over the place, and a stench like to make you throw up. Pardon me, ma'am. Sorry about that."

Cordelia Whateley struggled to stand up.

The trooper assisted her gently. "Can we take you somewhere, ma'am? Is there someone we should notify?"

"No." She shook her head. "I just want to leave. I just want to get back to Montreal and forget this -- this horror."

The trooper's face was visible in the reflected illumination cast by his flashlight. "Should a lady your age be driving a car?" he asked. "Do you still have a driver's license, ma'am? I mean, I know the laws are different there in Quebec. Your car has Quebec tags, ma'am. Are you from Quebec?"

She said, "Yes. Thank you. I'm perfectly all right. I just want to get home."

The trooper looked dubious, but finally he said, "All right, ma'am. If you're sure you'll be all right."

"I'm perfectly all right," she repeated, annoyed. The trooper released her and she climbed into her car. Her purse lay on the seat beside her and she found the cassette player and rewound the tape and hit *play*. From the player's speaker there emerged only a hissing and crackling, and the occasional hint of an indecipherable whisper.

Cordelia shut the player off. She tossed it into the back seat of her automobile. She switched on the engine. This time it started without hesitation. She reached up to adjust the rear-view mirror, but on an impulse turned it first toward herself. by the domelight of the sedan she studied her image. Her hair was white and her visage was the withered, wrinkled, desiccated face of a woman three times her age.

Keeping Festival

By Mollie L. Burleson

Snow crunched underfoot as Paul alighted from his car at the tiny mall. Marblehead on the twenty-first of December. The real Yuletide. He smiled. Wrapping his scarf tighter around his neck and pulling on his gloves, he headed towards the business area.

From the crest of the hill, the town spread out before him, and his artist's eye saw the beauty of the gabled houses that lay in various attitudes of disarray like a giant's toys scattered about. Lights were coming on in them one by one, giving an appearance of welcome to him. Somewhere off in the distance a dog barked and the wind blew flakes of snow about. The whole scene was reminiscent of the snow globe he had as a child. Beautiful.

As a mere lad Paul had read the stories of the writer H.P. Lovecraft and enjoyed them tremendously. But then he had grown up and had forgotten them in the world of trying to stay alive, trying to exist on the money his paintings brought. Not a rich life monetarily, but rich instead in the things that were real. He had forgotten those charming stories until the other day when in cleaning out his bookshelves he had come upon a few of those volumes and immersed himself for awhile in their otherworldness.

That was when he decided to come to Lovecraft's Kingsport by the sea - Marblehead - and find out for himself just what it was about the town that had captivated and influenced the writer so much. Where had he read that phrase - Only the poor and the lonely remembered? Well, he was poor enough, and lonely enough, and he *had* remembered.

The shops were still open and he entered a bookshop filled with ancient tomes and which served hot cider and gingerbread. The cakes were hot and fragrant, and the cider warmed his insides.

He walked the crooked streets, trying to see the town as Lovecraft had once seen it. It was little changed from the writer's description, especially now at night, when the small paned windows were unshuttered and open for all to view their lovely insides. Great Christmas trees stood in silent parlors, their lights blinking in the darkness; braided rugs lay at their feet, and presents abounded. A lone skier swished by. The setting was a more than one of horror. Still, Paul could imagine the spectral aspect of these seemingly untenanted homes, and the dark, narrow streets that led to even darker corners where anything could be waiting.

He climbed the hill to the cemetery then, looking over the town and the bay below. Ships in the harbor were strung with Christmas lights and rocked to and fro as the tide crept in. Now and then a ship's bell would ring; a lonely and forlorn sound, and even here high above the harbor, he imagined he could hear the waves splashing upon unseen pilings. He looked about him. The great old slate markers indeed looked more like the fingernails of some gigantic creature, clawing their way through the snow and out of their graves. He shivered involuntarily; that writer was quite a spellcaster.

He paused in his walk then, and listened. What was that sound? A great concrete slab grating against another? Surely it was a sound from the harbor, or a tree's limb rubbing against something. He shivered again.

As he cautioned his way down the steep path, he saw a dark shape before him. A man, similarly occupied, viewing the harbor on this night of nights. A tall man, almost completely covered from head to toe with overcoat, mufflers, and cap. Paul could barely see his face.

"Good evening," Paul announced.

"Yes, it is indeed a good evening," the man answered in a high voice and in beautifully enunciated English.

"There doesn't seem to be anyone else abroad tonight," Paul said. "You're the first soul I've seen."

The man said nothing, but fell into step beside Paul, who found it difficult to keep pace with him and his long-legged strides. He was so bundled that Paul could just barely see his eyes, which were dark and, in the streetlight's glow, sparkled as if with some secret amusement.

The man said, "I know this town well. I have trod these lanes many times, and each time I like them better; especially at night."

Paul nodded agreement, but said nothing, thinking that the man preferred a quiet companion.

"Would you care to go down to the harbor and watch the tide come in?" the man asked.

"I was about to do that very same thing myself, and I'm glad to have someone along for companionship. Somehow the water seems forbidding and strange to me now, and at this moment so does the town. The wind must have shifted."

The man made no comment, but continued down the shore. The water was indeed black and forbidding, and the tide hungrily lapped at the wooden pilings with a frightening sucking sound.

"According to some, this is the great Yuletide, the twenty-first of December. I've never really thought about it before, but I suppose it is. A celebration older than time."

The man nodded agreement and said, "Would you care to have me show you a special monument, a church on a hill?"

Paul heartily agreed, for he had grown accustomed to the stranger and his ways, so different from people one met today. A gentleman, he was; a real gentleman.

The man led the way down darkened and silent streets and up a slight incline to a church perched forthrightly atop it. Alongside was the usual New England churchyard with ancient slate stones marking the resting places of the forefathers of Marblehead's residents. A cold wind blew snow into their faces, and the man shuddered.

"I think it's getting colder," Paul said. "Colder and damper."

The man told Paul that he could not tolerate the cold for very long, that he preferred the summer's heat.

"But," Paul said, "there's something to be said about the cold, something primeval and humbling, and I feel that the Yuletide coming on a sultry August day would not be the same."

"Of course you're right; but nevertheless, I cannot tolerate the cold." As the man spoke, he wrapped his arms about himself as if for warmth.

"I wonder if others are observing Yuletide tonight, or are we the only ones?"

Some of the lights were beginning to wink out, and Paul saw that the hour was late. Then he heard, or thought he heard, voices far off. They seemed to be singing or chanting, and in the frosty air the sounds vibrated as surely as a bell would have when struck with its frozen clapper.

He turned to his companion to comment on the strange happenings, but found him gone. Where did he go? And how? Paul had not sensed his leaving. How very strange.

The voices were nearer now, and Paul left the church's steps and carefully went down the icy slope to the shelter of the houses across the street.

What he saw then amazed him, for hundreds of people, it seemed, came up the frozen walkway to the church. They were clad in long black robes and walked in a strange fashion. The first ones entered the church, followed by the next group and the next, and it appeared to Paul that the line of communicants would never cease. But finally, the last one entered the dark church and disappeared from view.

Paul's curiosity was aroused then, and he made his way back to the church and up the steps, trying to peer in at the locked door. All was silent and dark. And as he looked down at his feet, no footprints but his own appeared in the sparkling snow.

Was it all a mirage, a fancy brought on by his recent reading of the Lovecraft tales? And his strange companion, what of him?

Paul retraced his steps down the darkened streets, toward where he had parked his car, musing all the while. He could not justify the whole evening, the strange man, the masses of people near the church, the eeriness of the tide, and he did not wish to. It was the Yuletide after all, and he, too, had kept Festival.

FRANK THE CNIDARIAN

By Benjamin Adams

Frank Bruce had heard a lot of hooey in his time, but what Doug Davis was spouting took the grand prize.

"They's been a 'splosion at the school!" Doug babbled excitedly. "They says a monster did it!"

The other men in the Yellow King Bar & Grill nodded sagely at this news. Frank glanced at each of them in turn, incredulous. Why anyone would listen to Doug Davis in the first place was beyond Frank's comprehension. Everyone knew ol' Doug barely had enough smarts to tie his shoes in the morning, let alone wipe his perennially runny nose.

So Frank decided to stir the waters a bit, wake these Arkham townies up. "Monsters!" he exclaimed, halfway between a bark and a laugh.

Doug Davis turned his affably gooney face toward Frank. "Yessir -- they say it was darn near ten feet tall, it was!"

"Was it now?" Frank drained the rest of his Jenkin's Brown, adding it to the collection he'd already built up over the course of the evening, since he'd got off work at the hardware store at 5 PM.

Next to him, grizzled old Bob Watkins shook his bald, sunburnt head. "Yer still kinda new around here, Frank, so I kin understand yer a bit skeptical. But strange things happen in this town, 'specially around Miskatonic. May well be a monster over there, fer all we know. Why, I've seen some mighty queer things 'round these parts, ayup. Way back in '28, I think it was -- I weren't but a child, ye understand --"

Frank Bruce tuned the old man's babbling out. Sure, Frank had only been living in Arkham a couple of years, but hell, that ought to be enough so they'd quit trying to impress him with all of their tall tales about monsters and mermen and mysterious voices whispering in the woods. That stuff got old real fast.

At first he'd listened politely to such talk, figuring it was a good idea, getting used to the standard folklore and legends of the Arkham area. Soon, though, he realized that these people were only concocting an elaborate ruse designed to fool and embarrass newcomers like himself.

Dammit, it was all Liz's fault. She'd insisted on moving back here after they were married, since her mother had died and her father -- Moloch Waite -- was barely two steps from the grave. She said she'd never be able to forgive herself -- and by extension, Frank, though she cleverly left it unsaid -- if her father died and she wasn't by his side.

Frank liked thinking of himself as a progressive husband, so he'd put his promising career at Ben Franklin on hold, taking a job as assistant manager at Whately Hardware on Church Street. In Boston he'd have had his own Ben Franklin store by now.

Some of his old girlfriends had complained that Frank was too self-centered, but how could that be true when he was here in this lousy burg, just for Liz's sake? Hell, he was a saint. Stuck here in Arkham, slowly rotting by degrees while the best years of his life passed by, and his father-in-law, old Moloch Waite, didn't even have the goddamn good graces to shuffle off this mortal coil, why wouldn't he just come on and --

"-- die already!"

Frank gradually became aware that Bob Watkins had ceased his story, and no one else in the bar was talking.

Matter of fact, they were all staring at Frank. Doug Davis' face seemed even more slack-jawed than usual. He looked downright shocked.

Frank's face blanched, then quickly colored beet-red as he realized he'd spoken his last thought aloud.

He reached in his pocket and fished out a twenty-dollar bill, laying it next to the garden of Jenkin's Brown bottles.

Making his way past the gauntlet of Arkham townies, Frank kept his gaze straight ahead. He didn't even turn his head when Doug Davis said, in a voice so solemn it passed the verge of ludicrousness, "They's is *so* monsters, Mr. Bruce. They's *is*."

* * *

Liz wasn't home yet. Of course. She'd still be over at her old man's ancient, decrepit house, helping him through his evening routine, getting him into bed. There was something vaguely unhealthy and obscene about that, Frank thought. He wondered if Moloch Waite got off on having his daughter touch him, bathe him. Probably. The old man had a knowing twinkle in his fish-like eyes when he deigned to glance at Frank; a look of shared knowledge and male comradeship. Frank knew the look -- he'd exchanged it with his buddies in high school and college: guys who'd managed to fuck the same girl. The look was the non-physical form of a salacious wink, an elbow jabbed in the ribs. And getting the look from Moloch Waite, with his weird, lewdly bulging eyes, was enough to turn Frank's stomach.

He hated the old bastard. That son-of-a-bitch.

Were there any Jenkin's Browns left in the fridge? One good thing about Arkham; Jenkin's was a helluva good local brew. Supposedly every bottle was inspected by the brewer, the eccentric Marc Ranee.

Huh. Just one left. Frank popped it open and settled down heavily on the overstuffed couch. God, it was ugly. Red plaid -- not his choice.

He picked up the remote and zapped on the television.

A moment later, he found himself spitting his first mouthful of Jenkin's Brown across the room.

Goddamn! That drippy-nosed Doug Davis was right -- there *had* been an explosion on the Miskatonic campus. WAGL-TV, the local ABC affiliate, was all over it like flies on sherbet.

The explosion had apparently ripped a chunk out of Armitage Hall, the University's foreign language wing. Feared dead were two faculty members and a reporter for the Arkham *Herald-Tribune*. A couple of female students, so hysterical they were almost incoherent, claimed they'd seen someone -- or some*thing* -- gigantic and misshapen at the scene immediately following the explosion. "It screamed, like it was rilly, rilly angry about something, y'know?" claimed one of the co-eds. "And then it disappeared. It just, like, vanished."

This Goddamn town, Frank thought. They're all friggin' nuts. Doug Davis, Bob Watkins, those co-eds, Liz and her old man -- every last one of 'em oughtta be locked up.

He tilted the bottle back and drained it.

No backbone was the problem, he decided. He didn't have a Goddamn backbone anymore. It disappeared when he married Liz. Frank the jellyfish. No, he thought, remembering his one failed semester of Marine Biology -- Frank the cnidarian. Cnidarian. Yeah.

"Screw this," he blurted aloud. "Fuck it! I want out. There's a Goddamn Ben Franklin with my name on it in Boston. I need it, I deserve it, an' I want it."

The words sounded good, he thought. In fact, he'd say those exact words to Liz when she got home from . . . whatever she was doing with her old man.

He pictured himself proudly wearing the red-and-white Ben Franklin colors. And the little wood plaque with his picture laminated on it, a sparkling brass plate underneath announcing that *Ben Franklin Store #581 is managed by Frank Bruce. Please don't hesitate to ask Store Manager Frank Bruce for assistance. He's here to help you, the consumer, any way he can.* . . .

The clicking of the front door lock pierced his daydream. He stood, ready for a confrontation with Liz right here, this moment. Yeah, this was the time.

"Frank?"

She swept into the room, her slim, dark form reminding him briefly why he'd married her in the first place. But a glimpse of her hazel eyes -- looking bigger and bigger every day, almost a parody of her father's grotesquely bulging orbs -- made him resolute. He had to say it now.

"Liz," he said, "we gotta talk."

His words made no evident impression on her. She moved toward him and took his hands. "Oh, Frank, I'm so glad you're here!"

This was not going the way he'd hoped. "What?" he asked lamely. He sensed the moment vanishing, receding away like a train pulling out from a station. Heading to a new destination.

"You've got to come with me. Father is dying . . . and he wants to talk with you."

* * *

On the way, they passed the Miskatonic campus. There were still emergency vehicles parked out front, while a tired-looking policeman waved onlookers past. Frank remembered Doug Davis' excited babbling. *Monsters*. Yeah, right.

While Liz drove, Frank's head lolled alternately between the headrest and passenger window of their Saturn. He felt queasy. What could old Moloch Waite, on his deathbed, possibly have to say to Frank?

He wondered idly if it had anything to do with the old man's will. Liz was his sole remaining relative; everything would go to her upon Moloch's demise.

And that meant the Waite house, too.

Frank shuddered at the thought. He loathed that house with a passion.

Liz had told him how the house predated the Revolutionary War, and was indeed one of the oldest homes in the Arkham area. The Waites were among the first settlers in this section of Massachusetts; at one point they'd also been among the richest, with controlling interests in much of the sea trade coming in through nearby Innsmouth.

Something had happened to the Innsmouth Waites, though -- something Liz didn't want brought up. Frank thought the hint of ancient scandal wasn't worth pressing, and left her alone.

Now Moloch Waite was the last male descendant of that once-proud line, and he rotted away his last days in the ancestral house with its decrepit gambrel roof. The whole place stank of rot. Moloch's peculiar fishy odor didn't help. The place never failed in giving Frank the creeps.

"Things will be different," Liz suddenly offered.

Frank started at the sound of her voice, his eyes popping open. He'd been on the verge of falling asleep. Maybe that last Jenkin's Brown had been one too many. "Yeah? Different how?"

"You just . . . won't have to worry about anything, not anymore."

He turned toward her, trying to make out her expression in the car's gloom. He could barely even see the silhouette of her face, let alone gauge her emotions.

"It means more than you'll ever know that you came out here with me," she continued.

"Yeah, well. . . ."

"I just want you to know -- when father's gone, things *will* be different."

Ferchrissake, that was what she said in the first place. Bemused, Frank turned his gaze out his window. They were on Jefferson Road now, nearing the old Waite place. In this still-rural section of Arkham, streetlights obviously weren't a priority. The only illumination came from the Saturn's headlights, and the weirdly distorted gibbous moon hanging a few degrees above the horizon.

Watch that signpost up ahead, Frank thought. You are now entering . . . the Ugly Zone. What had ever possessed people to settle here? Probably the same urge that had gripped the first settlers in, say, Chicago. Or Newark, New Jersey. A bizarre, lemming-like drive to be miserable.

Well, he'd take Boston over all of them. Boating on the Charles. Frisbee on the Common. Ben Franklin stores *everywhere*. And now that old Moloch Waite was about to kick the bucket, Frank could finally take Liz back to Boston. That had to be what she'd meant by things being different.

They could sell the Waite house and make a killing. All of Moloch's crap -- the weird sculptures that looked like cuttlefish-headed gorillas, the stained-glass windows that looked like scenes from *Godzilla vs. the Smog Monster*, the brass-and-gold contraption with the big blue diamond at its center -- not to mention the thousands and thousands of books lining every possible wall in the place -- all of it would go.

Frank wondered what kind of condominium he and Liz could get facing the Charles. And to think that barely twenty minutes earlier, he'd been ready to scrap everything. The things he'd thought about Liz and her father -- must have been the Jenkin's Brown.

He grinned lopsidedly. Man, this thing could turn out better than he'd ever imagined.

Liz drove the Saturn through a pair of immense stone pillars, the wrought-iron gate that once barred the entrance between them now collapsed in rusty heaps on either side. And ahead, leprous in the car's high beams, the ancestral Waite home squatted like a toad at the end of Jefferson Road.

* * *

If ever a man matched the house in which he lived, Moloch Waite was that man.

Shriveled beneath his heavy bedclothes, Moloch Waite peered intently at his daughter and her husband, baring his tiny, sharp teeth in a filmy yellow smile. Those enormous bloodshot eyes looked almost ready to pop out of his head. His hair, sparse to begin with, had completely receded, leaving only minuscule tufts behind his almost vestigial ears. The fishy stench in the room was almost unbearable. It seemed to emanate from Moloch Waite's skin, which looked greenish and dry, almost scaly in places. It reminded Frank of a case of athlete's foot he'd once had.

"Ahhhh," Moloch wheezed. His needle-like teeth clattered together as he spoke. "I'm . . . gratified you . . . could come, Frank. My time here . . . is almost done . . . and you and I have . . . much of which to speak."

Frank nodded blearily. All those Jenkin's Browns were really catching up with him now. "Yeah, okay, Moloch. Can I sit down? I'm kinda tired. It's been a long time."

"But of course . . . you may," the old man whispered. He beckoned weakly toward a chair near the headboard of the elaborate four-poster in which he lay. "Please . . . sit."

Frank staggered toward the chair and collapsed in it.

By the door, Liz cleared her throat. "I'll wait downstairs, Father . . . Frank."

Moloch smiled again. "Thank you . . . my dearest."

She curtsied and left, closing the door behind her. Frank blinked. He'd never seen her curtsey before. It seemed so strange and old-fashioned -- like so much else in Moloch Waite's home.

"You're probably . . . wondering why I . . . asked you here," the old man said in his rasping voice.

"Well, yeah, the thought had crossed my mind."

Moloch stopped smiling. "Is it too much to ask . . . that you be . . . somewhat civil to me . . . while you are in my home?"

Frank wondered in what way he hadn't been civil. Maybe his tone of voice? Hell, he was having a hard enough time keeping his eyes open, let alone track of whether or not he was being *civil*, ferchrissake.

Just to be on the safe side, he said he was sorry.

Moloch's great eyes blinked slowly. "Very well. Frank, I must be . . . honest with you. When Elizabeth first . . . announced her intentions . . . of marrying you, I opposed the . . . idea of the union."

Big surprise, thought Frank. He couldn't fathom why the old man was telling him this. Trying to get a few good licks in before he died, maybe.

"You did not seem the . . . ideal mate . . . for my only child. But she has . . . convinced me . . . that perhaps you . . . and I . . . share some things in common."

And then Moloch Waite gave Frank that *look*. The same look that said volumes about the quality of the father / daughter relationship in the Waite home. Frank couldn't believe it. His head throbbed thickly with anger. If this old sonofabitch didn't die on his own in the next few minutes, Frank decided he'd help Moloch along.

The look vanished, and Moloch began speaking again, his voice seemingly gaining strength with each word.

"You see, Frank . . . the Waites are an . . . old family. Older than you might think. And it is very important that our bloodline not die out. Elizabeth knows her part in this. She is to help bring the new brood into the world, and help pave the way for the Great Old Ones to return. *Ïa! Ïa-R'lyeh! Cthulhu fhtagn! Hai ep fl'hur*!"

This was absolute insanity, Frank decided. He'd had enough of Moloch Waite and his daughter, this rotting old house, and the entire town of Arkham. He'd never have to hear garbage like this back home in Boston, behind the counter of his very own Ben Franklin.

But when he tried opening his mouth to tell Moloch Waite to shove his Great Old Ones up his scaly old ass, something funny happened. Frank couldn't move a muscle. Couldn't twitch an inch.

He tried wriggling around.

Nothing.

He attempted a scream for help.

Nothing.

This really sucked, he thought.

Moloch grinned again. "Now, where were we? Ah, yes. The history of our family. It was my uncle, Ephraim Waite, who learned how to keep the lifeglow flickering, and pass it on from body to body. For years I have pored over all his manuscripts and secret books of forbidden lore, learning his secrets. I have perused the fabulous *Necronomicon* in Latin *and* in Greek, studied the dreaded G'harne fragments, peered into the Catacombs of Kish.

"Now that I myself am nearly dead, I know how to send my lifeglow onward -- and I will place it in *your* body. And your body will impregnate my lovely daughter, but with the seeds of my mind.

"The Waite family will continue! And we shall return home to lovely, brooding, wondrous Y'ha-nthlei to live forever!"

Yeah, right, thought Frank. Here he was, having a stroke or seizure or something, and all the old bastard can do is ramble on about screwing his daughter. Frank wished his head wasn't so fuzzy. Damn that Jenkin's Brown, anyway -- after tonight, he swore silently, he'd never touch the stuff again.

Moloch Waite grinned that terrible yellow grin and began moving toward Frank, throwing the bedclothes off his withered form. The fishy scent suddenly grew stronger.

Oh, no, Frank thought as Moloch's face neared his, Moloch's sharp-toothed mouth opening wider and wider. Oh, no -- not that --

-- Don't let the old guy *kiss* me --

And then Moloch's head snapped back.

"You are . . . *drunk*," he hissed, horrified. His bulging eyes filled with seeping mustard-colored tears. "It will not work . . . if you . . . are *drunk*! I used all my . . . energy to freeze you . . . in place -- and now . . . and now . . . I cannot --"

Moloch Waite fell backwards onto the bed. "Ïa! Ïa! I am coming . . . oh Great Old Ones. . . ."

* * *

Liz's bulging eyes widened even further at the sight staggering down the stairs. "Father!" she exclaimed, moving toward him.

"I think he's dead," Frank said.

Liz stopped in her tracks. "Dead?" she whispered.

"Well, yeah, that's what I said." Frank scratched his head. "Things sure got weird up there. I think he was trying to reach out to me in some way at the end. By the way, he kinda told me about you and him -- uh -- *you know* --"

"*FATHERRRR*!" wailed Liz. She pushed past Frank and ran up the stairs. In a moment her anguished cries filled the halls of the old house, echoing through the Waite house like the screams of a banshee.

Frank Bruce shrugged and walked out the front door. Good riddance to 'em both, he thought. In a couple of days he'd have the divorce papers delivered to Liz. Give her that long to calm down over old Moloch's kicking the bucket. There was no way he'd stick around with her after this, though. Her old man had seriously fucked her over, and Frank knew he wasn't the one to try to set things right.

He patted his pocket. Good, he had his own set of keys to the Saturn. He could be in Boston by dawn. Within the month, he knew, he'd have his own Ben Franklin hardware store.

"So long, Arkham!" he called cheerily.

But first, he wondered if he might still be able to find Doug Davis hanging out at the Yellow King Bar & Grill.

That snot-nosed schmuck didn't know what he was talking about, and

Frank was looking forward to filling him in straight.

There weren't any monsters.

Only people, or something.

For John Layman and Brian McNaughton

Tuttle

By James Robert Smith

James Gardner and Lee Tuttle scandalized their families in 1968. Upon graduating from Miskatonic University, rather than enter into their fathers' respective businesses, they retreated to the hills beyond Arkham to form a commune. Their relatives, all blue-blooded and successful merchants from the earliest days of the colonies turned their backs on those two. Communications between respective families and the black sheep ceased to flow.

Initially, there had been Gardner, Tuttle and his family of three, and four other young men and their companions (some of them female). Tuttle had apparently made the decision of locating the commune. Most of the others, upon arriving, had immediately begun to voice concerns over Tuttle's choice. The place sat at the feet of the big hills that lead up to the high peaks. In fact, the White Mountains were easily seen from several vantage points, and while this made for pretty photographs, it meant that the soil was poor, at best, and the weather would be especially harsh when winter came around.

The others, after a few weeks, began to voice their concerns. Tuttle, a large man who had been captain of the Miskatonic basketball team, was in no mood for debate. When his friend, Gardner, failed to join in voting to move the commune to a more hospitable location ("out west" seemed to be the group's favored place), the commune collapsed and the others fled. Tuttle, angry, refused to see them off, but Gardner met them all as their little caravan loaded up and prepared to pull out.

* * *

"I really hate to see you guys leave, Jeff. We really could have made a go of it here. And this part of the country needs people like us." Gardner still had his hands planted on the door of the VW bus, leaning in a bit, his face almost on the plane of the window.

"We just don't think it's gonna fly here, Jim. I know you're real loyal to Tuttle and all that, but you ought to try to talk him into coming on out west with us. You know you guys would be welcome."

"I can't leave Tuttle and Susan like that. I gave him my word when we planned this thing."

Jeff sighed, a warm breeze tainted with marijuana. "Yeah, I know. But you really ought to push him on it. This place just really has some bad vibes, you know? Christ. Barbara and Tom had that really bad trip. Tom really hurt himself banging around in that barn. And even I was having nightmares until we decided to leave." He sighed again.

"Well, Jim, you've heard it all from us. I don't need to flog a dead horse, do I?"

James stepped away from the van as the motor revved. He smiled and waved goodbye. Well, now it was just the three of them, plus one infant.

"Peace, man." He flashed the sign and watched them go.

* * *

Gardner and Tuttle met at the rambling farmhouse that had served as the center of the commune. They sat with paper and pencil and decided after much debate and budgeting that they could hold fast to the lease and hope to attract replacements for those who had fled. They would work hard, prove the commune, and soon there would be others. Gardner knew that this would be difficult, at best, since Tuttle had proved so hard in his resolve to keep the commune at his chosen location. Word passed quickly in the Movement, and it wasn't likely that others would come to replace those who had left. Still, James Gardner was nothing if not loyal and optimistic. They were young. Worlds could be conquered.

Tuttle moved out of the smaller house which he had unselfishly chosen, and into the building that had been the commune's nerve center. That house had five bedrooms, so Gardner joined Tuttle and his family there, shutting up the place he had shared with another Miskatonic graduate, and took a bedroom in the downstairs of the larger house. They were all there: Gardner, Tuttle, Susan (Tuttle's wife) and their infant son, William. The other three houses they locked down tight and shuttered up. "Maybe we'll need them by summer's end," Tuttle had said.

It was the beginning of April. Gardner and Tuttle did their research and decided what crops would best be grown so that they might at least partially sustain themselves over the coming year. Initially, they had thought to utilise the big barn and make rustic furniture--several of the fled members had been quite adept at such handiwork. Now, though, they were left to count the money in their accounts and hope they could grow enough and sell enough to see them through.

They consulted their almanac, and had seen that the best time to break ground was early on April 20. The morning air was crisp, fog hanging in the low places and hiding the earth there. They chose a low rise that grew up from the scrubby pastureland that had been left to grow for several years--ever since the last tenants had vacated the place. They looked around, and then they began to work.

* * *

"This ground is like iron," Gardner said as he looked back. He was sitting astride their single tractor, a decrepit John Deere that still putted along although they knew it was at least thirty years old. Occasionally it spit out an acrid puff or two of dark smoke from its pitted muffler.

"Yes," Tuttle admitted. "I don't think it's been turned in a decade. He kicked at a lump of the white, hard clods. "You wouldn't think clay would be so hard, would you?"

"Well. You know they make plates from it. Draw out the water and fire it up good and its pretty hard. No different just because it's in a field." Gardner wiped the sweat from his face as he looked down at his old chum.

"Those discs have hardly made a dent. Look. You've made three passes over this plot and you've yet to turn the grass under. Damn." Tuttle straightened and drew off his shirt, revealing his hard, chiseled body. He still had his athlete's build after nearly a year of no collegiate sports.

"Well, all I can do is keep making passes with the tractor. Eventually it'll loosen up enough so that we can think about mixing in the manure." Gardner nodded toward the pair of dark mounds a local farmer had dumped for them: eight foot cones of dairy cow makings. The stench mixed with the gas fumes to form a singular odor.

Tuttle strolled to what remained of a rocky fence, built of the tons of stone former tenants had dug out of the field. There was a testament to hard work if there was any. He tossed his shirt on it, saw a field mouse scuttle into a crevice, and he hefted a maddock. His long legs took him quickly back to the field.

"What are you going to do with that," Gardner asked.

"You just keep on with the tractor. I'll see what I can do with this," he indicated the metal blade of the maddock with a nod.

As Gardner took the tractor round and round, Tuttle fought with the clay and did his best to break it up. From time to time, his friend would twist about in his bouncing perch and look back to see Tuttle, all muscle and sweat, hacking away at the ground; determination set his strong profile.

* * *

After a week of constant, backbreaking toil, the field was still not ready to plant. By then, the choice time of seeding the peas had passed and they were worried about missing double harvests. The plot was still full of great, white clods that stubbornly refused to be pulverized. Tuttle and Gardner both had taken to the field with hoes and maddocks to try to break them. Slowly, the plot was taking shape. But they knew their plans to see a pair of harvests would probably be missed.

They spent an eighth day there. From the rise above the field, at the band of pines that hid the big farmhouse from them, it appeared as if they were struggling with the Earth itself, as if they were astride some gigantic serpent, hacking away with their tiny blades. Of course, only Tuttle looked like Thor.

After six hours of this, they retreated to the farmhouse, leaving their tools leaning against the wall built up of the many rocks plucked out of that awful field. The imagery of that long, low wall was not lost on the pair. They staggered back, Gardner bringing up the rear.

"You two look awful," Susan told them. She rarely hid her intentions and was as tactlessly blunt as she was pretty. Her auburn hair was pulled back and tied in a tail so that she looked a bit more severe than either man was accustomed to seeing her. But, she had iced lemonade, in a tray held out for them. Her breasts, large and full of milk seemed on display upon the tray, straining against her white blouse. Behind her little William hustled along, crawling from the open door and onto the porch.

By the time Gardner shuffled to the stoop and sat, Tuttle was on his second glass. His tiny son had stood, using his father's hard shoulder for support, and he was gumming away on a trapezius muscle.

As Gardner took his glass, he looked down at the tray, seeing what else Susan had gotten for them.

"Acid," Gardner muttered.

"I picked it up in Arkham. I got it when I drove over to the university this morning," Susan told him.

"It's not from that batch that freaked out Barbara and Tom, is it?" James looked at it with suspicion, although he picked up the tab that was his.

"Well, yeah. I got it from that guy, that chem major at Miskatonic. Funny guy. Weird funny. He seems real curious we're out here, but he doesn't want to join us. Aside from making acid you'd think he was a Republican. I guess he's just making extra money while he works on his thesis."

"Any replies to our flyers?" Tuttle was referring to the notices they had posted at the college. They were hoping to attract recent grads to try the commune, or to lure disillusioned students tired of chasing an unwanted Masters degree.

"No. No one wants to join us here. We are a long ways out, you know."

"But that's what a commune is all about." He set his glass on the porch and lifted a tab of the acid on the tip of his forefinger. "You guys want to drop?"

Gardner was staring off, through the trees, thinking of, if not seeing, that unyeilding field of clay. "Might as well." He sighed. "The day's not good for much else."

Susan nabbed hers and she lay it atop her pink tongue.

The baby gnawed away at his father's shoulder.

The world soon dissolved.

* * *

Tuttle stood at the edge of the field and pointed toward the hills looming up, their flanks clothed in dark green that was nearly black in its lush growth. Evergreen needles writhed like snakes, but he wasn't smiling.

"Jim, you're the geology major." He breathed and could see colors like a rainbow. It must have been his essence. He still did not smile. "What did you say about this rise we plowed our field on?"

Tuttle's voice boomed and echoed twice and Gardner did not reply until he'd heard the question an unvoiced second time. "You see," he said, "when the great ice sheets retreated at the end of the Ice Age, isolated glaciers still remained here and there all around New England. Whererver there was a mountain high enough to calve one." His own voice made little white bubbles in the air that floated away. He watched them one by one, each a syllable.

"Now, those two big hills there: the locals call them Big Head and Little Head. Their sides are so steep because they were carved out by a localized glacier that had its origins way up there on those bare peaks we call Mount Gaunt and Whatley's Peak." Jim's finger blurred across his field of vision as he moved it. He could feel the rocky top of Mount Gaunt on his fingertip. "Well, that glacier led down and down and gnawed its way through what used to be a long ridge but is now Big and Little Heads. And its terminus was right about here some 8,000 years ago. It spit out clay vomit and little doo doo balls of gravel and rocks and what we are carving a field out of is really a terminal moraine."

Tuttle laughed and both men were surprised to see the noise take wing and spin off into the green sky. Black scales. Not feathers. "Lucky for us some poor bastards already pulled all of that rock and gravel out for us."

"Yeah," Gardner hissed. "Lucky for us."

* * *

That night, Gardner came quickly awake. Little William was crying, not in pain, but it seemed in fright. Susan, too, was calling out. She was at the back door that opened on the small mudroom that led out to the back yard. She was yelling, "Tuttle", over and over. *Bad trip*, thought Gardner.

A little groggy, James stood up and pulled on a pair of jeans. He threw on the dirty flannel shirt he'd been wearing before he'd showered and he was aware of his own body odor he'd left behind on it. He noted for the first time what his personal scent must be. Without pulling on his shoes he went through his already opened bedroom door and passed through the kitchen to the where Susan stood and called. Little William was at her legs and in the moonlight Gardner could see her bare breasts and he wondered why she didn't stick one in the baby's mouth to make it shut up. Even with his heart pounding with some slight fear he noted how attractive her naked body was and an erection stirred.

"What is it," he asked her, trying to make himself heard above the baby.

Susan flinched and then turned, facing him. She seemed not to care that she was completely naked. He'd never seen her naked. "Tuttle went out of the house. I think he's having a bad trip." She turned her eyes back to the night.

"Are you still tripping?" Gardner bent and lifted up William and handed him to Susan. She took him and damned if he didn't latch fast to her right nipple.

"No," she said. "I came down couple hours ago. But Tuttle didn't. He kept seeing things and hearing things and about an hour ago he got...agitated."

"What do you mean?" James began to button his shirt. It was cold. Gooseflesh stood out on him and on Susan's flesh. The baby seemed as soft as ever.

"He said he knew something now. He said..."

"He said what?"

"He said 'I can grow it. I know how.'"

"Damn." Gardner went to the mudroom and pushed the door completely open and stepped out into the night air. It was even colder there. His breath fumed out before him as he called Tuttle's name. Susan said something about *the barn like Tom when he had that bad trip*, but Gardner was already going that way. He sucked in a breath of surprise as cold, wet dew met his bare feet.

Tuttle wasn't in the barn. He'd been there, because James could see Tuttle's big footprints everywhere. It looked like he'd been rummaging in one of the old horse stalls that had been so full of junk they'd decided to just leave them that way. All of the junk in one of them was now scattered about the barn as if everything there had been little squeak toys and Tuttle had been a big puppy. Some of that stuff was really heavy. He recalled that Tom had hurt himself trying to move some of it.

Gardner went back into the yard and listened. The baby was quiet now. Susan couldn't see James and had stopped calling for Tuttle. He listened.

Tuttle was in the field. His whoops and yells were all but masked through the swatch of trees. Gardner trotted that way, wishing he'd put on his shoes, but glad at least for the pants and shirt.

When he got to the field, Tuttle was a black mark dancing upon all that pale clay. He had something large and pendulous in his corded arms, and he was reaching at it and flinging his right arm and reaching at it and flinging his right arm. Over and over. His movements seemed almost like dance. Gardner was about to step onto the field.

When.

Tuttle turned in his direction. Even in the moonlight Gardner could see madness like a rictus grin on Tuttle's face. There was a slick sheen of drool all down his chin and on his big, bellowing chest. "Grah! Grah," he said. And other sounds that might have been words through a mouth mashed in by stone clubs but that certainly should not have been uttered from Tuttle's jaws.

Gardner flinched back and that seemed to make Tuttle happy; happy enough so that he went back to his dance, his face now smiling crazily. And James could see now that Tuttle had a big burlap or canvas bag in his left arm and he was reaching into it with his right hand and flinging some small *somethings* round and about the field. "Raaaaahhh! Raaaaaa 'n' rahhh gunt," said Tuttle.

Gardner's foot touched the edge of the field and he could see hundreds, thousands of little black spots all over the white clay. In the moonlight, it almost looked as if the spots were tiny beetles, aphids, maybe, and they were jittering atop the clay, as if in some obscene ecstasy over contact with the earth. He was thinking that maybe he was tripping again when he looked up, saw a blur of Tuttle's amazing physique.

And he never saw the forearm smash that sent him off to a painful oblivion of dreamland.

* * *

"orry about"

"What?" Gardner was lying in the tall grass. He was flat on his back and he was looking up at the dawn sky and his face hurt, the left side of it, anyway.

"I said I was sorry about running into you last night." It was Tuttle, and he was lying there on his back, too. "I was still tripping, I guess and I ran at you when you came out here. I didn't mean to hit you. I think my elbow got you. Real sorry about that."

James turned his head and he could see Tuttle lying there naked in the grass with him. Tuttle he had seen naked many times. Even in a grassy field once. He sat up and felt the side of his head. It was tender and he made a sound something like *ouch*.

"I'm really sorry, man." Tuttle stood and began to walk toward the farmhouse. "Come on," he said. "Let's go get some breakfast."

When Gardner got up, Tuttle was already vanished through the trees. He stood and went to the edge of the field, trying to recall what he had seen. Looking down, there was only clay. No little bugs, no little black dots. There was a canvas bag at the edge of the field, but when he looked in it there was nothing there. "What the Hell," he muttered, and then he walked stiffly back to the house.

* * *

"The peas are coming up." Gardner was surprised. "I didn't think the field was really ready, but they came up really nice. Thick, too. We may even have to trim some of them back. Don't want them crowding one another out, you know."

Tuttle sat at the table with a mouthful of oats tacked together with honey. It took him a moment to make an intelligible sound. "No. We don't have to trim them back. Let them go wild. We won't have to weed them and we won't have to fertilize them and we damned sure won't put any bug spray on them. They'll do fine." He attacked another mouthful of Susan's patented cereal. Baby William said, "Dah!" And he punctuated it by smacking his little palm on the table.

"Well, you're right about the bugs. I haven't seen one aphid or anything else on our peas. And the squash and melons are starting to vine out. But there are some weeds in the middle of the field. I should probably..."

Tuttle pointed and swallowed hard to get the food quickly out of the way. "You leave the field alone. Don't mess with it." His stare was not as friendly as Gardner might have hoped.

James just nodded and worried about Tuttle doing all that acid. Gardner had stopped dropping it, but he and Susan did a tab almost every few days now. It was getting out of hand. Susan just sat and stared half the time and had stopped reading. The only time she showed any interest in anything was when she drove over to Miskatonic to buy some more acid, occasionally some pot, although only James seemed to be smoking *that* lately.

"Sure, Tut. No problem."

At night, he always listened as Tuttle left the house. If he raised his window, he could even hear his chants drifting in from the field.

* * *

The peas bore early, very early. Tuttle came back to the house with a sackful of them, the narrow, greenish pods jutting toward his madly grinning face. "Look," he yelled. "Look! They are beautiful, aren't they?" He halted, barefoot, at the table and dumped the bag amidst the breakfast dishes.

Garnder stood and picked one up. He had to fight off the sensation that the pod had moved under his fingertips. Peas didn't writhe. "Well, the color is a little strange. But they look plump. They *can't* be ready to harvest, though. It's too early. Way too early."

"But they are. They are!" Tuttle grabbed a handful and jammed them in his mouth and chewed until yellowgreen saliva oozed through his lips. He grinned and then swallowed. "Ha, haaaaaaaaaa."

"Eat some, *Gardner*." His big right mitt was full of pea pods.

"No thanks. I like to cook my vegetables. And you really should wash those, you know."

"Screw that," Tuttle said. "I don't have to wash *these*. These *want* me to eat them just the way they are. You eat some. You'll see."

He watched a listless Susan drop a few in a dish where she cut them with a fork and began to chew. A thick fluid oozed out of the vegetables where she had broken them. She giggled a little and swallowed. At least she was eating *something*, thought Gardner. She had lost about fifteen pounds, he figured, which was a lot for a woman as fit as Susan had been. She really didn't have fifteen pounds to spare. Her face was growing gaunt and her eyes were looking sunken. If she let herself go much more, she was going to look starved: Buchenwald starved.

"Come *on*," she pleaded. "You won't drop acid with us. You won't eat our peas."

"Maybe for supper."

"You aren't good for *much*, are you?" Susan wasn't smiling.

Gardner got up from the table and left the room. Little William crawled silently around the kitchen, poking here and there among chair legs and corners. James had been Tuttle's closest friend for better than ten years, but loyalty could only go so far. And what kind of friend was he if he let Tuttle destroy his health? If things didn't get any better, he was going to go into Arkham and phone up Tuttle's folks and get them out there. He hated to do it, but it might be his only option. He would give them a few more days. If things didn't look any better, he would make the call when it was his turn to take the garbage out to the dump station. It was only another twenty minutes past there into Arkham. He could always say he'd gotten a weakness for a burger or something.

* * *

The next day, Gardner was in the woods above the barn, where the slopes of Big Head come down to the farm. He was marking some dead trees for felling so that they would have enough firewood for the winter. It was dark in there, but he was enjoying being away from Tuttle and Susan. And little William, too. It had occurred to James that all that acid she was dropping could very well be affecting her milk, and William certainly enjoyed latching onto his mother's ample bosom. He was marking a big, but very dead blue spruce with a yellow chalk "X" when he heard Susan's screaming. There was pain evident in her voice. He dropped the chalk and raced downhill, gravity and fear lending speed to his feet.

By the time James broke the cover of the woods and the farmhouse came into his line of sight, he could see Susan as she staggered onto the side porch and collapsed. He ran even faster, leaping over the ditch that carried runoff away from the barn. In a breathless moment he was by her side, lifting her up in his arms, his chest heaving with the exertion and with fear.

As he pulled her up he realized that his hands were bloody. For a second, he thought that her head was split, but then he saw that it was just her nose. Still a steady stream of bright red blood flowed out of both nostrils. Her left eye was blackened and already beginning to swell shut.

"Tut-Tut-Tuttle," she said between sobs.

The bastard.

"Are you going to be okay, Susan? How hard did he hit you? Do you think you might have a concussion?" He had to get a hold on himself. That wasn't how you concluded such things. James held his breath for a moment, then put his hand on Susan's nose. *It wasn't broken*, he decided. But it sure was bleeding. "Can you stand up?"

"Yes. I think so."

Going into the kitchen, they left a crimson trail of droplets throughout the house. Once there, James put Susan in a chair and made a compress of wet towels. He put the towels against her nose and on her eye and sat beside her.

"How old are you, Susan? How many fingers am I holding up?" And so on until he had decided that she did not have a concussion. As they both began to calm down, he thought about William.

"Where is your son," he asked.

"Right here with me," said Tuttle. His voice was thick, as if he were drunk. James turned and looked. He choked.

"What's wrong, little boy? Cat got your tongue?"

Tuttle was covered in boils. He had some kind of skin growths virtually all over his body. They were everywhere James could see, for Tuttle was standing there completely nude. There were even small nodules all over his genitalia.

"He was like that when we woke up this morning," Susan tried to whisper. "And he started to hit me when I said I'd go for help."

"SHUT UP, YOU!" Tuttle advanced, and for the first time James noticed that Willaim was cradled in his father's left arm. The boy looked perfectly fine, except for the way the baby was staring, with some kind of clinical observance at Susan and James. James wondered if babies could suffer shock.

Gardner stood up.

"Tuttle. Um. Can I have William, please? Can I hold William?"

Tuttle turned his attention to his old friend. His face, the vague outlines of his Nordic good looks all but vanished, was awash with fleshy spheres. "You don't have to talk to me like I'm some kind of idiot, *Gardner*. I'm not sick, you know."

"You sure look sick to me, Tut."

"I'm not sick. I'm just becoming like the Goat."

James edged forward an inch or two. "Goat? What goat, Tuttle? What are you talking about?"

"The Goat with a thousand young."

At that, Susan screamed.

"That's me, for sure." Tuttle began to laugh. "You shouldn't have stopped dropping acid with us, Gardner. Then you'd know what I'm talking about. Then you'd know."

"Well, you can tell me all about it, Tut. But can I hold William, first?"

"Yeah. Sure. Take him." He handed the child over to James.

And then Tuttle, moving so quickly that James had no time to react, smashed Gardner flat-handed on the side of the head so hard that he went straight to the floor, with barely enough control to hold William away from him to protect the baby. He landed solidly on the hardwood planking. He actually blacked out for a second, then came quickly to, pushing William away from him.

Susan was screaming again, and probably bleeding, too, but James had no time to check on her. He went to one knee, then as fast as he could he gripped the legs of the straight-backed chair in which he had been sitting and he hefted it with him as he stood. With Tuttle watching, seeing what was happening, yet doing nothing to stop it, Gardner drew back on his unweildy club and he brought it down on Tuttle's head.

The chair broke apart on impact, the force of the meeting shimmying down Gardner's wrists and into his arms. It hurt. Tuttle laughed.

"Can't you do any better than that, boy?" He slapped Gardner again, this time spinning the smaller man completely around.

James did not rise then, but began to crab toward the mudroom which he made without being attacked again. Once there, Gardner did stand and look back, but Tuttle was not there. He looked in the corner, and saw the length of metal pipe that he'd brought from the barn to replace a leaky section. It was solid, about four feet long. Hefting it up, he opened the door to the back yard and went out. Tuttle was already there, hiding by the mudroom and he grabbed James by the collar and threw him a carlength down the yard. James rolled with the impact and did not lose his grip on the pipe.

When he heard Tuttle coming for him, he went to his knees again, and then took the pipe and brought it up with both hands behind it. The end of the pipe made contact with Tuttle's big chin and Tuttle did go down, all six and one half feet of him. He was out.

"Oh, God," James said. He staggered back and went into the house. "Susan. We've got to take the truck and go into town while Tuttle's out. Come on. Get William and we'll go. Susan?"

Susan, holding the towel to her face with one hand, was ahead of him. She had her big purse and was throwing it over her shoulder. "Get the keys," she said. They kept them on a hook in the kitchen: three sets.

"They're gone," Gardner said, both of them staring at the bare brass hooks. Tuttle had obviously taken them.

"Ask...ask him where they are," Susan said.

Gardner went to the window and looked out in the yard. Tuttle, like the keys, was gone. Gardner doubted that he'd really been knocked unconscious. The length of pipe was still in the yard, about four inches of it showed from the lawn where Tuttle had jammed it barehanded.

* * *

They'd decided to stay the night. It had been too late to walk into town before night caught them, and he didn't know if Susan could do so after such a beating. He certainly couldn't have left her alone there.

It was getting dark and Gardner had arranged lamps so that they shone into the yard around the house, enabling them to see out so that they could see if Tuttle was coming. They'd need that when it got dark.

"Susan?" He looked at her, at the livid bruise on her face. Her nose hadn't really been injured much. It had just bled a lot. Her eye, though, was swollen shut.

"Yes?"

"What was he talking about? About the Goat with a thousand young?"

"We've been praying to it, James."

"*Praying* to it? What are you talking about? What is it?"

"I can't explain it to you."

"Why not? Why not try?"

"Because you stopped dropping the acid. You can only hear it when you drop the acid. It talked back to us."

"When, Susan? When did it talk back to you?"

"Well. It talked when we chanted in the field at night. And you can hear it if you eat of the field." She stared at him through her one eye. "You don't eat of the field, either. You weren't going to join us, were you?"

He grabbed her by the shoulders and shook her. "Stop it, dammit! You're scaring me. Don't go spacey on me. I'm the one who's *protecting* you. Tuttle is the one who's out there. He's the one who busted your face."

"Yeah. Yes. Tuttle's the one." She sighed, going silent. Nearby, baby William sat and moved only a little. In a moment, Susan was snoring, sitting up in the easy chair he'd brought into the kitchen.

Now he'd have to stay up and watch on his own. The moon came up. His body ached from the thrashing Tuttle had given him. He watched the moon arcing in the sky until it reached the top of the window sash and vanished.

He woke up.

"Damn," he cursed himself. "Susan? SUSAN!"

"I'm right here," she said.

He looked. The lights had been switched off but he didn't want to argue with her about it. The moon was still up, though, and it offered more than enough light to illuminate the yard. They'd see Tuttle if he came toward the house.

Gardner stood and and went to where Susan was standing. She had her blouse off and was holding William in her arms, breast feeding him. Even by moonlight, James could see that she was covered in those boils. "Susan." He groaned.

"It doesn't hurt," she told him. William made sucking sounds.

"Susan. Let me have William, please." He made to take the child and she gave him up. As he pulled the boy off of her nipple, he could see that her breast was black, wet. If there had been enough light he knew that it would be red. "Susan?"

"Oh. That." She giggled. "It's little William. He's begun to bite. Teething, you know." James tore his eyes from the sight of Susan's ruined nipple. He looked down at the baby in his arms. Those eyes were not the eyes of a baby. There was something cold in them as they calculated James and sized him up. It grinned, pulling wide babyflesh to reveal a mouth full of white points. Before he could drop William, the child had gripped his arm and bitten down. Gardner screamed and tore the thing from him.

Backing away, he watched to make sure that neither made a move to follow him. "Don't. Don't come toward me," he warned them. There was a shuffling noise near the door to the den and he could see that Tuttle had been there all along, ever since he'd awakened. "No," he croaked.

"Don't worry yourself, James. We're not going to hurt you." Tuttle's voice was thick, deep, like a record played too slow. "We're becoming like the Goat, we told you. You can stay and watch if you want to. If you want to."

Frozen in place, Gardner could only do just so, watch as Tuttle spread his arms wide. Those boils were huge now, impossibly huge and gravid, rolling in his flesh. One by one, they began to open, each one spewing those dots of black onto the floor. Dots that might have been beetles, might have been aphids, but weren't. Dark little things that came down onto the floor and began to jitter, as if in obscene ecstasy. "A thousand young," Tuttle slurped just before his face exploded in a cloud of black motes.

Screaming. Sreaming and running. Those were what he thought of. He paid no mind to the night. He did not acknowledge the thick, inhuman chanting that came up from the field beyond the house. James did not see that a weird, cold light shone from the field and illuminated the farm like electric fire. Gardner just ran, screaming, his legs taking him up slopes and down hills and through branches that slapped at him but which he did not feel. His throat went raw and his legs turned dead and wooden.

* * *

And when he woke up he did not recognize the face that peered down at him. Coke bottle lenses. Black hair. Large eyes and soft chin. Pale skin. Very pale. But the smile was real.

"Whoa, Gardner. Settle down, my friend. I wouldn't try to sit up just now."

James looked around. He was lying in the grass by the side of the drive that led up from the farm to the gravel county road. At least they were away from the farm.

"Who are you," he managed through a laryngitic throat.

"Well. I guess I'm what you might call *your connection*. I was providing you folk with the acid."

James tensed, but knew he was too weak to do anything.

"Just be at ease," said the strange face as it began to melt. "I jammed a few down you while you were sleeping. In fact, you ought to be feeling the effects about...anytime now I'd say. Just relax and"

Gardner could hear the Goat, now.

It spoke to him. It wanted him to deliver up a thousand young. He would sit in the wood like the Goat and he could do it. *You can DO it, Gardner*, it told him. And more than that, James wanted to. He *wanted* to do it. He *wanted* to be host to a thousand young.

* * *

In the house, the man with the strange face lay on the floor and sang to the thousands of new ones. They heard him and came out from where they hid, marching to him, knowing others were arriving soon.

On the floor of the den, little William sat amidst what remained of his parents, and he gave up as host...

The Horror at Columbia Terrace

By C.J. Henderson

"Well, pal," sighed the balding man, staring into the mirror on the back of his office door, "this is another fine mess you've gotten us into."

Paul Morcey's reflection did not answer. Turning away in frustration he brushed his near foot-long pony-tail back off his shoulder and then crossed the room, heading for his desk. Sitting in his chair, he threaded his fingers behind his head, then tipped his chair's front legs up off the ground. It was his favorite position for thinking. And, at that moment, he had a lot to think about.

With his two partners, Lisa Hutchingson and Theodore London, he ran the London Agency, an investigations firm that had attracted more than its proper share of unusual cases. In their time they had done combat with all manner of horrors--flying monsters, mass murderers who lived forever, interdimensional travellers--even Satan itself. The agency did not advertise its unusual "specialty," did not encourage that type of business. As it was, a number of their people had already died in the handling of the few of those cases which had come their way so far.

Thinking about the job he had just accepted, the balding man found himself wishing his partners were not out of town, that he was not alone in the office--the only person on staff who believed in things most others only encountered in books and films. Paul Morcey believed in the supernatural. Together with London, he had wrestled with it, filled it with lead, battered it with axes--stared it in the eye and smelled it up close. At London's side he was willing to brave anything--even the gates of Hell itself.

But, he thought, that's just it. The boss ain't here, now. Just you, wise guy. Just little ... fat ... you.

A woman had come to him with a hysterical plea. Find her son. He had disappeared--one of eight children from the neighborhood to do so in a month. He tried to tell her the police were her best bet--that she would be wasting her money hiring a private agency. He had explained that the police had far greater resources--more manpower, more equipment--more of everything.

The woman had not cared. She had shown Morcey a picture of her boy, a healthy, strapping youth, Nordic in his coloring. Almost unable to let the picture pass from her fingers, in a voice desperate to keep from cracking, she had said,

"My Steve. He's a good boy. I know how easily that comes from most parent's lips, but he really is. He didn't run away. He's not mixed up in drugs. He's not. Someth--one has taken him. I know. I can feel it in ... at night ... there are ..."

Stumbling over every other word, the frantic woman stopped herself before she could say anymore. The abrupt silence caught Morcey's ear. There was a dread attached to it, a fear that if she said what she wanted she would not sound rational to even herself, let alone to him. Most men would have been happy to let the moment go, to reaffirm that they could do nothing for the grieving mother and send her on her way.

But, Paul Morcey was not most men.

He had been a private detective for little over a year. Before he had been sucked into a nightmare that almost swallowed the entire world, he had been a janitor. He survived his first supernatural encounter by accident. Before he had known what he was doing, he had killed a monster--destroyed a man transformed into a winged reptile through its devotion to a nearly all-powerful being from another dimension. After that, he learned quickly to watch for clues and signs of what was really happening ... to watch for--as one of their group had put it--the things that are not there.

At that moment, Paul Morcey knew there was something more to what he was being told. Wishing he did not have to, he asked,

"Mrs. Peters, what were you gonna say?"

When she did not answer, he asked again. When she tried to put him off, he told her he could not take a case where he was not given complete cooperation. That had done it. Waving the meatless bone of hope before her, he had forced her to go the full distance--to tell him what she had not dared mention to either her husband or the police.

"Oh, please," she tried once more to divert his attention. Then, staring into his eyes--seeing who he was--she knew she had no choice. Breaking eye contact, unable to face Morcey with her suspicions, she rambled for nearly ten minutes, feeding him bits and scraps she hoped he could arrange into something coherent. It was a wild, disturbing tale, and half way through it the ex-maintenance man understood the courage she had needed to tell it. Once she had finished, he asked,

"Mrs. Peters, let me see ... you think, because of music you've been hearin', just sorta everywhere ... and dreams you've been havin', and just the way your home, ah, *feels* ... that Steve might've been kidnapped by, not someone, but some *thing*? Somethin' that ain't human?"

"I'm sorry," she said at once, her voice catching sadly--filled with embarrassed regret. "I shouldn't have ..."

"No, no ..." he said, his mind whirling. As he let time stretch out between them, his mind argued back and forth,

Don't. Who do you think you are? Someone that can handle something like this? You're no London. You're just his flunky--

This woman needs help. Help she's not gonna get from the cops ...

From you either, fat boy. This is one of two things--nothing, or something way out of your league. Best stick to tracking insurance frauds--

Help she can only get from us ...

Better yet, better go back to emptying trash cans--

Only from us ...

Cleaning toilets--

And then, his anger snapped. Without betraying his inner conflict to Mrs. Peters, he snarled at the negative voice within his head.

I don't clean toilets no more. I clean house. I cut up monsters with fire axes--remember? If I'm a janitor, I'm fuckin' Conan the Janitor.

Morcey raised his head a notch to look into the eyes of the woman across the desk from him. Taking in her despair, he told himself,

Besides, it don't matter what kind of job this is. The world's fulla evil. There's all kinds'a beasts everywhere, and every one of them is human as I am. The ex-maintenance man took a deep breath, adding,

Things don't have to show up on the Sci Fi channel before we can call them monsters.

And then, finding his voice, the detective took Mrs. Peter's phone number and address. Having never heard of Columbia Terrace, he jotted down directions to her Brooklyn home. After that he took the picture of her son, found out where he went to school--everything his mother could tell him. Finally, he quoted her a price, accepted her check, and told her to go home, assuring her he would arrive there later.

That had been an hour earlier. For sixty minutes he had sat leaning back with his hands behind his head, his chair balanced on two legs. Finally, he shifted his weight, allowing the other two legs to find the floor. Then he stood, made sure his wallet had a sufficient supply of business cards, and headed for the door. Stopping long enough to stare into the mirror again, he muttered,

"A great, big, fine mess."

And then, his reflection scowling at him, he headed for the hallway, wondering if he really was as stupid as he felt.

* * *

Columbia Terrace proved to be a small neighborhood. It was a rebuilt community bordering the much older Red Hook area--a horrid maze of squalid, rotting buildings along the waterfront opposite Governor's Island. Morcey cruised the gentrified collection of refurbished townhouses and low-rent, government subsidized condominiums, trying to get a feel for the vicinity. He noted the sharp differences in the pair of neighborhoods--two worlds at war--one shining and new with lanes of planted trees and lawns, the other a desolate rat heap of dirty highways and even dirtier buildings, each more dilapidated than the next.

At a sort of halfway point between the two, he was forced to reduce his speed to a crawl. The reason soon came into view--a huge excavation site, one that appeared to take up roughly the dimensions of four, even five, of the surrounding buildings. His curiosity aroused, he parked by a nearby hydrant where he could keep an eye on his car, then sought out the project's foreman.

The idea that had seized him was one that went back to his childhood. Construction sites had been the scene of a number of injures amongst his schoolmates--even one death. With such a large dig so close to the area where eight children had already disappeared, he found it impossible to not ask if the builders had experienced any trouble with youthful trespassers. He was surprised at the foreman's answer.

"Tell you the truth, we had to get security. Normally, we wouldn't bother, you know? Just erect a cyclone barrier, put a dog inside at night. Usually all you need. Not here."

"Why?" asked Morcey. "What's so different here?"

"I wish I could tell you. We don't leave anything behind at night to steal. We're not building anything, we're just digging a hole. But for a while--at first, before the Suydam's ..."

"Who?"

"The owners. Before they brought in the guards--there were footprints every morning. Everywhere. All around the hole--inside it--crazy."

Wondering at what he was being told, he asked what size the footprints were--if they might be children's--and if it were possible any children could have been hurt, perhaps buried in some kind of accident. He knew the foreman would be defensive and explained his reasons for asking as thoroughly as he could, implying he wanted to prove to his client he was tracking all possible leads, no matter how outlandish. After a few more minutes of putting the man at ease, he got him talking again.

"Guess I can't blame you for asking. Cops were by with the same questions. All over the site--twice. Think they were down from Butler Street--if they found anything, you might be able to ask them. They didn't seem to think anything was wrong, though."

Watching the foreman's eyes, Morcey wondered at a slight catch in the man's voice as he had spoken his last sentence. The detective knew the man was hinting at something further he wanted to say--a subconscious desire to speak about some note made by the back of his mind, but one that needed to be prodded forward. Prompting him with several conspiratorial remarks, the balding man finally got the construction boss to admit,

"Know it sounds crazy, but a couple of times ... I mean, I work in dirt and mud ... all day--have for twelve years--I know how it moves, how it lies ... know what it's telling me ..."

"Yeah?" asked Morcey, goading the man on.

"Now, I don't want to sound like a nutcase or nothing, but," the foreman made a long pause, then finally admitted, "I'd swear a few times I found tracks only leading up out of the hole."

The detective asked the construction boss if he could possibly remember the dates he had found the impossible tracks. The foreman apologized, admitting the task was beyond him. Morcey thanked him for his time and made to leave, then turned back at the last second, asking,

"Sorry--just one thing. Do you remember how *many* times you found footprints only comin' out?" The foreman counted in his head for a moment, then answered with assurance,

"Eight."

At that point, the balding man returned to his car. He wondered at what the foreman had told him, at whether or not it really was a coincidence he stopped at the construction site. He had been driving around the neighborhood for the sole purpose of getting its "feel," to see if anything about it stood out to him.

"Well, what'daya think?" he muttered as he started his car's engine, "Is there any connection or isn't there?"

His partner, London, was a far more seasoned detective with many more years in the business. He had cautioned the more excitable Morcey early on to take care not to see things just because he wanted to see them. And yet, if London had opened himself to the ether and just driven around the neighborhood, finally pulling up to the same spot, they would have been certain the looming dark hole was connected to the disappearance of Steven Peters.

"Yeah, well," said Morcey aloud, working his car out of his illegal parking space, "he's pulled off a lot more of this hoodoo stuff than me. He's earned the right, I guess."

The words *and you haven't* chuckled through the balding man's brain, making him curse. What exactly he was cursing, he did not bother to make clear.

* * *

As he drove on through the area, Morcey wondered which of the two neighborhoods would affect the other in the future--would Columbia Terrace shame Red Hook into cleaning itself up, or would the latter ooze out over the former and drag it down into hopeless ruin. He still had not formed an opinion by the time he arrived at Steven Peters' school. Parking his car, wrapping its length of bolted chain around the steering wheel and locking it, he left off wondering about the future and went inside what appeared to be the main building, hoping to find some clues about the present.

Unfortunately, the school was of no help. Its officials flatly refused to cooperate in any fashion, even when he offered to prove he was working for Mrs. Peters. The administration's answer to all questions was that the police had instructed them to not give any information to anyone--no matter what. Morcey took the hint and found his way back to the front door.

On the way however, he noticed something that gave him a moment's pause. Having left his Manhattan offices close to eleven, he had arrived at the Brooklyn school during lunch hour. Junior high-aged youngsters were everywhere, huddled in small groups throughout the halls, in doorways--anywhere, the balding man figured, except where they should be.

Only one of the groups attracted his attention, however. Just as he was nearing the front entrance, a blear-eyed procession of nine young men came toward him, playing eerily on cheap musical instruments. What was bothering him he could not say at first. True, it was unusual in an electronic age to see boys making music by blowing wooden pipes and banging carved sticks one against the other, but that was not what he had noticed.

As the line drew closer to him, he gave his full attention over to them. And then, when they were near enough for his conscious mind to hear the words their leader was chanting, he realized what had caught his attention.

"Friend and companion of the night," the pock-faced boy started again. "You who rejoices in the baying of dogs and the spilling of blood. Who wanders in the midst of shadows and graves." Each word was intoned coldly, flatly. Part of Morcey's brain dismissed the entire parade as just another childish fad. Another part, however, riveted him to the sight, focusing all of his powers of observation on the disturbing line.

"Who longs for blood," the leader called lifelessly. "Brings terror to mortals. Gorgo, Mormo, thousand-faced moon, look favorably on our sacrifices."

And then, the chant started over again--the same words--same dull litany. The line passed Morcey, heading into the school. None of the boys seemed to notice the balding man staring at them. None of them varied their tone, lost their beat, or missed a step. As they went by, however, Morcey noticed that the last boy was neither chanting nor playing. He had a thick stack of cheaply printed cards in his hand, one of which he passed out to each student he passed.

From what the detective could see they were black on one side with a white-lettered paragraph overlaid, the other side adorned by only a large black circle with a white background. Something stronger than curiosity prompting him, the balding man stuck out his hand. The boy almost put one of the black squares into his grasp, then held it back at the last second, saying,

"Too old."

After which, the procession disappeared into the school. Morcey stood for a long moment, staring at the door. Finally, he turned back toward the street, pausing only long enough to bend down and retrieve one of the squares which someone had discarded. Looking it over, he mumbled,

"So's your mother."

Then he stuck the card into his jacket pocket and headed off, only the back of his mind vaguely aware of the eighteen hate-filled eyes drilling into his back as he walked away.

* * *

"So, Mrs. Peters," asked Morcey, "what part of the house feels so bad?"

"You tell me." The balding man stared at the woman, the hostility in her voice throwing him for a moment. Before he could say anything, however, she said, "I'm tired of sounding crazy … feeling crazy." Stepping closer to the detective, she said,

"I haven't told anyone else what I've told you. I don't know why I went to your agency, Mr. Morcey. I don't know why I told you things I didn't tell my own husband. Maybe you're just humoring me."

"Mrs. Peters … all I want to …"

"No!" The woman's voice was shrill and taut. She was near the breaking point, lost and alone in a world she was beginning to fear was one of her own making--a feeling the detective understood all to well. With a pitiful desperation clawing at her words, she told Morcey,

"I want you … I need you to, to go through my house, on your own. I want you to discover what I'm talking about without me being there." When the balding man just stared, she begged, "Please. If you find the spot I'm talking about … without me being there … that would prove … don't you see …"

Morcey stepped closer to the distraught woman, one hand raised in a silencing gesture. He knew what she meant--knew how she felt. He had been there himself and could not refuse her. Asking her to take a seat in the living room, he moved off into her home … searching for her torment.

The Peters' home was nothing special. A railroad flat in a brownstone on a street filled with railroad flat brownstones. As the detective moved from room to room, he tried to open himself to the dread feeling that had invaded his client. Passing from one area to another, he emptied his mind as best he could, trying to put aside any preconceived notions that might distract him from whatever subtle current Mrs. Peters had tapped into.

He found nothing--anywhere. Bathroom, bedrooms, kitchen, dining room, hallway and living room--nothing. Walking back toward his client, he wondered at what the problem might be. He had become convinced the woman was not crazy. Although he could not feel the disturbance she had described, did not know her boy well enough to have her mother's faith in him, still ... he *knew* something was amiss. And then, as he reentered the living room, ready to admit his lack of discovery, suddenly he thought,

Wait a minute. She's the only one feeling this, this ... whateveritis ... *she*. Mom. You might have opened yourself up to whatever's here--but you did it as a guy.

Looking into Mrs. Peters' eyes, the balding man told her,

"Ah, I think I'm goin' to need a few more minutes, ma'am. If that's all right ...?"

The woman nodded her head sharply several times, her lips tight, eyes frightened. Giving her a calming look, the detective took the picture of her son from his jacket pocket and then stared into it. Letting his eyes lock into Steven's, he dug his way down through the paper, trying to reach the boy beneath.

Flooding his mind with concern, letting his imagination run wild with fear, he stripped away his own identity, searching for a connection to the face in the picture. His eyes closing, he expanded outward into his own mind, searching the dark ether for a trace of Steven Peters.

I know you're here somewhere, he whispered. *I'm worried about you. We're all worried about you.*

Images of the black hole in the ground rushed through his brain. So did flashes of Mrs. Peters, her eyes, her worry, her gnawing, acid terror.

Come on, Steve--we're looking for you--we need you--

Morcey felt sweat beading on his brow, could feel his lungs constricting, could feel Mrs. Peters' fears seeping into him, filling him with the crushing anxiety she had carried within her heart since her son had vanished. The shaking force of the cold pain building within the detective cried out to the woman, lifting her from the couch. Before she knew what she was doing, the woman had crossed the room to where Morcey was standing.

Steve--where are you? What happened to you? Why can't we find you? Come back to us.

Her hand shaking, fingers trembling, unable to speak she reached out, her terrified spirit forcing her to fold her hand over Morcey's, over the tightly-clasped picture of her son.

Steve--you have to come back.

No--came a sibilant hissing--*he is gone--he is ours.*

Mrs. Peters screamed, her hand releasing its hold of the detective's as if it had been burned. Morcey's eyes snapped open, his fingers dropping the photograph at the same time. Spinning around, he scanned the room, almost expecting to find the owner of the voice they had heard there in the room with them. And then, he understood.

Suddenly there was a chilled itch eating at his spine--a dull noise in the background of his head, thin, screeching, like the sound of squealing car brakes off in the distance. It was a disquieting sound--akin to the noise of determine insects digging away at the back of his brain--and, now that he had noticed it, he could not shake it away. Turning to Mrs. Peters, he said,

"What you've been feeling ... it's the whole place ... it's everywhere. Isn't it?"

The woman gave out a mournful cry and then collapsed into the balding man's arms. He held her, whispering quiet assurances, finally admitting to himself what he had known from the first moment she had walked through his door--that horror was walking the land again. That it was stealing children, and not with one of its typical face-behind-a-mask, sweetly seductive lures, but openly, defiantly--challenging the world to find it and engage it once more.

But, he thought, the world ain't stepped up to bat. I'm the only one here.

A sinister laughter flooded Morcey's brain. It was a mocking, piteous sound, and for the life of him, the detective could not tell if it were part of the numbing evil whisper he had stumbled across in the Peters home, or just his own cynical side chuckling over his now, seemingly inevitable destruction.

* * *

"My boy," the lanky, bearded man said, rubbing his hands together, "It is always such a pleasure."

The speaker was Doctor Zachary Goward, head of Columbia University's philosophy department, one of the world's leading theologians and occult researchers. Morcey had barely finished relating the saga of Mrs. Peters when the professor had jumped up and headed for his bookshelf. Picking up the black card he had taken from Steven's school, the balding man looked at the white words printed on its black side. When he had first read them, he had thought them merely a string of gibberish words--

* HEL * HOLOYM * SOTHER * EMMANVEL * SABAOTH *

* AGLA * TETRAGRAMMATON * AGYROS * OTHEOS *
* ISCHYROS * ATHANATOS * IEHOVA * VA * ADONAI *
* SADAY * HOMOVSION * MESSIAS * ESCHEREHEYE *

But Goward had known better, recognizing the evocation immediately. As he searched his shelves, Morcey asked,

"Lookin' for somethin' that'll tell ya what this means?"

"Oh, heavens, no, my boy. That all is easily translated. For instance, Agla is a Cabalistic term formed from the initial letters of the Hewbrew--*Aieth Gadol Leolam Adonai*--God will be great forever. Tetragrammaton, that's another one from the Cabalists--supposedly the most effective word in their magical performances. Now, Athanatos ... that ..."

"Doc," interrupted the balding man, "I don't need a play by play. Can you just tell me what the whole thing's about?"

"Certainly," the professor threw over his shoulder, still busily searching through his thoroughly disorganized library. "It's a sort of Hebraised Hellenistic Greek. Someone's put together a fairly terrible demon-call there. They've hit a suggestion of Alexandrian decadence, the likes of which ..."

"Doc, save the lecture and just tell me, if you're not tryin' to look up those words ... what are ya lookin' for?"

"This," answered Goward in triumph. Turning back to his guest, he held up a thin, well worn, leather-bound binder. When Morcey inquired as to what it was, the doctor answered, "This is a manuscript found on the Yucatan coast. It was penned by a Lieutenant-Commander, ah," Goward opened the binder carefully, then read, "Karl Heinrich, Graf von Altberg-Ehrenstein. German navy--he was in charge of one of their U-boats back at the end of World War I."

"What's he got to do with this?"

"Hummm?" The distracted professor looked up from his slow thumbing through the yellowing manuscript's fragile pages, then added, "Oh, nothing."

The balding man closed his eyes in frustration. Goward was a distracted man who lived much more in his own private reality than the one he shared with the rest of humanity. Choking back his temper, Morcey asked,

"Well then, Doc, what're you doin'?" Dragging out each word, the professor answered,

"Looking ... for ... ah, here it is." Closing the binder, Goward set it aside on top of one of several wildly teetering pile of papers and books his secretary had yet to refile. What the professor had located was a sheaf of papers covered in notes made in his own hand. Turning back toward Morcey, he said,

"I purchased Herr Heinrich's manuscript at an estate sale, oh, twelve years ago. The estate of Robert Suydam." As the balding man's interest perked up, the professor added, "Yes--the Brooklyn Suydams." As Morcey warmed to his tale, Goward continued, half-reading from his notes, half-talking from recollection.

"I bought a number of books there ... figurines, some other bric-a-brac, et cetera ... lot of good information on Persian devil worship and the like, but the main reason I went was the story behind the sale. You see, about 1925, Robert Suydam, of Flatbush, married Miss Cornelia Gerritsen of Bayside. On their honeymoon voyage, however, Suydam and his wife were murdered by what the ship's company could only describe as a 'thing.'"

"A 'thing,' huh?"

"Oh, yes. The only crewman who got a good look at it went mad. The ship's doctor didn't see it, but did claim to see the word 'Lilith' glowing on the wall in red letters."

"'Lilith?'" asked Morcey. "Like in Adam's first wife--the one that got bored and went off with Satan?"

"Yes, you are Jewish, aren't you, Paul?"

"What'daya mean?"

"It's usually only people of Hebrew extraction that seem to know that slant on the legend. Generally Lilith is thought of as the daughter of the devil, or more commonly, merely a female demon who dwells in deserted places and assaults children." As Morcey's eyes reacted to the last bit of news, Goward added,

"Yes--starts to fit together, doesn't it?" Morcey nodded. Skimming over his notes, the professor continued, saying,

"Suydam's will left everything to his wife--hers, everything to him. In case of mutual death, everything was left to her sister. The sister never allowed anyone to look into the affair, kept all Suydam's possessions private--rumor is she destroyed a great deal of his books. When she died, however, her children held the sale where I got the manuscript."

"All right," said Morcey slowly, "I'm followin' ya, but I'm not gettin' the big picture. Yeah, we've got some interestin' connections, but how does it all pull together? I mean, okay--fine--this guy sees the word 'Lilith' on the wall, and you say that's a demon that attacks kids, and ..."

"One thing at a time, Paul," answered the professor. "First off, I wouldn't accept 'word on the wall' too literally. It was 1925--Freud was still alive. The world had yet to discover most of the tricks the mind can play."

"What'daya mean, Doc?"

"Think about it. The lower caste seaman--the sight of whatever killed the Suydams drove him insane. The member of the upper class--the doctor--swore he didn't see anything ... anything except a glowing word on the wall." As the balding man stared, Goward explained,

"No one else saw the word, Paul. Just the doctor. This has always led me to believe that the doctor actually did see the same horror as the seaman, but that being a bit more urbane, he was able to repress whatever it was about what they both saw that drove the other man mad. But, what he did glimpse struck him in some fashion as relating to the legend of Lilith. So, his mind, out to protect his sanity, visualized merely the name of the child-stealing demon, instead of seeing the demon itself."

"But, how does it add up? Back then, the thing didn't steal any kids--it only iced the Suydams, and it did that at sea."

"Only partially correct," answered Goward. "The thing killed the Suydams on the boat, but according to the reports, a tramp steamer arrived bearing a load of disreputable mariners with a message from Suydam. It instructed the captain to turn his body over to them if anything happened to him." Putting his papers back into the binder, the professor said,

"The men took the body away--back to Brooklyn--where, at the time, quite a number of children had disappeared. They were found shortly after the incident on the launch when a number of Red Hook apartment buildings caved in. Some children were discovered in an old church nearby. Most of them, however, were found dismembered--their bones sawed apart, sucked dry and chewed on--along with what was left of Suydam's corpse. All of it in an secret subterranean chamber at the site of the cave in."

* * *

Morcey twisted his steering wheel, easing his car to the curb. Pieces had begun falling into place in Goward's office. Driving down from the Bronx, he had stopped at the agency's main office to pick up some things, and then headed back to Brooklyn--more specifically to the Butler Street police station. As he killed his ignition and chained his steering wheel, he rolled the bits of the puzzle he had over in his mind.

In 1925, kids disappear in Red Hook. Now today, they start disappearing again right next door in Columbia Terrace. The first bunch are found underground. The new ones disappeared near where someone is digging a hole.

But, he wondered, *why move from Red Hook to Columbia Terrace? What's the difference? And, what's this Lilith thing? Did it come back? Did it never die? Is someone callin' it back?*

Morcey pulled the black card from his pocket.

Goward said this was a chant for callin' demons. Is someone tryin' ta resurrect this thing? Are they feedin' it kids? The balding man stopped for a moment, staring at the card, frowning. And what kinda sense would that make? If you're tryin' ta raise demons from Hell, ya don't go around advertising it. Do ya?

Do ya?

Morcey shuddered. He had thought to try and contact London. Had reached for the phone when he was in the office. More than once. He made it as far as picking up the receiver, but he had not dialed, merely gathered what he had come for and then left.

Deal with what? the back of his mind sneered, laughing as he sat motionless in his car. *How? You? You're a chump, fat boy. This is beyond you. Go home and have another sandwich.*

Why am I doing this to myself? he wondered, staring out at the police station. *The only place I can learn anything else is in there. So why don't I just go in?*

'Cause you're wisin' up, fat boy. 'Cause you know you can't do this without London. And you know why ... 'cause you're too old ...

Morcey bit at his lip, dropping his head, eyes half closing.

Too fat and too stupid. You--figure this out? Save kids? Protect innocence? Avenge grieving mothers? You? Don't make me laugh.

The balding man fought the fear snaking through his system. Fear that the back of his mind *was* right--that he wasn't good enough, smart enough, fast enough ... enough of a man to do the simple things men were supposed to do.

That's right, his vicious streak snarled. *You're not. Look at you, stuck to your seat, sweat in your shorts--scared little pig. Squeal like a pig, you little shit. Squeal, squeal, squeal and then run away home.*

"No."

Coward. Slob.

"Shut up."

Moron. Jerk--Idiot. Fat, disgusting idiot.

"Shut up!" Morcey roared, slamming his fists against the dashboard. Pounding on the molded plastic, he sent cracks shattering outward from the screws bolting it down, splintering it as he screamed,

"Leave me alone, Goddamnit. *Leave ... me ... alone!*"

And then, suddenly, he was calm. His body was trembling, but his mind was clear. Whatever his doubts had been, they were suddenly gone. His will had unified behind more than just the idea of going into the station house and getting on with things. He had dispelled the idea that he was helpless without the rest of the London Agency.

In less than a minute, he was at the front desk of the station, asking for someone who might be able to help him. Of course, it took a great deal longer before he actually received any of the help he was looking for. Since the balding man could not claim emergency status, he was shuffled from the front desk to a duty officer, to the duty officer's partner, to a detective, to another detective, then finally to Lieutenant Hawkes, an older, heavy-set, stocky detective who functioned as the station house's unofficial historian.

Morcey had picked up bits of useful information along the way, but he had yet to get everything he needed. As he explained to the cigar-chewing Hawkes,

"The other officers helped me with the questions I had about ownership of the excavation. But, they thought you might be able to help further. I do appreciate your time, sir."

"Hey--anything that lets me do my duty and stay right in this chair is okay by me. I'm retired in four months." He held his cigar aloft, joking, "That's why I only chew these anymore. Nothing's cheating me out of forty years worth of pension." Then, looking the balding man up and down, he added,

"You only look about forty yourself."

"Forty-three, actually."

"Forty-three, huh?" Hawkes smiled. "Okay, kid, what can I help you with?" Morcey smiled back at the man, feeling some of the pressure of the station house run-around lifting away.

"Well, as I was sayin', bein' a private ticket, I appreciate the help."

"So'kay," Hawkes responded. "The force wants to see these kidnappings stop more than anyone."

"Right. Well, I've been checking out a ... more bizarre aspect of the case, one that might tie into something that happened here a long time ago." Morcey showed the older man the black card. "One of the other officers said it was a Rave pass."

"Yeah. Kids pass them out to let each other know where the next big dance party will be. This black circle ... whatever that means ... that's the address."

"Right. Well, I was more concerned with the other side." The city detective turned over the card, studying the Cabalistic chant with intense interest. Shaking the card, he said,

"I've seen this. I know it." The man went back to studying the words before him, searching through the files of his memory for a match-up. Then finally, he said,

"I know what this is."

Getting up, Hawkes went to the back of his office, returning in seconds with a tattered, grey-cloth bound ledger. Flipping through it as he walked, he said,

"I just read up on this last year. God, how could I forget this one for even a moment? There was this case, back in the twenties. Really shook people up--course, the biggest crime then was rum smuggling. This was a thousand times worse--devil worshippers, cultists, whatever--they were stealing kids, feeding them to 'something', maybe each other ... no one ever did know for sure ... down under the city."

Hawkes rolled his cigar from one side of his mouth to the other, shredding it as he did so. As bits of tobacco tore free, sticking to his teeth, he sat down, announcing,

"Yeah, here it is ... Tom Malone ... he was in charge of that detail. He and ..." And then, the older man stopped suddenly, shocked awareness filling his eyes. Holding his place with one hand, he closed the ledger over saying,

"You said you're investigating the kids that're disappearing *now* ... but that it connected to an older case."

"Yes ..." answered Morcey slowly. Then, remembering what Goward had told him, he asked, "Lieutenant, did Malone's case end with a number of apartment buildings in Red Hook collapsing?" Hawkes went numbly cold. Morcey could see it in his eyes. Still needing one piece of the puzzle, the balding man pushed further, asking,

"But why the shift out of Red Hook? If this is the same thing ... why did it move?"

"Who says it did?" When Morcey questioned what he meant, the older man explained, "Red Hook used to be a lot bigger. But, as the yuppies cleaned up areas of it, they changed the name. What used to be parts of Red Hook is now twenty new little places."

"Like Columbia Terrace?"

Hawkes nodded. As his unlit cigar bobbed up and down, Morcey gave him the address of the construction site. Hawkes checked the old ledger, then nodded again. Holding up the Rave card, the balding man displayed the side with the black circle, saying,

"You know, I think that Rave is suddenly going to be easy to find." Then, hit by a sudden leap in logic, Morcey asked softly,

"What day did the buildings collapse?" The lieutenant consulted his file, then answered,

"August, 2nd. Today."

* * *

The two cars stopped at opposite ends of the block, the Suydam construction site halfway between them. After Morcey's revelation, the two had pulled together everything they had. The balding man had wanted to know why the Suydam's were digging up their old property. It turned out that after the original cave-in, a trio of cheap houses were thrown up by Robert Suydam's sister-in-law. She had wanted the entrance to the rum smugglers caverns under her property sealed and the Gerritsen family name protected. After her death, however, her heirs were anxious to tear down the cheap tenements and cash in on the revitalization of the area.

Apparently, what had taken them so long to get started was a court battle over their plans. Since the city records showed the area was honeycombed with underground passages, the heirs had to agree to fill in the space beneath their lots entirely before any permits would be issued.

"In other words," Hawkes had sneered, "the city forced them to open that charnel pit up."

"Yeah," agreed Morcey, his mind racing ahead into dread possibilities. "And let whatever's down there out again."

The lieutenant had stared at the balding man for a long moment. He asked no questions, made no threats or pleas, said nothing at all. Morcey waited--knowing something important was happening within the older man. Finally, Hawkes had simply said,

"Guess we better get going."

And Morcey, who had seen all too much of the kind of thing they were headed into--who knew the thousand different reactions the knowledge of such realities could inspire--had merely nodded his head in relieved gratitude and followed the older man out of the office. They made only one stop--at a locked and guarded room. When Hawkes was asked what he wanted, he had told the rookie on duty,

"Me? I don't want anything. You ain't even asking me this question because you ain't seen me all night." Then, the lieutenant had gone in and come back out with a long duffle, the shape of which suggested only one thing. No one had questioned them when they left.

Now, on the street, the two men approached the black hole in the ground from opposite directions. The closer they came, the louder grew an annoyingly rhythmic clatter coming from the dig. Scores of children, the oldest maybe sixteen, the youngest maybe nine, were swarming over the area. All of them were in the pit or around it, digging, kneeling in the cold, sallow clay, tearing at it with their fingers. Silent handfuls were passed from one to the other up out of hole, then dumped on the site or into the street.

Morcey searched the site for the source of the leaden music crawling through the darkness, soon spotting the same set of musicians he had seen at Steven Peters' school. Behind them the detective saw the rent-a-cops who were supposedly guarding the site. The two men sat against the over-sized wheel of a back-hoe tractor, their eyes glazed, lips bright with foaming drool.

Hawkes shook his head sadly. Only in New York, he thought, could this many children gather in the middle of the night, and not have anyone think anything of it. Not the neighbors--not their parents. Pushing his hate of the city back down with practiced ease, the older detective rolled his cigar to the other side of his mouth, then said,

"Let's nip this." Kicking open the gate, Hawkes growled,

"All right, everybody out of the hole. Now!"

Nothing happened. None of the children broke their rhythm, none even noticed him. None except the dark-eyed musicians. Realizing what was happening, Morcey nudged him, saying,

"It's the band. They're the ones we gotta stop."

Instantly Hawkes strode forward, heading toward the musicians from the left side of the pit. Morcey followed suit, taking the right approach. Both men could see that all nine of their targets realized they were coming. And yet, none of them did anything except to blow on their pipes and bang their sticks all the harder--all the faster.

Around them, the two men noted the children suddenly working harder, moving faster, matching the gnawing beat in hideous synchronization. Reaching the line of musicians first, Morcey grabbed the pipe out of the nearest one's hands, shouting,

"Gimme that, ya little monkey."

The beat shattered. At the same moment Hawkes knocked two of the stick bangers over into the mud. And, the measure thus ruptured, nothing on Earth could stop what followed. Instantly, the children and the two security men sitting against the tractor began to regain their senses. But, that was not the only reaction to the abrupt interruption.

Inside the pit, it's extreme center suddenly began to tremble. The rumbling spread outward with a fearful slowness, sending the children into a frightened, stumbling panic. Ignoring the musicians, both Hawkes and Morcey made their way into the massive pit as quickly as possible, pushing children upward, yanking them out of the mud and sending them on their way.

Many of them, too greatly confused by the passing of their stupors to move, simply sat where they had awakened, crying or screaming. The two men worked as fast as they could, calling to the security men to join them. The pair stumbled forward to help, only to be set upon by the musicians. No longer silent, the nine had transformed into howling, frenzied maniacs. The two guards would no sooner throw one back when two more would be at them, kicking, punching, slapping, biting.

And then, suddenly, a phosphorescent probe broke through the skin of the hole. Its radiant presence terrified the children remaining in the pit, sending many of them into screaming conniptions. Morcey and Hawkes redoubled their efforts, no longer trying to help the children to walk, but hurling them bodily up over the edge of the rim.

At their feet, the crack widened around the probing member pushing against the earth, As the slash in the mud grew larger suddenly, a howling tumult of ice-cold wind was freed from below. It carried a sickening, ghastly stench at its fore, convulsing the children still in the pit, gagging the men. And then, a wrenching force split the ground wide apart and a monstrously powerful sucking force collapsed the hole and exposed the ancient vault below.

Morcey and Hawkes landed in an ink-black pit along with the security men and a dozen children, their falls broken by the oozing, soggy clay which filled the chamber below. The darkness they should have fallen into was repelled by a cold, corrupt light--the shimmering off-cast of the phosphorescent horror which had broken through to the surface and dragged them down.

"It's the thing!" wailed Hawkes. "The thing in Malone's report. But they said it was just a dream! Just a dream!"

"Well," said Morcey, unlimbering his sidearm, blinking as he tried to take in the vast bulk of the monstrosity, "The dream got bigger."

The long dead Malone's report had spoken of a glowing humanoid form, one maybe no bigger than a large ape. The monstrosity confronting them, however, was the size of at least a pair of elephants. It was also no longer man-like in any fashion. The nightmare was nothing more than a pile of phosphorescent flesh, misshapen lumps twisted and piled atop each other in no recognizable pattern, all of them sprouting thick, lashing, claw-ended tentacles.

And, it was not alone.

From out of the shadows, rotting forms dotted with eyes shambled forward, heading toward the mass of humanity that had fallen into its midst. As the glowing pile of reeking corruption before them began to titter madly, Morcey took dead aim on the closest of the approaching figures, saying,

"Oh, man, I'm seein' things beyond me comprehension again."

And then he fired. The blast from his Auto-mag ripped through the first form, passing through a second and third as well. The blast of the powerful hand cannon echoing through the subterranean cavern, he fired again and again, doing massive damage to the nearing ranks. Then, he turned back toward the glowing thing, swearing,

"Fuck no, ugly--I didn't forget you!"

His eyes unblinking, he emptied a fresh clip into the dead center of the beast. The nine tremendous blasts tore deep into the bloated horror, exploding vast chunks of gory, glowing flesh away from its bulk. Tentacles writhing madly, the shapeless insanity spewed forth a dark green ichor, horrendous screeches bellowing upward from somewhere deep within it.

At the same time, Hawkes pulled the weapon he had taken from the properties room--a large, heavy automatic weapon Morcey could not identify in the shadows. The lieutenant swept the underground with fire, mowing down a half dozen of the smaller approaching forms. As they flopped about, he bellowed over his shoulder to the security men to get the children clear of the pit.

The two, frozen in gibbering horror, seemed not to hear the screams of the terrified youngsters all around them--nor even the deafening gunfire filling the chamber. Recognizing the state, Morcey turned and back-stepped until he was within reach of the nearest man. Slapping him resoundingly, he shouted,

"Do it! *Do it!* Get these kids *out of here!*"

At the same time, Hawkes had turned his weapon on the shining monster. The smaller slugs opened up a score of new wounds on the creature's side, heightening its maddening screams. His attention away from the monster's minions, however, the lieutenant was suddenly seized by three of the bounding shapes which had circled through the darkness to come up behind him. Instantly two of them sunk their fangs into him--right arm, left leg--forcing his lips apart in howling pain and curses.

Morcey froze for an instant, torn between emptying a fresh clip into the phosphorescent thing in the distance and helping his companion. Then he charged ahead, using the butt of his Auto-mag as a club. He brought the heavy weapon down squarely on the head of one of Hawkes' attackers, going completely through its thin-boned skull. Wrenching the butt free, he gripped the gore-covered handle and turned back toward the glowing thing even as the lieutenant threw off his remaining two attackers.

The phosphorescent horror had started oozing forward. As Morcey emptied another clip directly into it, Hawkes reloaded his own weapon. Jumping atop the pair of bodies he had just flung off him, he broke their bones with his bulk. Then the old man sent one burst through each body, saving his firepower for the next wave of dark figures he could already see rising up out of the water lapping at the distant edge of the mud.

A tentacle shot out from the central horror. As Morcey and Hawkes separated to let it pass, the festering length encircled one of the security men and one of the children. Before anything could be done, they were whipped backward at a dazzling speed and sucked down into the creature's abnormally shaped maw.

Something snapped within the other security man at the sight. Turning he screamed and then hurled himself madly across the muddy distance between himself and the glowing terror. Climbing its side, he slammed at it with his hands alone, driving his naked fists deep into its fungoused hide. Hawkes grabbed at Morcey's shoulder, screaming,

"Come on! Come on!!"

"We gotta get those last two kids!"

The two men staggered across the pit, pulling the two dazed children to their feet. As the lieutenant started the girl for the hole to the surface, Morcey grabbed the boy and jerked him to his feet, only to find,

"Steve!" The ex-maintenance man hugged the boy to him as if he were his own son. Behind him, Hawkes screamed.

"Fer Christ's sake, man--*move*!"

Instantly Morcey snapped out of his surprise and started Steven clambering up the muddy slope toward the surface. The lieutenant used his weapon as a crutch, digging it deep into the sliding earth--choking its barrel and rendering it useless--but nonetheless making his way bit by bit with the screaming girl under his arm. His arm and leg bleeding freely, the older man was panting, his chest moving in and out frantically. Next to him, Morcey sunk to his knees in the grasping mud as he pushed the Peters boy up toward the lip of the pit.

Once Steven had the edge, the balding man shouted, "Climb!" and then turned away from him, dragging his Auto-mag upward to the ready once more. Already, glimmering tentacles were sliding upward toward himself and the lieutenant. Taking aim on the largest, he blasted away. The slug struck dead center, severing the limb in two, but the cannon's fierce recoil finally drove the weapon from Morcey's aching grip.

Then, before the ex-maintenance man could move, another tentacle snagged forward, wrapping itself around Hawkes. The old man dropped the girl he was carrying. She tumbled a few feet, then managed to catch herself. At the same time, Hawkes drove his teeth into the corrupt flesh of the tentacle encircling him, pulling away a deep tearing strip. A howl erupted from below and the tentacle buckled, slipping down Hawkes' body, seeking to catch his legs and drag him down. As Morcey pulled the girl upward, however, the lieutenant fell on his back, evading the loop of flesh which only managed to suck his automatic rifle down into the darkness.

The two men struggled up into the man-made pit, both of them breathing in ragged gasps. Above them, they could see scores of children as well as the gathering curious. Their hearts thumping, chests heaving, both men wanted to collapse, to cry, to scream and howl at the stars laughing above them. But, something within them drove them onward. As they tore their way up into the construction site, Morcey shouted,

"Hawkes--you're the law. Get these damn people out of here."

Trusting the balding man, the city detective fumbled out his badge while screaming orders for everyone to get back. In the meantime, Morcey staggered to the bright yellow back-hoe. Pulling out his pocket knife, first he broke open the tractor's fuel cap. Then, he turned his attention to its control box. As he shattered his heaviest blade trying to pry it open, he could hear Hawkes screaming behind him.

"It's coming! The motherfucker's coming!"

Morcey, forcing himself calm, cursing his trembling fingers, pulled free a tangle of ignition wires from the ruptured panel.

"It's up in the pit! Move, move, man--*move!*"

Cutting through two of the wires, praying his sweat-filled eyes were seeing correctly in the scant light available, he peeled back their plastic coatings. He had spent all his life before the London Agency at heavy work.

"It's on you! Get out of there! *Get out of there!*"

Flooding his actions with memory, pushing aside the horror eating at his nerves, the balding man made his final connections. As the nine tons of diesel-powered tractor sputtered, then roared, three glowing tentacles broke through the glass cab, grasping for Morcey's life. The ex-maintenance man threw himself behind the wheel, screaming,

"*Eat* me? Eat *me*? Eat steel, cocksucker!"

Morcey spun the control wheel, and then brought the tractor's trenching arm down--hard. Instantly, two of the tentacles were severed. Following up the move instantly, he started the tractor rolling backward, away from the pit, forcing the phosphorescent horror to come to him.

In the silence formed by the cacophony of maddened screams all around him, blending with the noise of the engine in front of him and the wailing of the beast below, Morcey pulled together all his will. Forcing forward an energy that deadened the pain in his arms and legs, that stilled his rampaging heart and calmed the flooded message centers of his brain, he whispered,

"Come on, asshole. Come on, come to Daddy."

Pushing the tractor back from the pit slowly, inches at a time, the balding man watched calmly as the bulk of the nightmarish creature pulled itself up out of the pit. Raising the entrenching arm, he teased,

"Come on, another few feet. Daddy's got candy."

A monstrous bleat echoed outward from the slithering horror. Morcey gunned the four tons of engine he was riding, revving it hotter and hotter, but keeping the brake in place. The creature that had driven Tom Malone to madness a half century earlier moved toward the sound of the engine.

"That's right--come and get me, ya big turd!

And then, at the sound of the balding man's voice, the entire bulk of the glowing thing from the pit began to flop and vibrate. Shoving itself across the surface, the creature moved out toward the back-hoe. In the streets, people screamed in mindless terror. Chaos reined as children and adults ran into each other, over each other, desperately clawing and kicking at anything or anyone in their way.

Ignoring it all, however, Morcey sat his place atop the roaring back-hoe, waiting for the exact moment to strike. He knew what he needed to do, he merely had to force himself to wait for the right moment to do it. Watching the glowing thing before him, he whispered,

"I'm right here, ugly. Come and get me."

As if in response to the balding man's words, the creature made its move. It's sickeningly corrupt skin erupted, sending a volley of tentacles flying in Morcey's direction. Staying calm, the ex-maintenance man waited with one hand on the hoe-controls, the other on the gear shift. He watched the pulsating growths slide along the ground--watched them disappear from out of his field of vision.

And then, when he felt them encircling the rear axle, he reversed both the diesel's entrenching blade and its drive. Instantly the digging arm came down, burying itself deep within the phosphorescent horror. At the same time, the tractor shoved itself backward, rolling into and across the monster. Morcey waited for the crushingly large wheels to do as much damage as possible, then he reversed the direction, rolling the giant digger back over and into the horror.

A sonic wail bled from the creature that shattered glass in every direction. Morcey ignored the piercing noise, reversing direction again as if trying to pull away from the beast. At the same time, he began working the massive hoe arm back and forth, breaking it free from the body of the glowing thing. The monster's screams grew louder, more deafening. Morcey noted a wave of tentacles forcing their way up the side of the cab. Knowing he had run out of time, he tried the last trick he had left.

Jerking the hoe arm up to its full height, he released it, bringing it down with street breaking force. It's claw end broke through the phosphorescent skin of the thing, sinking to the very center of the monstrosity. At the same time, Morcey locked the forward control in place. At once the massive diesel started rolling, pushing and pulling the creature back toward its pit at the same time.

A tentacle caught the balding man's ankle. Without hesitation, Morcey threw himself from the cab, dragging the rotting length behind him. He hit the ground badly, knocking the breath from himself. The diesel kept pushing its way forward, grinding its way over the monster from below, pulling it back down into its hell. Unfortunately, it was pulling Morcey along as well.

As children and adults both ran screaming into the night, the tangle of machine and nightmare neared the edge of the pit. dragging the ex-maintenance man along with them. He reached out desperately, catching hold of a bracing pipe sunk into the ground near the gate. Locking his fingers, he kicked at the tentacle holding his left leg.

The pain in his hands flooded his senses. Tears splashed down his cheeks, but he refused to let go. The length of glowing flesh wrapped around his ankle stretched thinner and thinner, and then, suddenly its grip was lost. At the same instant the growling tangle of machine and monster toppled backward over the edge of the pit, slamming downward out of sight.

Morcey staggered to his feet. He could not feel his fingers. Could barely move. Pushing his way past the pain pounding at him, he stumbled his way to the cyclone fencing. Behind him, the thing thrashed in the pit with the still roaring back-hoe. Pulling down a NO TRESPASSING sign from the fence,

Morcey forced his way to the edge of the muddy lip, crumpling the thin cardboard as he moved.

He stared down into the hole, watching the tractor's still spinning wheels tear bits of flesh from the monster, seeing the still active tentacles ripping into the guts of the machine. Then, he set the ball afire and tossed it toward the fuel spilling from the still growling tractor.

Instantly flames shot up from the pit, surrounded by thick, tarry clouds. Staggering away from the hole, Morcey headed toward Hawkes. The old man had managed to stay upright only by hanging onto the other side of the cyclone fence.

As a reeling explosion tore through the night, sending a burning shower of flesh and steel through the night, Morcey held his lighter up toward Hawkes face, asking, "Need a light?"

Panting, grinning, the old man rolled the tattered remains of his cigar to the other side of his mouth, saying,

"Sure. Why the Fuck not?"

Agreeing, Morcey clicked up a flame, igniting the soggy cigar. The lieutenant took a deep, satisfying drag, pulling down as much smoke as he could. Releasing it, he said,

"You know, you kick some pretty good ass, kid."

"You're not bad yourself," answered Morcey weakly. As he worked at catching his breath, the older man said,

"Yeah, but I'm getting ready to retire. You ever think of becoming a cop?"

"Naw," said Morcey. Spitting out a wad of phlegm, he wiped his mouth on his torn shirt sleeve, then added, "I already got a job." Hawkes took another full, rewarding drag on his cigar, then asked,

"You like it?"

Morcey rubbed at the pain in his back, dabbed at the blood he could feel running down his face, his arm and leg and side. He had hit the ground so hard when he had leaped from the cab of the back-hoe that his vision had not completely refocused. Seeing well enough to look the lieutenant in the eye, however, he said,

"Yeah, actually, I do." Hawkes studied the detective's smile, then answered,

"Yeah, I probably would, too."

Morcey called out to Steven. The boy, still somewhat dazed, made his way to the ex-maintenance man's side. Then, the boy in tow, the two men pulled themselves together and walked off into the night, ignoring the retreating screams behind them and the nearing sirens ahead.

The Hitch

By Gary Sumpter

Les dieux ont soif.
CAMILLE DESMOULINS: *Vieux Cordelier*, 3 Feb., 1794

Martin leaned over and rolled down the window on the passenger side of the Honda. "Where are you headed?"

"Oh, it dun't really matter," the girl said with a smile. "Kin yew tek me?"

Her accent was vaguely familiar, one of the many quaint Yankee dialects so typical of rural New England.

He cleared his throat. "Sure; hop in."

Martin Phillips was not in the habit of picking up hitch-hikers: it was just too risky. Sure, he himself had thumbed his way from one coast to the other - without incident - during the summer of his sophomore year at college, but times had changed; there were too many crazies around, and he had a wife and two kids to think about. Still, there was... *something* about the girl standing, thumb extended, on the gravel shoulder of the Aylesbury Pike, that caused him to reconsider. Had it been the way she carried her willowy frame? Or the cut of her faded denim shorts and pale yellow t-shirt? Was it simply the way her long brown hair blew unfettered in the breeze?

The girl looked about eighteen, and as she climbed into the passenger seat, Martin was suddenly conscious of her aroma: the smell of sun and sweat and something else, something he could not place - some exotic perfume, perhaps.

Martin guided the car back onto the road. He glanced over at the girl and offered a friendly smile. "What's your name?"

"Abigail Perkins," she said, wrinkling her nose with obvious distaste. "But yew kin call me Abbey. Whut's yore name?"

"Phillips; Martin Phillips." He caught movement out of the corner of his eye; her substantial breasts, unencumbered by a bra, seemed to sway as he drove. She caught his sidelong glance and winked. Embarrassed, he looked away.

"Yew dun't usually pick people up, dew yew Mr. Phillips?"

He shook his head.

"Please, call me Martin." His mouth went dry, and he wondered what he'd gotten himself into. Fields and forests whizzed past, and it was all he could do to keep his eyes on the road.

"Kin we stop fer a bit?" Abbey suddenly asked as they approached the cut-off to Witches Hollow.

Martin felt a knot in his stomach. He cleared his throat again, pondering a suitable response. "If you like."

He pulled off the pike, and onto the road to Witches Hollow, with Grady's Filling Station standing at the junction. They had driven only a short way along the bumpy gravel road when Abbey indicated a spot just ahead: "Thes'll dew jest fine."

No sooner had Martin pulled over to the side of the road when Abbey was out of the car, running and skipping through the tall grass of the adjacent field. Cautiously, he followed. Laughing and turning, she led him through the field and plunged headlong into the woods beyond. Martin was forced to run to avoid losing sight of the girl. The trees soon gave way to a rock-strewn clearing overlooking a small body of murky water.

"Thes hyar's Black Pond," she announced with a casual wave of her slim hand. "Tain't no good fer swimmin', mind, but sometimes I like tew cum down hyar an' jest set a spell. Papa dun't like me comin' hyar after sundaown, he says it's sacret an' shouldn't oughter be disturbed."

Given the amount of rocky debris littering the area, Martin deduced that Black Pond was actually a glacial kettlehole. Thriving in what must be highly acidic water, an unusual sphagnum bog covered part of the pond with a floating, spongelike mat filled with orchids, pitcher plants, sundew, and other vegetation. There was something odd about the place; something that Martin could not identify, yet found vaguely disquieting.

Abbey sat down on a mossy rock overhanging the pond. Martin joined her. "Do you live around here?"

"Not far," she said, drawing her knees up under her chin.

"Do you live with your parents?"

"With Papa and my brother, Eben." Abbey lowered her gaze and dropped her voice. "Mama died a couple uv years ago. Papa wudn't let no docter look at her - 'til it 'uz tew late."

Martin nodded sympathetically and fished a pack of Marlboros out of his shirt pocket. "Were you born here?"

"Oh, to be sure. The Perkins have allus lived in the Holler, I reckon."

"Do you go to school?" He slipped a cigarette from the pack and offered it to Abbey.

"Uster go in Arkham," she replied, accepting the cigarette. "'Til I was old 'nough tew stop goin', that is. Papa says they's a lot yew can't larn in no school. I bin mostly eddicated at home, but I reckon even city folk still got a lot tew larn."

Abbey tossed back her head, brushed the blonde curls from her face, and slipped the cigarette between her lips. Martin struck a match and lifted it. "Your father must be a very intelligent man."

"Oh, Papa knows a lot - abaout the stars, an' all." Abbey lit her cigarette, then watched as Martin lit one for himself. "He kin tell ye which ones are up thar any night uv the year. Certain stars is special, though, an' when they's out an' shinin' bright, it's magic. Papa knows all abaout the ol' legends - ye know, uv the Injuns an' them ones who was hyar afore."

Martin watched the discarded match disappear into the pond. He cleared his throat. "Do you... have a boyfriend?"

Abbey giggled. "Oh, Papa says that's all taken care uv. When my time comes, I reckon I'll marry one of the Whateley boys, or mebbe Nate Talbot's son, Will."

"Do they live nearby?"

"Oh, sure, they's all from the Holler. The Whateley's got relatives out in Dunnich, though. Papa would never let me take up with a city feller." She thought for a moment, and then her lips curled into a grin. "But I like *yew*, Mr. Phillips, yew're real nice."

Martin felt his jaw go slack. Abbey leaned closer; the impish smile had disappeared, and she was searching his face. He struggled for an excuse to escape, and found it when he felt a drop of rain on his hand. The sky had darkened overhead. "It looks like rain; shall we go back to the car?"

"No, I'm goin' tew set awhile," she answered. "I kin walk from hyar. Thanks fer the ride."

"How... do I reach you?" he asked, his words faltering beneath a sudden sense of impending - and permanent - loss.

"Ye kin't," she answered, offering him a half-hearted pixie smile. Martin started to protest, but she put her fingers to his lips. "I'll see ye again, Mr. Phillips. I promise."

And she was gone.

* * *

Everything about the encounter with Abbey had been enigmatic. Martin manoeuvred the Honda back down the road from Witches Hollow, but his mind was elsewhere. She had been flirting, as girls often do, yet Martin perceived that there was something more to it than that. Abbey herself was an enigma: despite her bucolic accent and limited education, she was plainly no simpleton. Her eyes belied an intelligence far greater than one might expect of a girl raised under those circumstances. Martin wondered whether

Abbey's upbringing dictated a front of naivete around men. He had heard of many fundamentalist sects that required a more "traditional" role for women - traditional in that they should always defer to their menfolk. Although he found something oddly appealing in Abbey's modesty, Martin was glad to live in an enlightened age.

It wasn't until he had returned to the Aylesbury Pike, however, and heard the noisy cry of crows overhead that Martin realized what had been so disturbing about Black Pond. It hadn't been the pond at all, but the area around it: the sounds of nature had been completely absent.

* * *

Martin's schedule was such that a return visit to Arkham could not be arranged until the following week. When at last he found himself approaching Witches Hollow on the Aylesbury Pike, Martin hoped - and half-expected - to find Abbey standing by the side of the road again, looking for a ride.

She was not there. Martin felt a twinge and wondered if it was disappointment. Still, the road to Witches Hollow loomed ahead; it beckoned to him, pulling the car toward it. Martin tried to convince himself that the girl's absence should be taken as some sort of sign; he struggled against the urge to follow what was surely the road to moral destruction, the violation of everything he held sacred. Common sense told Martin to abandon this reckless diversion: he was getting in too deep, far too deep. It was, however, the depth of his involvement that prevented common sense from dictating his actions, and in the end, it came down to taking the path of least resistance. Arkham could wait.

He pulled into Grady's Filling Station, triggering a bell. An old man in greasy overalls and a shabby baseball cap nodded wearily from a bench beneath the canopy of the adjacent general store and started to rise. His bloodhound raised its head briefly, then went back to sleep. Martin got out of the car and approached the fellow.

"Excuse me; do you know a family by the name of Perkins?"

The old-timer - whose name was Nahum, according to the oval badge sewn onto his uniform - removed his cap and scratched his head. "Zeb Perkins? What wud ye be wantin' *him* fer?"

"I'm looking for his daughter, actually."

Nahum's lips curled into what was a toothless but apparently knowing smile. "Wal, sarr, ol' Zeb's place is abaout a mile further along. Tek the dirt rud to yore left. The haouse is jest a ways past the bridge, an' set back perty deep in the woods. But I reckon ye waon't miss it."

Martin thanked the old-timer and turned to leave.

"If ye're lookin' for Mis' Perkins," Nahum called, "ye'd be a fool tew go up tew the house. Ol' Zeb daon't take kindly tew fellers messin' with his girl." He glanced over at Martin's Honda. "'Specially city fellers."

Over his shoulder, Martin called: "Thanks for the warning."

* * *

The road through Witches Hollow was in perpetual shadow - or so it seemed. The oak trees, having attained prodigious size through immeasurable years of growth unchecked by hatchet or saw, spread a canopy of green above the roadway and groped for the heavens. Witches Hollow seemed unwilling - or unable - to part with the past: the tide of progress slowed to a trickle here, among battered clapboard houses and rusting hulks of ancient automobiles. There were other roads, little more than dusty tracks, spreading like veins up into the hills, but Martin was not inclined to explore them. The people seemed a bucolic lot, probably full of strange superstitions and queer prejudices. They appeared happy to eschew the outside world - or did the outside world avoid *them*?

About a mile from the gas station, Martin turned onto the dirt road. Had Washington Irving lived in Massachusetts, and not New York, the Headless Horseman would have haunted Witches Hollow; of that, Martin was certain. He did not relish the thought of negotiating these narrow, rutted lanes by night; but soon reached the bridge of which the old-timer had surely been speaking. It was a wooden structure, wide enough only for a single vehicle. From the remains of a wooden frame, Martin presumed that this had once been a covered bridge: now he wondered whether it would bear the Honda's weight.

Martin slowed the car to a crawl and proceeded gingerly onto the bridge. Wooden planking creaked and groaned beneath the strain, but did not break. After what seemed an eternity, he was safely on the other side.

The Perkins house was dilapidated, a ramshackle clapboard affair like something out of an old photograph. The yard was littered with old furniture and patrolled by cantankerous dogs. In the driveway, a mountain of a man was working under the battered hood of the pick-up truck. He heard Martin's footsteps on the gravel and turned his bearded head.

"This hyar's private prop'ty, mister. Ye got business hyar?"

"Abigail: is she inside?"

The man scowled. "Ye got no business with Abbey, stranger. Git on yore way afore I turn my dogs on ye."

Martin decided that there was no point in testing the fellow's resolve and returned to the car.

Martin started for the pike, but changed his mind at the last moment. He wheeled the car around and back down the road to Witches Hollow -

toward Black Pond, where he pulled off the road and made his way on foot. There was no one in sight - but, standing at the edge of the pond, Martin sensed that he was not alone. Slowly he turned and Abbey was there, wearing the same thin yellow t-shirt and cutoffs, and the same pixie smile.

She padded toward him, bare feet making no sound, and took his hands in hers. "Told ye I'd see ye agin."

He closed his eyes; he could hear Abbey's calm breathing, and her warm breath upon him. She reached out and stroked his cheek; he leaned over to kiss her. Abbey shrank away from him, but he thrust his arms around her, pressing his body insistently against hers. Abbey struggled and tried to pull away from him, but her cheeks were flushed, and she was breathing heavily through parted lips. Her firm breasts strained against the thin t-shirt, erect nipples betraying her.

"Mr. Phillips," she said at last, "they's suthin' I got tew ast ye."

"What is it?"

"Dew ye think I'm perty? As perty as one uv them city girls?"

"You're every bit as pretty, Abbey. Even prettier. You'll make someone very happy one day."

Abbey leaned forward and kissed him. "I want tew make ye happy right naow, Mr. Phillips." Her voice was a whisper.

Her scent, warm and dark and musky, clouded his senses. Abbey reached slowly for the bottom of her shirt, pulling it over her head with one fluid motion. Martin caught his breath and gazed at her, full breasts now free in the warm sunshine. She took his head in her hands, drawing his mouth down first to one breast, then the other. Her eyes were cloudy with desire; she moved her hands to the top of her cutoffs and slowly she lowered the zipper. The cutoffs fell to the ground. Naked now, she put her hands on Martin's shoulders, pressing him to his knees. Abbey grabbed his shirt, jerking it out of his pants; she clawed at the buttons then, impatient, ripped the shirt open, sending buttons flying. She unfastened his belt and unsnapped the top button of his pants, roughly parting the zipper.

Abbey put her hand on his bare chest and pushed him back to the ground. She pulled off his shoes, then his pants. He lay on his back on the moss, naked but for the ruined shirt. Abbey put her fingers on his eyelids, closing them; she kissed him softly on the lips and chin, then moved to his chest, kissing and licking and nibbling on the way down. He stirred impatiently; she grasped him with surprising firmness. His world was hazy with pleasure.

At last she lowered herself onto him, her knees were drawn up close to her shoulders and her eyes rolled back, showing the whites. Impaled, she jerked back and forth like a worm on a hook. She was wailing and screaming now, gyrating and bucking wildly. Locked together, they writhed on the carpet of moss, breathing as one, gasping for breath; Abbey began to give out short cries, rising in pitch as she reached a climax. She cried in response, an animal sound that must have come from deep in her throat, because her teeth were bared.

They dressed and, sitting in silence, shared a cigarette.

Abbey had been an enthusiastic and capable lover: Martin realized, with a strange regret, that he hadn't been her first. Why had he assumed - or hoped - otherwise? Perhaps one of the Whateley boys, or Will Talbot had beaten him to it.

He had been expecting feelings of incredible guilt in the aftermath of his infidelity, but these did not materialize. Nor did he hate himself, like he had once assumed he would. He felt good - about himself, about the world, and - most of all - about Abbey. She made him feel *alive* again, awakened feelings that had lain dormant for too long.

Abbey gazed down at the unbroken water of the pond. "We best git goin'," she said at last. "If Papa ketches us hyar..."

"I suppose you're right." Martin tossed the cigarette into the pond, where it hissed out its existence. "When can I see you again?"

"Friday," Abbey whispered, taking one last drag. She tossed the cigarette into the pond, where it hissed out its existence. "You kin meet me hyar, at sunset."

* * *

The screen door slammed. Perkins stomped across the porch, a shotgun in his beefy hand. He glared at Abbey. "Git in the haouse, girl."

Abbey threw her hands up. "Have maircy, Papa; warn't like thet t'all! Mr. Phillips hyar just druv me down the rud apiece - tew Arkham."

"Dun't ye lie tew me, girl. I know whut ye done. I had Eben foller ye daown to Black Pond."

A look of terror came over Abbey's face.

"Git in the haouse, girl. I'll deal with ye later."

Martin began to protest; Perkins scowled at him. "Jest shet up. Hain't nuthin' ye kin say. I told ye onct to mind yore own business, mister." He shifted the shotgun menacingly. "I reckon they's no law aginst me usin' this if ye've been warned."

Martin slowly backed toward the car, careful not to make any sudden moves; he had no doubt about Perkins' intention to make good on his threat.

"You can't keep her here forever, you know. You can't force her to live like this."

"Mister, ye got some nerve comin' hyar an' tellin' me how tew raise my kids. Jest git in yore car and git clear off my prop'ty, or I'll blow yore fool head off." He pumped the shotgun and took a step forward. "Ye hear?"

Martin bit back his anger and retreated to the car.

* * *

There is a time in all men's lives when the line between right and wrong becomes blurred by the influence of self-interest. Martin now found himself on the other side of the line, never having realized he had crossed it. He had sinned, betrayed the trust of those he loved, yet - strangely - he felt no remorse, no shame. Sin had not left a bad taste in his mouth; he was surprised how easy it was to carry on as though nothing had happened.

* * *

Martin found himself turning off the Aylesbury Pike and into Grady's Filling Station with less than a quarter of a tank showing on the fuel gauge. It was Friday night; the sun had set, leaving the western skies charged with golden hues.

Both of the pumps were in use. He waited impatiently while the driver of a dusty Pontiac with New Jersey plates made his way to the rest room and back, then pulled the car up to the now unoccupied pump.

Martin stepped out of the car and the old man in the overalls, glancing over from the other pump where he was checking the oil of a flatbed Ford, seemed to recognize him. "Did ye find the place alright?"

Martin nodded. The bloodhound emerged from beneath the canopy of the general store long enough to embark on a foolhardy chase after a motorcycle speeding along the pike.

"Git back here, boy!" the old man yelled at the dog. "Crazy son-uv-a-bitch dun't knaow whut's good fer him."

The driver of the Ford, a young fellow in jeans and a Boston Bruins jersey, returned from the general store with a bottle of Coke. "Everything alright, Nahum?"

"I reckon so. Ol' Zeke, bless his soul, he wouldn't waste his time chasin' no motorbike."

"What happened to Zeke?" Martin wondered idly.

"My best bloodhound," Nahum replied. "Lost ol' Zeke in Black Pond."

The reference startled Martin; it gave him a sudden - and unexpected - shiver. "Black Pond?"

"Yessarr, Ol' Zeke caught scent ef suthin' one night an' tore off down tew the pond. I cud heer him yelpin' - an' mister, if it warn't the wuse noise I ever heerd. Never did find ol' Zeke. None ef the other hounds wud go near the place."

"A fox, I suppose." Martin wasn't really listening; he was lost in his own thoughts, but he heard the old man's words. "Surely there aren't any wolves left in these parts."

"Sheriff said it 'uz prob'ly a wild animal, but I know better. 'Twarnt no animal what tuk ol' Zeke - *not no animal of Gawd's airth.* They's suthin' daown thar what ain't got no right to be hyar."

The younger fellow chuckled as he climbed into his truck. "Pay him no mind, mister. Nahum's an old man and his memory's not so good. Still, I wouldn't suggest going to Black Pond after dark - not without a flashlight, anyway. One false step and you're liable to find yourself up to your ears in mud."

* * *

Martin switched on his flashlight and headed into the woods. As he stepped into the clearing, there arose such a cacophony of sound - the first time he'd heard anything of the sort here - that he felt a sudden chill. Frogs croaked; crickets chirped - and above them all, the whippoorwills cried. Would Abbey still keep their date? *Yes*, Martin realized with relief when he saw her shadowed form ahead.

Until he saw a second, larger shadow by her side. It was, unmistakeably, her father.

"Ye hear them whippoorwills?" Perkins gloated. "They allus cry like thet when they's fixin' to ketch a soul."

Martin heard something - a gurgle. The surface of the pond was bubbling, as though someone were breathing underwater. The mat of spongy vegetation was *alive*: it hissed and heaved as though it were boiling. The narrow beam of Martin's flashlight revealed only a portion of what was now emerging from the pond; the moonlight hinted at the rest. Here was an abomination, something that should not - *could* not - exist. It was unlike anything Martin had ever seen - or imagined: a mountain of sentient vegetation, well over ten feet high. He was sick with terror and revulsion, for the thing reeked of rot and decay. When the beam of his flashlight fell upon the middle of this mass of writhing muck, Martin saw its horrible sucker-tipped maw, gaping and eager to sate some unearthly appetite.

Martin took a step toward Abby, who shrank back behind her father. "I'm sorry, Mr. Phillips." she said, a faint smile upon her lips. "Yore a nice man an' all, *but city folk got a lot uv larnin' tew dew.*"

* * *

At Grady's Filling Station, the old bloodhound cowered at Nahum's feet as the cries of the whippoorwills reached a crescendo - and a terrible silence fell once more upon Witches Hollow.

The Shunpike

By Robert M. Price

Business brought me to North Central Massachusetts, as it had many times before. I make my living in the admittedly inglorious profession of grocery supply and field supervision for a medium size chain of food stores sprinkled throughout the Commonwealth with another few franchises in Rhode Island and New Hampshire. It is my task at appointed intervals to visit and inspect these establishments, to check on their managers, their supplies, and to diagnose the problems of failing stores. Our chain was once considerably more widespread, having since lost business to burgeoning competitors, so it behooves us to keep a finger on the pulse. Like the circuit-riding preachers of old, I knew my rounds well and could almost have driven them, in my capacious Packard, blindfolded. Aylesbury, Arkham, Ipswich, Fenham, Wilbraham, and others: they were almost like the furnishings of a great room to me, so familiar and, generally, comfortable were they to me. Despite harsh driving conditions during certain parts of the year, I rejoiced to circle the New England countryside and viewed my unspectacular employment primarily as an excuse to tour my beloved homeland.

Thus it was that surprise, no, shock overcame me as I approached a toll station along an oft-traveled stretch of road leading to the Berkshire region; I spied for the first time a crude and weathered signpost, peeping out from behind a shock of recently pruned foliage. It's haggard letters spelled a single word: SHUNPIKE. It was one of those old rutted paths, invisible on any printed map, creations of the ingenuity of the poor who lacked even the small sum to pay the modest toll and yet could not drive their burdens overland through open country. As my automobile approached more closely, I slowed my pace for a better glimpse. The dense roadside growth had been cut back much more drastically that usual, and I found that a significant stretch of the makeshift road was visible before it began to make its inevitable bend to rejoin the main road somewhere on the other side.

On a whim I pulled the Packard over to the side of the road. I was still yet some yards from the toll station and could not tell whether my pause had excited the notice of the toll collector, or whether he might be asnooze, not unusual for this section of road where the press of traffic was not great. I quickly reviewed my schedule of appointments and decided that I could indeed spare some time. I had no fixed deadline in such a leisurely part of the countryside where grocery proprietors habitually passed the days with friends around the cracker barrel. And besides, how much time could it take? The only danger might be to my tires, for who knew what degree of desuetude might afflict the neglected road beyond my field of vision? So, as my patient reader must have at once surmised, I made for the unofficial turn-off, feeling my way carefully and possessed of a sense of adventurous expectancy.

What I anticipated finding I could not then have explained, and probably I felt more of idle curiosity than aught else, but as I have said, the wonders of the New England countryside, as well as its small towns, are the refreshment of my spirit, and I am always willing to try for a look at some new corner, cove, or glen I have not heretofore seen.

The road surface was surprisingly smooth, as if heavier traffic of an earlier day had succeeded in packing the ground and smoothing it. Subsequent muddying rainstorms had apparently done little to erode it. And thus I found I had actually to slow down in order to take in the adjacent scenery. Driving presented no real difficultly. I had struggled along paved roads with more trouble from time to time.

Another thing I had not counted on was the sheer extent of the thoroughfare. While it would be natural for the tributary to linger before rejoining the mainstream, so as not to make the illegitimate circuit too obvious, the duration of the drive along the shunpike seemed a good deal longer than necessary, almost like a real back road. In a few moments I began to worry about getting lost. I considered simply turning around and retracing my path, paying my toll, and being on my way to my next stop. But something bade me continue on, just a little and ever a little more.

I carried on for what must have been twenty minutes in this trajectory when I again felt the electric jolt of total surprise, for before me appeared another signpost, this one unobtrusively pointing the way to the town of Foxfield some undisclosed distance from the road I was driving. A turn-off from a turn-off? This struck me as very singular. I had to assume that what I had discovered, including the shunpike itself, represented the vestiges of an earlier and largely effaced road system swept away by the construction of the highway on which I habitually traveled.

And yet it was hard to imagine the people of a town permitting themselves to be so completely cut off from common traffic. True, there might be some connection between the settlement and other open roads on the other side, but I felt sure that in all my travels and on all my maps I had never seen a town of Foxfield.

Almost fearing to look at my fuel gauge, I was relieved to see that I had a fair safety cushion providing the town were not far away, for of course I had determined to seek it out. I made the turn and motored down the road. This one suffered as little from encumbrances as the last, surely an oddity in both cases, given their little use over so many years, but the gravel with which it was covered made for a bumpier ride. Nor did I relish the sounds of impact as tiny gravel missiles ricocheted off the recently repainted side surfaces of my automobile. And yet I kept on.

Though I knew the place must be a ghost town by now, I rationalized this waste of company time with the vain scheme of searching out the viability of recommending a new franchise in Foxfield should the hamlet still somehow manage to thrive. Why should the natives, if there proved to be any, not welcome the prospect of reestablishing closer contact with the outside world? I could think of no reason.

My heart sank as I saw a gasoline station coming up on my left and, nearing it, found it a weed-grown relic. Only then, at the pang of disappointment I felt, did I realize how strongly I had harbored the folly that the town might still flourish. Now it seemed plain that it could not. And yet I continued. I can give no real account why. I suppose I simply felt stubbornly inclined to see the thing through to the end, unspectacular as that must now surely be.

It turned out to be a day of surprises, since not five minutes later I slowed down to a stop along a cobbled street of a small but living and active town!

My arrival made me the magnet of ill-concealed stares from adults and open gaping by the gathered children who had been playing amid the leisurely progress of their elders down the street of the place. They gaped openly at my automobile as if they had never laid eyes on one. While trying to appear friendly and inoffensive, I did not at once try to speak with anyone as my eyes were involuntarily drawn to the architecture of this, apparently the main street. I began a leisurely stroll down this thoroughfare, bare of cars though liberally sprinkled with fresh-faced villagers. I crossed one bridge over the rushing river below, the Miskatonic, I imagined, and noticed the crumbling remains of another, older structure which had once spanned the waters further down their course.

Foxfield looked like a living fossil from a previous generation. There was evidence of modern amenities here and there, but on the whole the place had the air of the turn of the century. The same was true of the costume of the natives, as I was soon to notice. Yet nothing suggested any conscious attempt to preserve or to affect the past out of a sense of nostalgia such as I myself felt. It seemed rather that here one might visit another time just as we are accustomed to visit other places and to observe there a fully-formed world of fashion and custom consistent in detail and yet without conscious artifice.

To my request for direction to a good restaurant, a young man, whose dress suggested unmistakably a member of the cloth, perhaps returning from lunch himself, replied with a stammered recommendation punctuated with a pointing hand. I thanked him and proceeded down the block, smiling at those few who made eye-contact and otherwise taking in as much as I might of my surroundings. I became aware that the clothing of most around me attested the same anachronistic design. Most of the clothing, however, partook of the banal functionalism of the dress of most working people and was little distinguished as to style or period.

I will not dwell on the unexceptional decor of the eating establishment I had chosen. I need only note the puzzling character of the menu and of some of the items on it. For one thing, no prices accompanied the entries. This detail usually denotes the exorbitant prices left diplomatically tacit in the most expensive New York restaurants, but this place, really little more than a pleasant cafeteria, could scarcely be charging so much. Or so I hoped as I made to choose between a number of enigmatic dishes. There was a surprising percentage of orders involving venison, even bear meat, very little in the way of beef. And some of the vegetable items bore names utterly unfamiliar to me. Feeling in an adventurous mood, I finally settled upon one of these and waited to discover what familiar greenery the local names "starflower" and "angelroot" might conceal. As I waited, I could not help but notice the inquisitive looks aimed in my direction by most of the other patrons. None seemed hostile, only curious, no, perhaps apprehensive might be a better word.

My lunch was not long in arriving, and I greeted it ravenously. I was intrigued to see that on the salad plate rested at least two vegetable species with which I was wholly unfamiliar, though they looked edible enough. So I set to. Starflower and angelroot were tasty enough, quite distinctive in fact. And here my head for business began to return. Could not my own grocery chain regain some of its dulled edge in the competitive field if we could arrange to become the unique distributor of some canned variety of these delicious and unique treats? Our own label, and the profits to be split with local farmers? More than another local franchise might be at stake here. I made up my mind to seek out some greengrocer in the town and make some inquiries.

I had gotten no further with mercantile speculations such as these when my gustatory reverie was interrupted, pleasantly enough, by a visitor. It was the very man who had only half an hour earlier directed me to this very lunch counter. His face was unreadable, but his manner was polite as he asked if he might join me. I rose and extended a hand of welcome. Then we both sat down. I am, I suppose, naturally friendly, but many years in my profession have reinforced my belief that friendliness is the best policy, smoothing many a feather and soothing many a brow.

"Pleased to know you, Reverend... Or is it Father...?"

Shaking his closely trimmed, brown-haired head, the young cleric corrected me. "Actually, I am called Elder, Elder Renfrew. And may I know your name, stranger?"

"Of course. I should have introduced myself. My name is Howard, Howard Willet. I am a traveling field supervisor for the N______ chain of grocery stores, and I am delighted to have discovered your fine municipality."

This seemed to set my interlocutor at ease, just a bit, but he retained the air of unease. "I should say that 'discover' is quite the word, Mr. Willet. Few outsiders find their way here. Few even know of Foxfield any more. May I ask how you made your way here, and why?"

It took only a moment to supply him with the details of my story, and I did see no reason to hide my business interests. All this he took in without remark. I took advantage of the lull in conversation while he thought over what I had said.

"Elder Renfrew, I suppose you could say I am something of an antiquarian, and I must say the aspect of your town charms me immensely. I should much enjoy a tour of your church if you can spare the time this afternoon."

His eyes brightened, and he almost smiled, as if by some word I had unwittingly made things easier for him. "That would be a splendid idea. In fact, Mr. Willet, I might as well tell you, it's not my church. I am only the assistant there. The Presiding Elder is Elder Thorndike. I told him of your arrival. As I said, it's quite an event when an outsider visits us in Foxfield. And Elder Thorndike asked me to invite you to his study. I was afraid you might think it a bit queer, your only having arrived in town."

"Not at all, my good man. By the way, precisely which Christian denomination do you and the Elder Thorndike serve?"

At so simple a question the young clergyman hesitated. "I think you would not have heard of us. And besides, we don't really have a name. There are no other churches to distinguish ourselves from in Foxfield. But Elder Thorndike can explain all that better than I can. As I say, I am just his assistant. Pretty green on fine points theology, I'm afraid."

Knowing the name of one's sponsoring religious body did not strike me as a particularly fine point of theology, but I elected not to press the point.

"I was just finishing up anyway, so we might as well leave," I said, rising and reaching into my vest for my billfold. But my companion forestalled me with a gesture of his own, saying. "No, you're our guest. Let me pay it."

I thanked him and couldn't help but notice that the young man seemed to place himself between me and the woman at the cash register in such a manner that I would not be able to see the actual exchange. Had the meal indeed been prohibitive in its cost? I feared he did not want me to know how much his courtesy, to which he may have felt obliged, had burdened him. Knowing that most rural clergy live like church mice, I could not allow this. So I stepped forward and retrieved my billfold.

"Really, Elder Renfrew, it's most kind of you, but I can't let you..." My eyes fell upon the notes in his hands which I at first took for some antique issue of the Treasury Department, but were not. He rapidly passed to the woman two or three pieces of odd-looking scrip which almost looked to have been hand-drawn. Did the isolated village have its own system of currency?

I had no choice, then, but to let him pay, thanking him again for his generosity, and politely pretending I had seen nothing out of the ordinary. Whatever the reason for it, alternate local currency would certainly complicate my embryonic plans for a profitable relationship with the town of Foxfield. I realized I had a lot to learn about the strange settlement. As we exited the building and made our way down the block I realized I would very soon have an opportunity to satisfy many of the questions that assailed me.

The outward aspect of the church, a white, wood-frame structure typical all over New England, was unusual in one respect only. Indeed it bore no name board, though two signboards stood at either front corner of the lot, one announcing the title of the week's sermon, the other bearing a scripture quotation, though I could not at a glance identify the source of the text: "Secret things shall be made manifest, and hidden things shall come to light." A good Congregationalist layman myself, though my travels forbid me regular attendance in a single local church, I have committed many portions of scripture to memory and tried my best to memorize this one as we passed it.

The front doors of the church were open, and we proceeded quietly down the nave, trying not to disturb the two or three elderly parishioners who had stopped in for midday prayer. We turned left before the pulpit and, after another turn or two, arrived at the door of the pastor's study. Elder Renfrew's knock brought a swift response. The oaken door opened on a small cubbyhole of an office. The diminutive Elder Thorndike welcomed me in with a broad sweep of his hand. His battered desk bore opened and marked books, of which the wall shelves were full as well. Most seemed crudely bound, and the open volume was, I would swear, hand-written. But my eye was drawn to a strange contrivance of square gold or brass plates, each thin rectangle inscribed in strange glyphs, the whole stack being connected by two thin arches of iron wire threaded through two holes along the edge of each plate.

"I see you fancy books, Mr... Willet?"

I assured the parson that I did indeed, treasuring the library bequeathed me by my maternal grandfather, a collection of musty volumes dating from the last century, dear old books from which I had learned much in my precocious youth. Some of these tomes looked to date from about the same period, I suggested, indicating one of his full cabinets.

"And so they do, Mr. Willet. Sit, and let us talk, shall we? Good. Now I would very much like to know how you chanced to come among us." My story was repeated at no great length. And again, I saw no reason to conceal my hopes for reopening commerce between isolated Foxfield and its Novanglian neighbors.

"That, I fear, would be a problem," commented the parson, as if the idea were a foregone impossibility. "You see, Mr. Willet, it's not as if we are so completely shut off as you might think... It isn't easy to explain to someone who's not one of us. Well, Foxfield people decided a long time ago to try and protect ourselves from the worldly influences beyond our borders." His jowled chin rested, cupped in one hand, elbow propped on the table. I could tell the man was choosing his words judiciously, as if trying to satisfy me without really telling me anything.

Perhaps I might get somewhere by changing the direction of the conversation. "Elder Thorndike, would it be possible for you to introduce me to the mayor of Foxfield? I mean no disrespect, but it might be that he would have a different perspective on the matter."

"I'm afraid that would be impossible, or rather, I should say, unnecessary. You see, sir, I am the leader of the community--the civic leader, I mean, as well as the spiritual leader."

I replied that this arrangement was certainly unusual, though not entirely unprecedented, and that I had not intended any discourtesy by my request. The Elder only laughed pleasantly.

"Our ways must seem queer to you, I know. And that's part of the problem here. Too much time has gone by. We're too out of touch with the fast-paced world out there. Oh, we tried it. The machine age reached us here in Foxfield, and we played with its toys for a time. But in the end we decided we liked things better the way they used to be."

I thought of the Amish and Hutterites of Pennsylvania, not to mention the derelict gasoline station I had passed earlier. But he had not finished speaking. Rapidly I sought to regain his train of thought.

"Besides, it's not as if we're ingrown or anything, no inbreeding, God help us." Even so, I had noticed no marks of that taint among the fine-looking people of the little town. There was something slightly exotic in a feature here or there, perhaps a trace of immigrant blood, but nothing more.

"I surmised that you must grow and hunt a great deal of your own food, but you don't even seem to use Federal currency..." Here the older man shot a glance of dismay at the younger, the latter subtly flinching. "And I am quite sure the name of Foxfield appears on no current maps of the area. How do you manage?"

"Actually quite well, thank you, Mr. Willet. Much better than we would manage if we were once again to risk contamination by the world. We cherish our ways, our faith, and there are some things the common run of mankind just does not understand. Alma says it well enough, "O ye workers of iniquity; ye that are puffed up in the vain things of the world, ye that have professed to have known the ways of righteousness nevertheless have gone astray." Of course, not you personally, Mr. Willet! I simply mean to..."

I reassured him that I took his point, and that it was hard to deny it a large measure of validity. I thought to ask how much the younger generations of Foxfield even knew of the outside world, as well as how many of them might make their way there, but some prudent instinct bade me forbear. Instead, I thought it better to salve my itch of curiosity on another point.

"I fancy myself a student of scripture, Elder Thorndike, and yet the text you quote is unfamiliar to me. Oh, the sentiments are common enough throughout Holy Writ, but I cannot quite place the words. Would you be so kind as to enlighten me?"

Here young Renfrew caught his eye with a look of grave concern which made the older man hesitate as he reached up to the nearest shelf. But:

"I'm sure it will be all right. Aren't we commanded in scripture itself to make the truth of scripture known like the pealing of a bell?"

His stubby finger tapped several spines in near-sighted scrutiny till he found the one he sought, and handed it to me.

"It's an extra copy. Take a look at it, though I'm afraid I can't let you keep it. You'll find the passage in there; here, I'll mark the page. But let me tell you a bit of history."

Something seemed to have changed the old parson's mind about telling me what I wanted to know. Now he seemed fully as eager to enlighten me as he had been only a few moments ago to keep me in the dark. This fact made me a bit uneasy, but at the moment my curiosity was uppermost and I did not think his sudden garrulousness as odd, indeed as ominous, as I might have.

"Mr. Willet, the New York State border is no great distance from here, as I'm sure you know, being a great traveler and all. Unlike us shut-ins, I mean. You asked about our religion here in Foxfield, and I'm going to tell you. In fact, it's something you'll be needing to know. Now where was I? Oh, yes. Along about the mid-eighties the whole region was ablaze with the fire of revival. The evangelists and preachers were through here one after the other, criss-crossing the map like travelling salesmen--no implication to be taken, you understand. Folks were getting saved, sanctified, filled with the Holy Ghost.

"Only they didn't all cleave to the same church. Families were split as to who got converted by the Methodists, who got dunked by the Baptists or the Holiness. When the preachers left to go elsewhere, the region was fairly busting with religion. There wasn't a town in Eastern New York or Western Massachusetts that hadn't got religion--and lost it again--two or three times over. In fact they took to calling the whole area 'the burnt-over district.' Ah, I see that rings a bell with you. Good. Well there was a lot of strife, I'm sorry to say. You know how it is with religious folk: sometimes they're so busy being Christians they lose sight of how unChristian they're being to one another. Well, about that time, there must have been several of the younger men in the towns of the burnt-over district that just couldn't see strife as the handiwork of the Lord, so they betook themselves to quiet places in the hills and took to praying for hours at a time that the Lord would show them the way. Which church to join."

I had indeed heard of the notorious "burned-over district," and things began to fall into place. What the clergyman had just recounted was the beginning of the tale of Joseph Smith, the controversial seer of the Mormon Church. Having had a cousin convert to that faith, I had had ample occasion to learn more than I wanted to know about his religion.

"I see it in your eyes. What I'm telling you isn't unfamiliar. But let me go on. One man, named Phineas Hoag, a Foxfield boy much taken with the use of seer stones and water-divining, used to go out to the megaliths on the other edge of the town--you'll be wanting to take a look at them, I'll warrant. And he fasted for forty days, beseeching God all the while. And at the end of the forty days, a great shining Being revealed himself to Phineas. He announced himself as Moroni, from the men of Lomar. He entrusted to Phineas a set of plates, like these; they're a copy, of course. What you're holding is a translation. It's called the Pnakotic Manuscript.

"And it told the history of the Land of Lomar and its fair-skinned people, how they built a mighty citadel in the lands far to the north, and how they were finally driven south by the squat, hairy Gnoph-kehs. Also calls 'em Voormis, which is a little easier to say. These critters, ape-men, I guess you'd call them, kind of like what those evolutionists talk about, they caught up with Moroni's people hereabouts. There was great bloodshed, but the men of Lomar called upon the Lord, Avaloth, they call him in the Manuscript, and he delivered them. He showed them the Place Between the Rocks, the very place Moroni appeared to Phineas Hoag. And there the people of Lomar found safety in a hidden world, preserved from their enemies."

I couldn't help interrupting him with a question, "But Elder Thorndike, isn't this the story of Joseph Smith you're telling me? The Book of Mormon, the war between the Lamanites and the Nephites? Are you telling me you and your people belong to the Mormon Church?"

"No, my friend, I am not. You see, Moroni appeared to several who took refuge in the hills. Some were not worthy, others failed to understand. Some confused the revelation they heard. But, yes, there is a connection. It was only Phineas Hoag who proved a fit vessel for Moroni and his people. Only Phineas was vouchsafed the secret of the Place Between the Rocks, where the men of this earth we know may commune with those of Lomar. I told you we're not exactly shut off. It's just that we seek higher company. We hold truck with the Old Ones, we eat the bread of angels, if you will."

I had never heard of this sect, but I knew enough about that period of fervent revivalism he mentioned not to be surprised at most of what he said. It was plain that I had stumbled upon the source from which young Joseph Smith had derived most of his mythology. Skeptics had long pointed to something called the Solomon Spaulding manuscript, an old religious novel in handwritten draft, as the basis for Smith's artificial scriptures, but here was surely the actual fountainhead of his creed. So he had pilfered it from a local rival sect! I had here discovered something of real historical value, and I resolved to feign only casual interest. Later I would try to contact a scholar at the Miskatonic University with whom I might share what I had learned.

But the Elder was talking again, "I know I've given you a lot to think about, Mr. Willet." He looked out his window and continued, "The sun's about to set. I hope you'll accept our hospitality for the night."

To do so would put me behind, though not seriously; but in fact I was by now fairly certain that I should not be allowed to leave the village of Foxfield in any case. My stay should be an extended one, most likely a life sentence. The town, as I have said, held distinct attractions for me. It was a place a man of my tastes might even consider as a retirement home. But to be detained there against my will was another matter entirely. And yet I knew discretion for the better part of valor.

So I thanked the good parson for his offer and promised to take especial care of the borrowed volume, which, of course, he had supplied as part of my orientation to my new life in the pious community of Foxfield. He dispatched his young assistant to accompany me to the Manor House, the largest and perhaps the only hotel in the town.

During our walk to the hotel, I was quick to observe what I could of the reactions of the townspeople we passed. This time, seeing me freely accompanying the well known Elder Renfrew, most faces seemed less uneasy. One or two even smiled or nodded. Despite my position, I could feel nothing against these people, who, as far as I was concerned, shared my plight whether or not they knew it. Even young Renfrew was hardly to be blamed. His mentor, the Reverend Thorndike, no doubt acted from sincere motivation as well, but then so had Torquemada, I did not doubt.

I thanked Elder Renfrew for his company and bade him good night. He seemed to hesitate a moment, as if on the point of saying something, a warning perhaps, but then he must have thought better of it and departed. As I unpacked my valise and lay half-clothed upon the comfortable bed, it occurred to me to wonder at such a state of careful preservation of a structure for which there could be no conceivable use in a town in which visitors were feared and shunned.

Shrugging off this curiosity, I deemed it best to pass the time absorbed in the book Elder Thorndike had given me, the Pnakotic Manuscript. Mark Twain had once characterized the Book of Mormon as "chloroform in print," and I hoped its apparent prototype might not be the source of its soporific quality. I opened the book and began to read. There did seem to be a fair amount of dreary dogmatizing, which I quickly decided to skim superficially. Various pithy sayings were quite striking, though, especially those attributed to a prophet named Kish of the Land of Mnar. As in the canonical Bible, there was no dearth of ceremonial instructions, and even though these had been translated into familiar English, some terms had simply been transliterated, there apparently being no appropriate English word for this ritual instrument or that sacrificial beast. The implication, of course, was that the text did in fact stem from an alien time and setting. Or at least some forger had been clever enough to include such artifice.

What interested me the most, once I finally located it, was the historical account to which the Elder had referred, not that of Phineas Hoag, a modern figure, of course, but the saga of the men of Lomar and their epic struggle with the degenerate Voormis. The habits of these latter were hinted at with euphemistic reserve which did not manage to conceal terrible depravity and bestiality. Who either of these peoples were and how they might have been harmonized with orthodox ethnology I could not guess. But then it was all quite likely fantasy and fiction, though the more I read, the more often I had to remind myself of this fact.

The loathsome Voormis, it seemed, had worshipped a particularly repellant demon called Tsathoggua, whose ultimate origins were not of this world. It was this foul Being, described in the Manuscript sometimes with the features of a great bat, other times as more nearly a massive, tentacled toad, who had raised the loping Voormis from their original animal state into a shambling parody on the clean lines of true men. The Lomarites, on the other hand, were presented in terms suggesting the Greek demigods of the Iliad and the Odyssey.

The stilted prose did nothing to silence the ringing echoes of tales in which strapping swordsmen of Lomar sank their blades and axes deep into stinking Voormi flesh defending their homeland in a doomed attempt to whelm the invading tide of the pelted half-men. Of any eventual fate of the detestable Voormis there was no hint, something only natural, I supposed, the rest of the chronicle being written from the standpoint of the men of Lomar, whose miraculous deliverance severed any contact with their subhuman opponents. It was fascinating. And despite the superficial Christianization of the whole business implied in Elder Thorndike's monologue, I could find in the text no attempt to connect this mythology with the biblical tradition. It was quite a puzzle.

By this point it is clear I had indeed become enthralled with the remarkable book. Some portions did indeed merit a Twainian reproach, while others, no doubt the work of unknown bards and poets, gave me to believe I had discovered a genuine, though hitherto unknown, epic tradition having barely survived the fall of some prehistoric Northern civilization. Had the book done its intended work upon me? For, though still disinclined to believe in any present-day Lomarians locked in an unseen dimension adjacent to rural Foxfield, I had about come to the conclusion that the Pnakotic Manuscript must represent an ancient tradition, albeit mythical.

So absorbed had I become in the book that it took me a few moments before I realized someone was knocking insistently upon the door. Reaching for my shirt, I wrapped it about me, stuffed its tail into my trousers and approached the door. Without stood my assigned companion, Elder Renfrew. I welcomed the agitated man in, indicating the single chair in the room, while I seated myself upon the edge of the bed. At first I thought he had returned only a few minutes after his departure, perhaps to add some final, momentarily-forgotten detail of his mentor's instruction. But then I noticed his dripping overcoat, which he hung on the closet door hook. There had been no rain earlier, and suddenly I realized that nearly three hours must have passed while I had paged through the Foxfield scripture.

"I see you've been reading it." Elder Renfrew said, with a nod toward the volume. "What is your impression?"

"I must confess I am quite impressed with your Pnakotic Manuscript. It appears to be a genuine discovery of some importance. I wonder that your Phineas Hoag did not try to make it more widely known. Was he perhaps overshadowed in his effort by his more successful rival Joseph Smith?"

"I'm not sure I would call the heretic Smith successful. He was, after all, lynched in the end."

I laughed. "Yes, there's a point!"

Only a hint of a smile relaxed the man's face, which then returned to an expression clenched with foreboding.

"I expect you have surmised that you are never to depart Foxfield, Mr. Willet." This he stated quite matter-of-factly. In the same tone I replied.

"Yes, that was my inference. I see I was not mistaken. Will you tell me why I am to be detained? And how? Will they make room for me in the Foxfield jail? Or is my life sentence to be a short one?"

"Neither. They hope in all good conscience to win you over so that no coercion will be necessary. But none is needful in any case. Foxfield is quite small enough that any attempt by you to escape would be noticed and stopped. Elder Thorndike has already alerted our roaming hunters to keep close surveillance. There are a number of armed men in the surrounding fields most of the time anyway, you see, so guarding you presents no problem, not even any special effort."

"I see. Then at least my confinement would be more in the nature of house arrest. But I must warn you I cannot abide being kept against my will. And I am beginning to suspect that you are tired of it, too. Am I anywhere near the truth, Elder Renfrew?"

His eyes widened and he hunched forward in the creaking chair. He said nothing but waited for me to continue. I did. "I thought you employed the word 'they' a bit too often, Mr. Renfrew. And now please tell me why you are here."

He seemed confused, vacillating between hints of despair and of renewed hope. "I hope I am not a book so easily read by Elder Thorndike! But I think he cannot suspect. It is moot, though. I will tell you that I had planned on returning to see you with a plan of escape. You see, it was I who contrived to have the underbrush trimmed back so that it would no longer obscure the entrance to the shunpike. I hoped someone would come, not knowing exactly what to do if anyone did. It would have been better if a large group came. Frankly, that's what I had hoped, that it would be your police. It is possible that a large armed force might make the difference.

"You see, Mr. Willet, as a clergyman here I am privileged to know certain things about the outside world that others never learn. Ironically we must know about the outside in order to remain ignorant of it, isolated from it at any rate. Still... it must be futile. I have stooped to grasping at straws."

"Don't be so quick to despair!," I sought to reassure him. "It is not impossible even now that, my presence being missed, a party will be sent to find me. My itinerary is known, and witnesses will remember having seen me at my last stop. So surely there will be a search party in the area. Once they discover the shunpike entrance as I did they are sure to explore it."

"It's no good. Your presence here will lead our leaders to make sure the entrance is somehow hidden again, and the highway authorities will probably not even notice. And suppose a party of outsiders did make it this far. There are the men of Lomar. You're not taking them into account."

My sense of bafflement returned. "What can they have to do with it, my friend? Surely you're talking about mere characters in a book. Forgive me if I seem to offend your faith, but the Lomarians, if they ever existed, are long dead."

At this he seemed to look over his shoulder nervously, but he went on, in lowered tones. "Mr. Willet, I only wish that were true. I can assure you, the men of Lomar are quite real. I mean physically real. I have seen them."

"What do you mean? In a vision?"

"No, they are as physically solid as you or I."

"But all this about their passing into some adjacent dimension of space. Surely that denotes heaven and angels."

He shook his head. "They are not angels, Mr. Willet, though there are devils worse than them."

The young man pulled his chair closer, drew himself up, and interposed a seemingly unrelated question. "Does it not seem strange to you that a town as xenophobic as our Foxfield should maintain so capacious hotel as the Manor House?"

"To tell you the truth, I had wondered that, yes."

"The rooms in this establishment are maintained for the occasional visits of those from Lomar." He could, I am sure, read the incredulity written broadly across my face, but I said nothing for the moment and let him continue. After a pause, he said, "They do not often venture outside their secret zone, nor for long. Where they dwell is a timeless realm, more akin to dream than to waking life. And outside of it they will age just as we mortals do. So they are loathe to leave it. Favored members of our community are allowed to enter their dimension at the Place Between the Rocks, but, again, not for long. They are permitted to take sparingly of the game and the crops of that strange world, but the possession of timeless immortality those of Lomar preserve strictly unto themselves. Only one in the town of Foxfield have they taken to themselves and allowed to remain among them, even Phineas Hoag, to whom they revealed themselves."

I shook my head in amazed disbelief. "Are you telling me that the descendants of the ancient nation of Lomar are alive somewhere outside of this town?"

"No, sir. I mean to say that the very men of Lomar themselves, those of whom the Manuscript tells, are alive on our borders."

"You know," I said impatiently, "you're only making it more difficult, not less, for me to believe any of this. For one thing, what could either party gain from the strange alliance you describe? A few vegetables? Immortality, I could see that; but that's not part of the package. Except for your prophet. And why not suppose even that to be anything more than a legend that grew up after he disappeared? For all you know, maybe he met the same end as Joseph Smith!"

"You have asked me two questions; I will give you two answers. It is true, the return for our fealty to the Old Ones of Lomar is not great. They manage to supply us with what we lack from the outside world, and to some they supply certain articles we would consider very valuable, though little esteemed by them. Gold, for instance, though our circumstances set certain limits to what can be purchased with it. There is an irony in that, but I can tell you, Elder Thorndike's private residence is quite something to see. Like the dwelling of a medieval king, for whatever good it does him.

"The town of Foxfield first kept to their bargain largely out of fear. The power of those from Lomar is very great. It is a power easily able to repel and destroy any armed force from the outside world, though they would hardly welcome the attention that would bring.

"The last few generations of Foxfielders, however, have never known anything different, and only rarely does a renegade like myself grow dissatisfied. The tales of those few, once they are discovered, are terrible to hear.

"Whether they met their whispered fates at the hands of the town's rulers or those of Lomar, we do not know. It does not matter. But by now the bond with Lomar is simply a fact of life, like the air and the water.

"As for what our unseen masters reap from our service, it is rather simple. Just as there is a Gate to their hidden dimension, there are other Gates to other dimensions.

"Foxfield's misfortune is to have been founded near one of the places where these Gates meet. It is our task to see that they are not opened contrary to the will of Lomar. There are certain secret keys, words of binding and loosing, known only to myself, Elder Thorndike, and a few others.

"And, as for the immortal continuing of Phineas Hoag, the revealer, the covenant-maker, I have as little choice to disbelieve it as I do the existence of the Lomarians themselves."

"Yes?," I challenged, still hardly satisfied. "And what is the source of your certainty, if I may ask?"

Elder Renfrew abruptly stood to his feet, startling me; he strode briskly to the door and pulled it open. Extending an open hand toward the hallway without, he said in exasperated tones, "Both Phineas Hoag and three of his ancient masters are elsewhere in this building at this moment. Come, I will take you to see them if you wish it."

I was galvanized with an unexpected current of fear. Reason told me that Renfrew must either be trying to hoax me with the aid of a handful of rustic impostors, whose pretense would be immediately exploded, or himself have been deceived by such cheap chicanery.

And yet, who could seriously hope to bring off such a trick? And why resort to it if my confinement were assured in any case? For the first time I began to feel creeping coldly upon me a terrible sensation that the absurd, the preposterous, might actually be substantial and terribly real.

The bare thought of the proximity under the same roof of fabulous immortals and, even more, the blasphemous survival through more than a century of a contemporary of Joseph Smith, chilled my spine.

I stood but remained silent, dumbfounded. Renfrew slowly and quietly closed the door again. We resumed our respective seats.

"I... your word is enough... for the present," I said, struggling to regain my composure. "But what are we to do?"

"Friend Willet, I said I had hoped to discuss escape with you, but now that seems past all chance of succeeding. Tomorrow, like it or not, you will be taken by myself and Elder Thorndike to the Place Between the Rocks. No, do not fear, you will not be harmed. Not physically. But you will be shown the inner realm of the Old Ones of Lomar. I cannot predict how the sight will affect you, but it is likely you will think no more of escaping the hospitality of Foxfield. Beyond that, I cannot tell you what to expect."

"But surely you have seen this sight yourself," I reasoned aloud. "You must be able to give me some idea of what is in store?"

"Mercifully, I have not seen. I have never dared. But I fear, should my insubordination after all be detected, that I may share whatever fate awaits you. I thought you should know. Try to prepare yourself. Perhaps there is little to fear. I only know that some have not returned sane from the encounter. And now I must go, lest the length of my absence itself invite suspicion. Good night to you."

There was nothing more to say, and in an instant, no one there to whom I might say it. Here I was, a shaking wreck, who had only ten minutes before relegated the whole fantastic business to the follies of religious delusion. And now, God spare me, I had come to share it. I strove all night, in lieu of sleep, to have reason regain the upper hand, to reassure myself of the reign of sanity and the security of the mundane. When these efforts failed, I merely sought to tell myself that the night fears which make us all children would vanish with the dawn. Even the usually calming monotony of the rain at the windowpane did nothing to soothe me. At last sheer fatigue overruled and mercifully threw me the crumb of a hour's slumber.

Waking again with the light, I dragged my aching body from the bed and washed myself cursorily. With an anvil of dread hanging over me, I dressed and sat down to wait. Vacantly I flipped the pages of the Pnakotic Manuscript for some unmarked duration, probably not long, till I heard a knock upon my door. I rose wearily, my limbs numb from insomnia and resignation, and reached for the knob. I hesitated a moment, suddenly imagining who or what might await me on the other side.

To my considerable relief the hallway held only the two black-frocked Elders Renfrew and Thorndike, as well as a burly town policeman, whose uniform shared the quaint signs of anachronism characteristic of Foxfield as a whole. I gathered from an overheard remark some minutes later that the personages whose presence I had dreaded had returned to their accustomed dwelling sometime during the night.

"From the look of you, Mr. Willet, I fear you did not sleep well," began Thorndike, with the unctuousness of the practiced clergyman. "For that I am sorry. I believe my young colleague has told you of our destination." Here he took my shoulder in what seemed to me a mockery of fatherly reassurance. "I can assure you this will be a morning to remember, for us all." With this remark he looked a moment in Renfrew's direction. I said nothing, having none of the energy needed to frame an adroit rejoinder. I simply accompanied the small party down the stairs, through the lobby, and up the streets till we reached the open fields on the edge of the town.

Not far away I could see the silhouettes of one of the massive rocks about which so ominous a cycle of legends, or even more ominous truths, had developed. When we had come nearer to it, I could see others nearby. One could not tell whether they were purely natural phenomena or rather some sort of artificial structures. But in either case, still closer proximity revealed the presence of somewhat faded but deeply carved glyphs. Those on the pair of megaliths we approached were evidently of the same type as I had glimpsed on the metal plates lying open on Thorndike's desk the day before. I reflected that it must be such relics as these which had given rise to the many eccentric theories about Norsemen or ancient Phoenicians visiting New England's shores. As if the truth were any less fantastic!

"This is," began the theocratic ruler of Foxfield, "the very spot on which Phineas Hoag first beheld Moroni and received the Manuscript. It is sacred to us, so I must ask you to remove your shoes before we enter the Place Between the Rocks." The whole party, myself included, then performed the incongruously quaint-seeming ritual of unlacing our footwear. Well, Moses had not scrupled; why should I?

As we took a few solemn steps forward, I confess I did feel an odd sort of atmospheric disturbance, as well as something more. I began to fancy that I could almost make out certain rushing shapes in the air about me, from the corner of my eye, so to speak, nothing to see straight on. Noting my confusion, Thorndike explained. It seemed he had the natural tendency of the preacher, to interpose commentary at every opportunity, requested or not.

"They are all around us even now. The Old Ones walk serene and primal, not in the spaces we know, but between them. But you shall shortly gain the gift of second sight, Mr. Willet, and you will be one of us. Come, there is nothing to fear."

I traded apprehensive glances with Elder Renfrew at these words. I still had no clear idea of what to expect, what might happen to me. But I was not eager to find out.

"Elder Renfrew, I believe it will be your task to open the Gate. I will, ah, stand back here so as to be out of your way. I believe you know the liturgy for the occasion."

The younger man stepped forward gravely. He bowed, then knelt on the ground without regard to the moisture and mud. He rose and made a slow progress back and forth between the two great stones which rested about fifteen feet apart. Under his breath he was chanting the words of some memorized formula. I could not tell whether the words were in English or in the unknown tongue of the Pnakotic Manuscript, though I supposed the latter.

The feeling of disturbance increased, and I felt a ringing in my ears, also some reverberation which I can only compare to thunder sounding afar off, though I cannot swear it was truly sonic in nature. And then, between the rocks, the light of morning began to take on a strange reddish tint, like one sometimes sees in the night sky above a great fire in the distance. I wanted to look away but could not. I fancied that between the rocks I could catch a hinted silhouette of several tall figures, mostly male, and with a suggestion of a great many more behind them. I began to feel the powerful tugging of an instinct to weep, perhaps from awe. There was something undeniably majestic to the vague but potent scene taking form before me.

I had lost the sound of Elder Renfrew's monotone chanting. I had even lost any sense of myself and my position, so overcome was I with the epiphany. But in another moment, there was an outburst of cries and shouts. And then gunshots! That must be the police officer who had accompanied us. Involuntarily I wheeled about, losing my balance and stumbling to the wet ground. I saw the form of Elder Renfrew collapsing to the earth as well. It was he who had been shot. Instantly I supposed his disloyalty had been discovered and punished, though in more mundane fashion than I had expected. But I was soon to realize there was much more at stake here.

Now the thunderous crackings had magnified in intensity tenfold, sending disabling echoes through my tortured skull. I saw that Elder Thorndike had given into the same sudden pain and writhed upon the damp earth, while the confused policeman wasted his remaining shots firing into the air, aimlessly, as I momentarily thought. But then the senses of some in Foxfield were keener than mine where certain matters were concerned, and I realized he might be seeing something I could not. I looked back to the Place Between the Rocks, where the glowing portal between dimensions had seemingly vanished again.

But the same aura of eldritch half-light now spread as if with the strokes of a great brush across the whole horizon. And in it the eye strained to fill in the implicit lines of a great mass of struggling forms. I knew not what to make of this mute pantomime of heavenly battle. Coming to myself, I regained sufficient presence of mind to make for the moaning form of Elder Renfrew. Knowing the dangers of moving an injured man, I nonetheless decided I must attempt to hoist him up and drag him as best I could back toward town, away from the wildly firing gunman, who had now brought a second weapon into play. The wild-eyed policeman must have known no mundane weapons could reach the target he sought but continued to obey the dictates of panic nonetheless.

Our pace was maddeningly frustrating as I sought to regain the town. Shoeless on the bare ground, my speed was even less than it would have been. Anxiety bore heavily upon me, as I knew not but that any moment might send down upon us whatever Entities strove in the heavens above us. I now moved as in a nightmare fantasy, especially as I experienced in reality the same molasses-slowness that retards the would-be runner in a dream.

But at length we did make it to town. The bleeding Renfrew was able to make me understand how to reach the local physician, who, it turned out, had already been roused, like the rest of the townspeople, by the celestial cannonade. There was not much to be done, alas. The policeman had had little danger of missing his shot at such close range, and Renfrew was fading fast. I begged him to tell me what had happened and, more important, what might yet occur. His blood-drooling lips parted in a whisper.

"I told you there were other Gates, other worlds... Last night I decided something had to be done quickly. Knew how to get access to secret portions of Pnakotic... Knew there was a way to open other... Voormis, too... Waiting all this... In the end, decided... let them finish the job... Chant... opened both... into each other... Thorndike heard... too late, though. Over soon... for me, too..." And this was the last of it. My ear had been close to his stammering lips, but now I rose to look into the baffled face of the fearful doctor. I closed the lids of my poor friend's vacant eyes. I tendered no word of explanation to the nonplussed country practitioner, but turned and ran for the main street of the town.

My automobile was not where I had left it the previous day, but it did not take me long to locate it. It reposed before a particularly opulent private home a street or two away, which I surmised must be the palatial residence of the Reverend Thorndike. I only prayed no one had thought to disable the motor. Climbing into the driver's seat, I saw no key but retrieved the extra set I always keep about my person. The machine shuddered into life, and with none of my usual automotive caution, I barrelled through the cobble-paved streets like Barney Oldfield, sending the pathetic Foxfielders scattering in every direction. I made for the shunpike, resolving that no recently interposed barricade should long detain me.

As it happened, I met no opposition. My guess was that all the roving hunters and patrolmen, alarmed by what was taking place in the skies above them, had rushed home to see to their families' safety. Once I regained the hard earth of the shunpike, I ventured to look back toward the town I had so precipitously abandoned. Most of the phantom Armageddon had apparently run its course, the long-delayed conclusion of an ancient saga of hatred between two races who had far outlived their appointed time.

Ahead of me, at long last, was the reentry point to the main highway. I rejoiced to see it, and as I turned the wheel to regain familiar paths, I craned my neck momentarily for one last glimpse in the direction of Foxfield. The horizon over that way seemed almost normal now, save for a rapidly dispersing shadow that might have been a vestigial storm cloud from the previous night's rain, or might have been something else, but which suggested the rough outlines of a vast, squatting toad.

Van Graf's Painting

By J. Todd Kingrea

Dennis looked up from his textbook and out into the gathering dusk. He could barely make out the bell tower in the center of campus. A few cars moved along slowly, their headlights jabbing ineffectually at the darkness. Trees raped by winter swayed in the icy wind, which howled and beat at the window like a living thing.

His gaze wandered across the living room to the painting lying on the kitchen table. It had arrived earlier today by special courier, a gift from his mother. Dennis shifted in the recliner, the art history book heavy on his lap. He really needed to get a little more studying done before Logan got back. But somehow the lack of tympanium sculpture on the west facade of the Rheims Cathedral was not making an impression on him. Tires squealed in the night and Dennis looked back to the window. Snowflakes dashed against the glass and vanished.

He thought he saw Logan scurrying toward the building. He knew once his roommate returned they'd spend the rest of the evening watching movies, and he wouldn't get any studying done. His final in Early Christian and Medevial Art History was next week, and it was a big one. Fifty percent of his final grade rested on whether or not he could identify a triforium gallery, or describe the artistic philosophy of the High Gothic. And try as he might, he hadn't been able to concentrate all afternoon--ever since the painting had arrived.

Setting the book aside, Dennis rose from the chair, stretched, and ambled over to the kitchen table. He looked at the painting for what felt like the thousandth time.

It was about two feet square, set in an exquisite, multi-panelled wooden frame. The painting depicted a tranquil village resting at the edge of a lake or river. On the far shore was the indications of another town or village, but it was vague and unformed. The whole picture was composed of slashing, invasive sweeps of reds, blues, yellows--and by mixture, green. There was a combination of Impressionist and Cubist influences in the work, particularly in the depictions of the sky, the water, and the land.

But what drew Dennis's attention again and again was the central village.

The townsfolk shown along the narrow streets were executed in precise, exacting detail, something unusual for either an Impressionist or Cubist painter. Every fold of cloth, every basket, every bit of jewelry was delineated with attention. In the village a boy clutching a package rode his bicycle past an old man on a bench. The vendors along the street had but a single customer - a woman purchasing fish, and in the distance a man with a cape and walking stick had just entered the street, walking toward the viewer. Stepping back to get a better look at the whole image, Dennis was once again amazed at how the specific details of the village melded so subtly with the splashes and broad strokes of color. He found it somehow mysterious that two styles so different could be unified in such a compelling way.

The door to the apartment opened, admitting Logan and a gust of icy-tasting air. "Hey man," he said, dropping his backpack beside the door and removing his gloves. "What's up?"

"Oh, just studying some, on and off," Dennis replied, feeling somewhat distracted by Logan's arrival. He looked back at the painting, to the caped figure at the end of the street. He wondered who he could have been.

"What's that?"

Logan crossed the kitchen and stood behind Dennis, peering at the painting. Dennis could feel the coldness of the night seeping off Logan's clothes.

"It's a painting Mom sent us. A friend of hers passed away and willed her some artwork. She didn't have room for this one, so she gave it to us." He glanced around at the movie posters and pin-ups. "I guess she figured we could use a little culture around here," he added.

Dennis could tell that Logan didn't care for the picture. Logan didn't like modern art. He teased Dennis about it, since it was one of Dennis's favorite art periods, but Logan himself had little use for it. When the curriculum made him take an introductory painting class, he'd set out on one project to make fun of modern art. He'd painted half of a brown paper bag on his canvas and called it "Night Sky with Red Stairway #5." His professor had loved it, and Logan had made his point that "if that's all there is to it, anybody can be an artist!"

The television blared out suddenly, invading Dennis's thoughts and irritating him. Logan had switched on a ball game. His study time terminated, Dennis snatched up his notes and textbook, trying to ignore the cheerless mood he felt himself slipping into.

* * *

"I said, what're you doing?"

The words filtered slowly into Dennis's brain. He blinked several times, forcing the world into focus. Logan stood over him. "Geez man, you in a coma or something?" he asked, flicking his baseball cap into a chair. "I've been talking to you for five minutes--ever since I came in the door--and you've just been laying there like a corpse."

Dennis rubbed his eyes as Logan tossed books out of his backpack. Logan was a little over six feet tall, only an inch or so taller than Dennis, but he was a good seventy or eighty pounds heavier. He flopped down in the recliner and pulled out a cigarette. "I see you hung our piece of culture today," he said, rubbing his sparse beard and nodding toward the painting.

"Yeah." Dennis's response was dull, morose. "I put it up this morning."

"Didn't you go to class today?"

Dennis rose from the couch, still looking at the painting, as if waiting for something to happen within its oiled panorama. "Huh? Class? Oh, no. I skipped class today. I spent most of the day in the library, researching the painting and the artist." Somewhere below a stereo came to life, the muffled bass lines of Pink Floyd trobbing dully.

"Do you know what that woman's doing?" Dennis asked abruptly, pointing to the lady in the painting who was purchasing a fish.

Logan squinted his eyes, focusing on the painting. "It looks like she's buying a fish," he deadpanned. A wraith of grey smoke twisted past his humorous blue eyes and dissipated.

"No. She's going to poison her husband."

"Huh? How do you know?"

Dennis was silent for a moment. He stared at the painting. "I'm not sure," he finally said in a quiet voice, "I guess I read it somewhere during my research." A thought nagged at his mind: had he read it somewhere? Or was it something he had been thinking while laying on the couch?

Logan's clear, deep voice interrupted the thought. "So, who painted that mess anyway?" he asked, flicking ashes into a cup in his lap. "Looks like something my little niece would do in kindergarten."

"It was done by an artist named Rainart Van Graf," Dennis snapped. He paused, taking a moment to collect himself. He hadn't meant to bite Logan's head off. His roommate was always poking fun at some aspect of modern art. So why had he reacted so aggressively this time? It must be the strain of the upcoming exam.

Dennis grinned, a gesture to show Logan he was sorry for his snappy remark. "He was a fringe member of Der Blaue Reiter--The Blue Rider--a German Expressionist group from the early twentieth century whose members included Vasily Kandinsky, Franz Marc, and August Macke."

As he talked, Dennis began to feel awake, free, more alert. The strange sense of lethargy and futility he had experienced earlier, his unusual irritation at Logan, it was all going away. No wonder Logan had thought he was in a coma. He'd lain down on the couch, reviewing his research material, when he'd started studying the painting. That's when he started feeling depressed. Thinking back on this, Dennis couldn't pinpoint why he'd felt so melancholic at the time. Maybe this art history final really was getting him down. Or perhaps it was just the weather.

He continued: "Van Graf exhibited several paintings with The Blue Rider, but was never really considered part of the group. Where they stressed symbolic and spiritual properties of form, Van Graf was still dealing with emotional distortion and impact." Glancing away from the painting Dennis looked out at the campus.

It lay covered in a thin layer of snow, like a burial shroud. The buildings across the quad all seemed faint and unformed in the swirling snow.

"He called the painting "The Kingdom." He painted it after returning from a trip to Paris, where he'd spent several weeks in various hedonistic pursuits. He returned to Germany in 1916, painted this picture and one other now considered lost, and died a few months later." Dennis had stepped into the kitchen while talking and returned with a glass of iced tea, pausing again to study the painting before setting down on the couch.

Logan crushed out his cigarette, spit into the cup, and kicked his shoes off. He sat on the edge of the recliner cushion as if trying to decide whether to get up or sink back into its worn embrace. "So is this thing worth any money?" he asked, grinning broadly.

"Probably. I'd have to get it appraised to know exactly. But the other one he did after leaving Paris--the lost one--now that one would be worth a bundle if someone had it. I'd love to see what it looked like. There's no surviving sketches of it or anything. Nobody would ever know he did it if he hadn't mentioned it in a letter to Kandinsky a few weeks before he died."

The wind yowled outside, rattling the window and obscuring the campus with powdery snow. Pink Floyd continued to throb unabated.

"What'd he die of?" Logan queried. He hoisted himself out of the chair and headed toward the bathroom.

"He committed suicide," Dennis answered, raising his voice to carry down the hallway. "He hanged himself." His gaze slid back to the painting, to the man with the walking stick and cape. His voice sank almost to a whisper. "Right after he completed the "Sign of the King."

* * *

Later that night Dennis lay on the couch in the light of a single lamp. Logan had gone to bed, his stomach upset from too many nachos and chili dogs. Dennis had welcomed the silence in which to study for his final.

He put his book down to rest his eyes and take a break before pushing on. He focused on the painting. That woman was going to poison her husband, he thought. And he knew why. In his mind he began to construct the events of the woman's life, as sure of them as if he had been there. Or had actually lived them.

Her name was Dominique, and Dennis could picture her perfectly. She was of medium height, with long brunette hair, wide hazel eyes, and a quizzical scowl. Her face was wrinkled around the eyes and lips, and had lost much of its former beauty through marriage. Once a beautiful, exquisite lady, she was now a middle-aged, greying woman with scars and pain.

The fish would be the perfect way to murder Amadour. She would apply the poison conservatively, so that it would not render him dead until several days later. When the authorities questioned her about his death, she could tearfully and honestly explain it as a bad piece of fish. Of course, she would have to be sure not to eat any of it herself.

The weight of her decision was heavy upon her mind, but she knew it must be done. Amadour, while romantic and passionate at the start, had soon turned into a beast. He had beat their two children countless times, bloodying and bruising their tiny bodies. He had nearly killed little Aurelia when she was but nine months old. And of course there were the broken bones, dislocations, and brusies that Dominique herself had borne from his brutal assaults. No, she decided, his murder would be best for everyone. At last they would all be free from his rage.

Dennis, lying in the silent, charcoal darkness of the apartment, saw Dominique and her children. He saw their terror, their pain, as Amadour slammed them into walls and punched their tender faces. He saw the futility of Dominique's attempts to get help--he saw people turn their backs on her and priests accuse her of bringing it upon herself because of her sins and lusts. He smelled the fear, heard the crack of bones, saw the blood-tinged tears of the children. It played out in his head like a movie that he was powerless to stop or turn away from.

He looked deeper. She had left the tainted fish, returning to the market for vegetables to help hide the acrid taste of the poison. Dennis saw her enter the kitchen and stop, her eyes widening. She opened her mouth and screamed.

Aurelia and Jacques lay crumpled on the kitchen floor, their little bodies locked into twisted death spasms, bits of fish still clinging to their frothy mouths. Their muscles were rigid and stood up beneath their pale skin; their eyes bulged, their silent mouths gaped. Dominique screamed hysterically and fell beside her dead children. It was enough poison to kill Amadour in a few days, but it was more than enough to still her children's hearts in a moment.

Dennis saw the burly Amadour come home. He looked at the children's bodies, the remains of the poisoned fish, and his wife, who was huddled in the corner. Dennis ripped his thoughts away from the final scene of the drunken, roaring Amadour advancing on Dominique, fists raised high.

Dennis opened his eyes and looked toward the painting. A deep anguish flooded his body as he saw the woman with the fish. The pain in his heart was real, the sense of loss profound. Dennis rose from the couch, turned off the light, and retreated to his bedroom, a very real grief burning in his soul.

* * *

The following day was Friday and Logan left to spend the weekend with his parents. He had expressed concern for Dennis before leaving, citing the fact that he hadn't shaved, had skipped class for the second straight day, and was overall not his usual, jovial self. Dennis had attempted a smile and chided Logan for his overprotectiveness. "It's just that art history final I've got coming up," he'd told Logan while loading the car. "I've been worrying about it, I guess, and not sleeping very much."

They had exchanged a little small talk, then Logan drove off, leaving Dennis alone in the snowy parking lot.

He closed the apartment door behind him and locked it. He then walked into the living room and sat down on the couch. The overhead light buzzed like an insect caught in someone's hair. Then it popped and crackled as it burnt out; the room was thrown into a hazy shade of dusk. Dennis didn't mind. He lay back on the couch, his eyes wandering over the painting. A dog barked outside, and he could hear laughter from the parking lot below. Without ever taking his eyes off the painting, he saw before him a young man on a bicycle, carrying a brown parcel.

For Marcel, today was a glorious day. He smiled into the bright cloud-peppered sky, his blue eyes dancing, whistling a bouncy tune. He pedaled his bicycle along the cobblstone street toward the house of his love, the captivating Nathalie Martine Briand. Martine was a beautiful girl, full of life and humor; she was tall and slender, with eyes the color of cut emerald, and curled black hair that fell to her waist. She was demure and cultured, romantic and intelligent. How she had come to fall in love with someone from so ordinary a lot as Marcel was something he still did not understand. But his heart was too light, too full of joy today to question why. He did not care that he was a common field hand and she was the daughter of a regional magistrate. They loved each other, and that was enough.

Marcel rode down the main street, passing vendors and flower girls, children and animals. The spring breeze blew his thick brown hair back and tugged at his shabby frock. He gripped his brown package tighter, as if the wind might try to steal it from him. Inside was a clay figurine of a dancer that he had sculpted to give to Martine, to commemorate their one month anniversary. It was somewhat crude and primitive-- Marcel didn't have the money to attend art school like he so wanted. But he had done the best he could and was quite pleased with the result.

A chorus of yellow and grey birds were singing sweetly among the budding trees when Marcel arrived at the Briand mansion. He parked his bicycle near the steps and bounded up to the door, full of youthful exuberance. He knocked, then shifted the package nervously to the other arm.

He could hear Martine's laughter on the other side of the door. There was a click, and the door swung open. Martine, having been looking over her shoulder, turned to greet him. The charming, fairie-like smile on her face vanished when she saw Marcel. The change was not lost on him.

"Martine, what's wrong? Is anything the matter?" Marcel asked, taken aback by her reaction. Surely she remembered that today was their anniversary?

A deep, powerful male voice came from somewhere behind Martine: "Who is it, my dear?"

Marcel did not recognize the voice. It was not her father, nor either of her brothers. Martine glanced over her shoulder, then back at Marcel. The door was pulled open the rest of the way by a broad, tanned young man who slipped his brawny arm around Martine's delicate waist. A perfect smile was spread across his chiseled features.

"Oh dear," she giggled, eyeing Marcel as a man of science might observe an insect pinned to a board. "I'm afraid the game is undone."

Marcel stood frozen, unsure. His heart pounded like a galloping stallion. "Martine, what's...who is this? What's happening?" He glanced at the blonde, handsome man beside her. "Did you forget about our anniversary today?"

Martine giggled again, her soft hair catching the light as she moved. "Oh Marcel...," she started, but couldn't finish. Laughter had overtaken her. The man continued to smile. Marcel felt a coldness settle in the pit of his stomach. He opened his mouth to speak, but Martine shushed him with a wave of her hand.

"Marcel, this is Andre. You remember how I spoke of Andre, don't you?" Of how we used to see one another?" Marcel felt the coldness beginning to spread throughout his body.

"He and I saw much of each other before you and I courted. As a matter of fact, you came along right after Andre and I had had a... disagreement." She stared hard into Marcel's eyes. "I decided to use you to make Andre jealous, to win him back to me," she gloated.

"And it seems to have worked, eh, my princess?" Andre smiled. He slid his arm around her waist. "I'll never be foolish enough to risk losing you again. Especially not to one such as him."

Marcel felt the last word sting him, like the bite of a whip across naked flesh. He wanted to lash out, to cry, to run away, but his body was held fast by Martine's laughter and that of her beau. He looked down and Martine caught sight of the package. "For me?" she asked coquettishly, snatching the parcel and opening it. She withdrew the small, clay statuette that Marcel had made and held it up to the light. Marcel wanted to rip the figurine out of her hands and flee but all he could do was tremble.

She gazed at the unrefined statuette, turning it over and over in her hands, staring at the clumsy, unfired piece. Then she looked at Andre, and both burst out in loud, comical laughter. Marcel was crushed. He retreated until his back was against one of the porch's corinthian columns. Their laughter--hers so soft and airy, his so abrasive and deep--pierced Marcel's brain like hot pokers. He could feel his eyes filling with tears, his face and neck flushing.

Martine held the statuette out in front of her and let it drop. Shards of clay exploded outward as it impacted on the marble porch. Andre continued to chuckle. Martine fixed Marcel with a hateful glare. "I will have none of your amorous gifts, nor will I have anything else to do with you. My purpose in being with you has been served," she stated, caressing Andre's hand. "Never come around me again, you miserable little wretch. You have nothing to offer me. If I ever so much as see you again, I'll have you arrested and thrown into the blackest prison in France!" With that she slammed the door, blocking out the chilling laughter that was shared between the two of them.

Tossing and turning on the couch, Dennis observed the final outcome of the incident. He saw the young man standing on a bridge over a swift, deep river. Marcel held the cracked remains of the figurine's head in one hand. His face was lined with tears. He hadn't eaten or slept in days. He looked down into the murky waters of the river, swollen by spring thaws. He ached inside as if someone had cut a piece out of him and thrown it away. Clutching his breast, he sobbed aloud as he pictured Martine's beautiful young face; of how he had pushed her in a flower-entwined swing in her garden. He pictured holding her tiny hand and he saw them laughing and talking as they walked along the banks of this very river. He saw the times they had shared lemonade, and walked beneath the night sky.

The wind blew fiercly, whipping at Marcel's smock, chilling him with its razored bite. He held the figurine's shattered head in front of him and looked at it through tear-stained eyes. He turned it loose and watched it disappear into the raging torrent. Then he stepped off the bridge and followed the shard into the river's numbing embrace.

* * *

Dennis lay on the couch all that night with the images of Marcel and Martine in his mind. He was unaware of the passage of time. Although he felt the need to relieve himself, he made no move to get up and do so. Hunger and thirst began to assail him and still he made no effort to satisfy his body's cravings. He simply didn't care. It wasn't worth caring about, was it? What were his problems, his discomforts, compared to those depicted in the painting? He lethargically raked at the stubble covering his jaw and with his tongue he felt the layer of film that had settled over his teeth in the night. Dennis's heart ached with loss and his head was filled with thoughts of despair. He felt the absence of Marcel in his soul like he would have felt the loss of a loved one.

Those poor souls in that painting. How was it that Van Graf had been able to depict their tragic losses, their depression, their grief so vividly? Dawn was breaking outside. Sunbeams with no warmth crept through the frosted windows and played on the carpet. Dennis heard a door slam somewhere, followed by a car starting up. He rolled over onto his side and drew his knees up to his chin. His head felt heavy, his unwashed hair gummy and stiff. Wrapping his arms about his legs, he lay there in the chilly morning sun and wept for Dominique and Marcel.

Late in the afternoon Dennis left the couch. He stumbled into the bathroom, weak with fatigue and grief, and attended to relieving himself. As he did so he looked in the mirror. His usually wavy hair was matted to his head, and his eyes were heavy and bloodshot. A thin trail of mucous had dried under his nose and his cheeks and forehead were shiny with oil. He thought about taking a shower and cleaning up, but couldn't see the point in it. Why bother? He wasn't going anywhere. Besides, grief cares little for appearance.

Returning to the living room, Dennis looked out the window toward campus. Judging by the way the people's breath held itself in tiny clouds, it was still cold outside. But that hadn't deterred the students from bustling about in the sunshine, which still possessed no warmth. The academic buildings on the other side of the quad all seemed so far away as to be in another world. Just like in the painting, Dennis thought. The faint, surreal, undefined city on the other side of the lake.

He watched the students for a few more minutes. A girl played frisbee with her dog. A game of football was underway with teams of shirted and bare-chested fraternity guys. Most people scurried in and out of buildings, moving rapidly from one point to another. On the sidewalk that separated his building from the quad he could see an old man shuffling along, head bent against the biting cold, black coat flapping wildly in the wind.

Dennis turned and shuffled to the painting. The sheen of its oily surface mesmerized him. It called to him. Standing before it, he saw the image of the old man sitting on the bench. The look of emptiness the man wore was poignant, and only seemed to be noticable when Dennis stood inches away from the picture. He could smell the heavy oils and laquers on it, as if it had just been painted. The cloying aromas reached out for him, invading him. He felt giddy. Gripping the edges of the frame, Dennis strained his aching eyes and stared hard into the old man's painted sorrow. A low, painful moan escaped his cracked lips.

Jean-Pierre sat motionless on the green bench in Carcoseaux's street of vendors. He stared straight ahead, his gaze fixed on the Rhone River which, from his position, he could see between two buildings. He thought of travelling her once again, all the way down to the Mediterranean, and the port of her delight, Marseille. It had been in that very city on a warm night laden with a million pinpoint stars that he had proposed to Marie.

The night had been alive with music and romance. He could vividly remember the smell of the sea and the lights of the city spread out before them as they stood on the balcony. He had taken her hand, gazed deep into her sparkling eyes, and asked her to marry him. Her response had been immediate. He could remember their embrace, their laughter, the perfumed scent of Marie's golden hair. He could even remember how his heart had been beating so fiercly with happiness he thought it would explode from his chest.

Now his heart pumped less vigorously, even when warmed by old memories. Jean-Pierre sighed deeply and stared down at the wrinkled, spotted hands that lay in his lap. The same hands that had held Marie close on that enchanted evening and stroked her hair as she lay her head on his chest. They were the same hands that had held their first born, Alain--with his deep brown eyes--and they were the hands that had laid the boy to rest only weeks later, the brightness of his eyes extinguished forever. These veined, creased hands had crushed his 11-year-old daughter's body to his own, in an attempt to force some of his life into her as she lay dying from the riding accident. They had carried the coffins of friends, and they had clutched Marie's frail, motionless hand as his companion for 49 years breathed her last in the darkness of their bedroom.

Jean-Pierre looked up again and the tears rolled down his wrinkled cheeks. He was utterly alone in the world. His family, his friends--all had preceeded him into Death's eternal embrace. He was a white-haired, palsied old man who had seen everyone he ever loved torn from him. The tears wet the corners of his quivering mouth before the spring breezes could dry them on his face. He felt the lonliness, the emptiness inside him like a yawning pit that could never be filled. He clutched his arms across his chest and wept until the Rhone overflowed its banks and filled his eyes.

Stepping back away from the painting, Dennis staggered and caught himself on the door frame. He had never in his life felt such depression and grief as he did now. His face was aching, the muscles tight from crying, and the space behind his eyes burned and throbbed. He felt so worthless, so unnecessary. He thought of his own problems and trials and could almost picture himself somewhere in the painting. But no, his tribulations were minor--no, not even that--they were inconsequential, and as such had no place in this masterpiece of pain.

He heard a voice in his feverish brain calling him, beckoning him. He sank to his knees and ground his fists into his eyes, trying to silence the voice within. But it raged and called, lied and cajoled, until he could do nothing but lift his weary head and stare at the final figure in the background.

* * *

The golden beams of day had been devoured by the approaching night, which brought with it large, lazy snowflakes that drifted aimlessly on the wind. The sky was a solid mass of pregnant, grey clouds that reminded Logan of unlanced boils.

The odor that greeted him when he entered the apartment made him choke. He held his nose to keep from gagging. It smelled as if the toilet had backed up and been left unattended. Crossing the kitchen, he saw why. Several dried puddles of vomit lay on the counters and the floor. Partially digested pieces of food were obvious in them.

"Dennis! You here?" he shouted after releasing his nose. He moved toward Dennis's room, side-stepped a urine puddle, then stopped. The painting was gone from above the entertainment center. A jagged hole in the plaster showed where it had been ripped from the wall. Logan continued down the hall, his pace quickening. "Hey man, are you here?" he repeated. "Are you okay?"

Maybe he's gotten food poisoning and had to call an ambulance, Logan thought. Or maybe he's too weak. Maybe he's been laying here all weekend, unable to get help. Logan hurried the last few steps to Dennis's door and shoved it open.

"Hey Denn--," he started, then choked.

Dennis's outstretched body lay upon his blood-soaked bed. The empty slits on both of Dennis's wrists were wide and deep, and gaped at Logan like the mouths of fish. The razor blade that Dennis had used was still stuck in the greying flesh of one wrist. The tangy, coppery stench of blood was still heavy in the air.

"Oh no," Logan gasped. "Oh God--no, man, NO...!"

Dennis's arms were lying neatly beside him, his eyes staring sightlessly ahead. His skin had started to take on a chalky-grey pallor, not unlike the wintery sky outside. The bedclothes lay jumbled in a pile at the foot of the bed.

Logan stood frozen. He couldn't take his eyes off Dennis's face. It was lined with grief and anguish, as if he had experienced a lifetime of loss. He stood there, staring, for several minutes, feeling the hurt beginning inside him. With trembling hands he reached down and closed Dennis's eyes.

Shaking, Logan turned toward the door, toward the telephone in the hall. As he did so, he noticed the painting hanging on the wall opposite Dennis's bed. Logan walked stiffly over to it. Dennis had clumsily nailed it directly onto the wall. The canvas was torn in several places where the nails had punctured it. Logan's eyes slowly drifted down to the table beneath the painting, upon which was a crumpled piece of paper. With numb hands Logan unwadded the paper. It was covered with Dennis's familiar, scratchy handwriting. Logan began to read:

Logan, I couldn't take the grief any longer. I tried to fight it. I really tried. But I wasn't strong enough. No one is strong enough to resist him.

My body no longer obeys my commands. I am hungry, but food won't stay down. I have no control over myself any more. All I can do is look at the painting.

If you are reading this, then I have not had the strength to destroy the damned thing and it has consumed me. I have no alternative; I cannot live with their pain and suffering. Mine is so trivial when compared to theirs. And their pain seeks me out, it invades me, it dwells in me. It MAKES me look.

Logan, you must destroy the painting. Shred it, burn it, do whatever you have to, but get rid of it! Don't look at it and don't ask "why!" Don't ask yourself who those people are! For as surely as you do, he will answer you. And he will fill you with all their unhappiness and sorrow and anguish and pain.

He's calling me again. I can hear him... I want to look away, to get up, to escape. But I ask myself, what's the use? I want to fight it, but it is inevitable. The stranger...he's calling to me, drawing me into that swirling, maddening vortex...he wants to show me more. And I do not, cannot care.

I'm sorry I'm not strong enough. My mother...don't let her know it was this painting...there has been...enough grief. I love her.

He's calling me...I can't look away. The depression--it washes over me. What's the use in fighting? There is no escape.

He is here. The stranger in the pallid mask, with his walking stick and velvet cape. With his twisting, spiralling sign. The herald of the Yellow King is here...

The Events at Poroth Farm

By T.E.D. Kline

As soon as the phone stops ringing, I'll begin this affidavit. Lord, it's hot in here. Perhaps I should open a window. . . .

Thirteen rings. It has a sense of humor.

I suppose that ought to be comforting.

Somehow I'm not comforted. If it feels free to indulge in these teasing, tormenting little games, so much the worse for me.

The summer is over now, but this room is like an oven. My shirt is already drenched, and this pen feels slippery in my hand. In a moment or two the little drop of sweat that's collecting above my eyebrow is going to splash onto this page.

Just the same, I'll keep that window closed. Outside, through the dusty panes of glass, I can see a boy in red spectacles sauntering toward the courthouse steps. Perhaps there's a telephone booth in back. . . .

A sense of humor -- that's one quality I never noticed in it. I saw only a deadly seriousness and, of course, an intelligence that grew at terrifying speed, malevolent and inhuman. If it now feels itself safe enough to toy with me before doing whatever it intends to do, so much the worse for me. So much the worse, perhaps, for us all.

I hope I'm wrong. Though my name is Jeremy, derived from Jeremiah, I'd hate to be a prophet in the wilderness. I'd much rather be a harmless crank.

But I believe we're in for trouble.

I'm a long way from the wilderness now, of course. Though perhaps not far enough to save me. . . . I'm writing this affidavit in room 2-K of the Union Hotel, overlooking Main Street in Flemington, New Jersey, twenty miles south of Gilead. Directly across the street, hippies lounging on its steps, stands the county courthouse where Bruno Hauptmann was tried back in 1935. (Did they ever find the body of that child?) Hauptmann undoubtedly walked down those very steps, now lined with teenagers savoring their last week of summer vacation. Where that boy in the red spectacles sits sucking on his cigarette -- did the killer once halt there, police and reporters around him, and contemplate his imminent execution?

For several days now I have been afraid to leave this room.

I have perhaps been staring too often at that ordinary-looking boy on the steps. He sits there every day. The red spectacles conceal his eyes; it's impossible to tell where he's looking.

I know he's looking at me.

But it would be foolish of me to waste time worrying about executions when I have these notes to transcribe. It won't take long, and then, perhaps, I'll sneak outside to mail them -- and leave New Jersey forever. I remain, despite all that's happened, an optimist. What was it my namesake said? "Thou art my hope in the day of evil."

There is, surprisingly, some real wilderness left in New Jersey, assuming one wants to be a prophet. The hills to the west, spreading from the southern swamplands to the Delaware and beyond to Pennsylvania, provide shelter for deer, pheasant, even an occasional bear -- and hide hamlets never visited by outsiders: pockets of ignorance, some of them, citadels of ancient superstition utterly cut off from news of New York and the rest of the state, religious communities where customs haven't changed appreciably since the days of their settlement a century or more ago.

It seems incredible that villages so isolated can exist today on the very doorstep of the world's largest metropolis -- villages with nothing to offer the outsider, and hence never visited, except by the occasional hunter who stumbles on them unwittingly. Yet as you speed down one of the state highways, consider how few of the cars slow down for the local roads. It is easy to pass the little towns without even a glance at the signs; and if there are no signs . . . ? And consider, too, how seldom the local traffic turns off onto the narrow roads that emerge without warning from the woods. And when those untraveled side roads lead into others still deeper in wilderness; and when those in turn give way to dirt roads, deserted for weeks on end. . . . It is not hard to see how tiny rural communities can exist less than an hour from major cities, virtually unaware of one another's existence.

Television, of course, will link the two -- unless, as is often the case, the elders of the community choose to see this distraction as the Devil's tool and proscribe it. Telephones put these outcast settlements in touch with their neighbors -- unless they choose to ignore their neighbors. And so in the course of years they are . . . forgotten.

New Yorkers were amazed when in the winter of 1968 the Times "discovered" a religious community near New Providence that had existed in its present form since the late 1800's -- less than forty miles from Times Square. Agricultural work was performed entirely by hand, women still wore long dresses with high collars, and town worship was held every evening.

I, too, was amazed. I'd seldom traveled west of the Hudson and still thought of New Jersey as some dismal extension of the Newark slums, ruled by gangsters, foggy with swamp gases and industrial waste, a grey land that had surrendered to the city.

Only later did I learn of the rural New Jersey, and of towns whose solitary general stores double as post offices, with one or two gas pumps standing in front. And later still I learned of Baptistown and Quakertown, their old religions surviving unchanged, and of towns like Lebanon, Landsdown, and West Portal, close to Route 22 and civilization but heavy with secrets city folk never dreamed of; Mt. Airy, with its network of hidden caverns, and Mt. Olive, bordering the infamous Budd Lake; Middle Valley, sheltered by dark cliffs, subject of the recent archaeological debate chronicled in Natural History, where the wanderer may still find grotesque relics of pagan worship and, some say, may still hear the chants that echo from the cliffs on certain nights; and towns with names like Zion and Zaraphath and Gilead, forgotten communities of bearded men and black-robed women, walled hamlets too small or obscure for most maps of the state. This was the wilderness into which I traveled, weary of Manhattan's interminable din; and it was outside Gilead where, until the tragedies, I chose to make my home for three months.

Among the silliest of literary conventions is the "town that won't talk" -- the Bavarian village where peasants turn away from tourists' queries about "the castle" and silently cross themselves, the New England harbor town where fishermen feign ignorance and cast "furtive glances" at the traveler. In actuality, I have found, country people love to talk to the stranger, provided he shows a sincere interest in their anecdotes. Storekeepers will interrupt their activity at the cash register to tell you their theories on a recent murder; farmers will readily spin tales of buried bones and of a haunted house down the road. Rural townspeople are not so reticent as the writers would have us believe.

Gilead, isolated though it is behind its oak forests and ruined walls, is no exception. The inhabitants regard all outsiders with an initial suspicion, but let one demonstrate a respect for their traditional reserve and they will prove friendly enough. They don't favor modern fashions or flashy automobiles, but they can hardly be described as hostile, although that was my original impression.

When asked about the terrible events at Poroth Farm, they will prove more than willing to talk. They will tell you of bad crops and polluted well water, of emotional depression leading to a fatal argument. In short, they will describe a conventional rural murder, and will even volunteer their opinions on the killer's present whereabouts.

But you will learn almost nothing from them -- or almost nothing that is true. They don't know what really happened.

I do. I was closest to it.

I had come to spend the summer with Sarr Poroth and his wife. I needed a place where I could do a lot of reading without distraction, and Poroth's farm, secluded as it was even from the village of Gilead six miles down the dirt road, appeared the perfect spot for my studies.

I had seen the Poroths' advertisement in the Hunterdon County Democrat on a trip west through Princeton last spring. They advertised for a summer or long-term tenant to live in one of the outbuildings behind the farmhouse. As I soon learned, the building was a long, low cinderblock affair, unpleasantly suggestive of army barracks but clean, new, and cool in the sun; by the start of summer ivy sprouted from the walls and disguised the ugly grey brick. Originally intended to house chickens, it had in fact remained empty for several years until the farm's original owner, a Mr. Baber, sold out last fall to the Poroths, who immediately saw that with the installation of dividing walls, linoleum floors, and other improvements the building might serve as a source of income. I was to be their first tenant.

The Poroths, Sarr and Deborah, were in their early thirties, only slightly older than I, although anyone who met them might have believed the age difference to be greater; their relative solemnity, and the drabness of their clothing, added years to their appearance, and so did their hair styles: Deborah, though possessing a beautiful length of black hair, wound it all in a tight bun behind her neck, pulling the hair back from her face with a severity which looked almost painful, and Sarr maintained a thin fringe of black beard that circled from ears to chin in the manner of the Pennsylvania Dutch, who leave their hair shaggy but refuse to grow moustaches lest they resemble the military class they've traditionally despised. Both man and wife were hardworking, grave of expression, and pale despite the time spent laboring in the sun -- a pallor accentuated by the inky blackness of their hair. I imagine this unhealthy aspect was due, in part, to the considerable amount of inbreeding that went on in the area, the Poroths themselves being, I believe, third cousins. On first meeting, one might have taken them for brother and sister, two gravely devout children aged in the wilderness.

And yet there was a difference between them -- and, too, a difference that set them both in contrast to others of their sect. The Poroths were, as far as I could determine, members of a tiny Mennonitic order outwardly related to the Amish, though doctrinal differences were apparently rather profound. It was this order that made up the large part of the community known as Gilead.

I sometimes think the only reason they allowed an infidel like me to live on their property (for my religion was among the first things they inquired about) was because of my name; Sarr was very partial to Jeremiah, and the motto of his order was, "Stand ye in the ways, and see, and ask for the old paths, where is the good way, and walk therein." (VI:16)

Having been raised in no particular religion except a universal skepticism, I began the summer with a hesitancy to raise the topic in conversation, and so I learned comparatively little about the Poroths' beliefs. Only toward the end of my stay did I begin to thumb through the Bible in odd moments and take to quoting jeremiads. That was, I suppose, Sarr's influence.

I was able to learn, nonetheless, that for all their conservative aura the Poroths were considered, in effect, young liberals by most of Gilead. Sarr had a bachelor's degree in religious studies from Rutgers, and Deborah had attended a nearby community college for two years, unusual for women of the sect. Too, they had only recently taken to farming, having spent the first year of their marriage near New Brunswick, where Sarr had hoped to find a teaching position and, when the job situation proved hopeless, had worked as a sort of handyman/carpenter. While most inhabitants of Gilead had never left the farm, the Poroths were coming to it late -- their families had been merchants for several generations -- and so were relatively inexperienced.

The inexperience showed. The farm comprised some ninety acres, but most of that was forest, or fields of weeds too thick and high to walk through. Across the back yard, close to my rooms, ran a small, nameless stream, nearly choked with green scum. A large cornfield to the north lay fallow, but Sarr was planning to seed it this year, using borrowed equipment. His wife spent much of her time indoors, for though she maintained a small vegetable garden, she preferred keeping house and looking after the Poroths' great love, their seven cats.

As if to symbolize their broad-mindedness, the Poroths owned a television set, very rare in Gilead; in light of what was to come, however, it is unfortunate they lacked a telephone. (Apparently the set had been received as a wedding present from Deborah's parents, but the monthly expense of a telephone was simply too great.) Otherwise, though, the little farmhouse was "modern" in that it had a working bathroom and gas heat. That they had advertised in the local newspaper was considered scandalous by some of the order's more orthodox members, and indeed a mere subscription to that innocuous weekly had at one time been regarded as a breach of religious conduct.

Though outwardly similar, both of them tall and pale, the Poroths were actually so different as to embody the maxim that "opposites attract." It was that carefully nurtured reserve that deceived one at first meeting, for in truth Deborah was far more talkative, friendly, and energetic than her husband. Sarr was moody, distant, silent most of the time, with a voice so low that one had trouble following him in conversation. Sitting as stonily as one of his cats, never moving, never speaking, perennially inscrutable, he tended to frighten visitors to the farm until they learned that he was not really sitting in judgment on them; his reserve was not born of surliness, but of shyness.

Where Sarr was catlike, his wife hid beneath the formality of her order the bubbly personality of a kitten. Given the smallest encouragement -- say, a family visit -- she would plunge into animated conversation, gesticulating, laughing easily, hugging whatever cat was nearby or shouting to guests across the room. When drinking -- for both of them enjoyed liquor and, curiously, it was not forbidden by their faith -- their innate differences were magnified: Deborah would forget the restraints placed upon women in the order and would eventually dominate the conversation, while her husband would seem to grow increasingly withdrawn and morose.

Women in the region tended to be submissive to the men, and certainly the important decisions in the Poroths' lives were made by Sarr. Yet I really cannot say who was the stronger of the two. Only once did I ever see them quarrel. . . .

Perhaps the best way to tell it is by setting down portions of the journal I kept this summer. Not every entry, of course. Mere excerpts. Just enough to make this affidavit comprehensible to anyone unfamiliar with the incidents at Poroth Farm.

The journal was the only writing I did all summer; my primary reason for keeping it was to record the books I'd read each day, as well as to examine my reactions to relative solitude over a long period of time. All the rest of my energies (as you will no doubt gather from the notes below) were spent reading, in preparation for a course I plan to teach at Trenton State this fall. Or planned, I should say, because I don't expect to be anywhere around here come fall.

Where will I be? Perhaps that depends on what's beneath those rose-tinted spectacles.

The course was to cover the Gothic tradition from Shakespeare to Faulkner, from Hamlet to Absalom, Absalom! (And why not view the former as Gothic, with its ghost on the battlements and concern for lost inheritance?) To make the move to Gilead, I'd rented a car for a few days and had stuffed it full of books -- only a few of which I ever got to read. But then, I couldn't have known. . . .

How pleasant things were, at the beginning.

- June 4

Unpacking day. Spent all morning putting up screens, and a good thing I did. Night now, and a million moths tapping at the windows. One of them as big as a small bird -- white -- largest I've ever seen. What kind of caterpillar must it have been? I hope the damned things don't push through the screens.

Had to kill literally hundreds of spiders before moving my stuff in. The Poroths finished doing the inside of this building only a couple of months ago, and already it's infested. Arachnidae -- hate the bastards. Why? We'll take that one up with Sigmund someday. Daydreams of Revenge of the Spiders. Writhing body covered with a frenzy of hairy brown legs. "Egad, man, that face! That bloody, torn face! And the missing eyes! It looks like -- no! Jeremy!" Killing spiders is supposed to bring bad luck. (Insidious Sierra Club propaganda masquerading as folk myth?) But can't sleep if there's anything crawling around . . . so what the hell?

Supper with the Poroths. Began to eat, then heard Sarr saying grace. Apologies -- but things like that don't embarrass me as much as they used to. (Is that because I'm nearing thirty?)

Chatted about crops, insects, humidity. (Very damp area -- band of purplish mildew already around bottom of walls out here.) Sarr told of plans to someday build a larger house when Deborah has a baby, three or four years from now. He wants to build it out of stone. Then he shut up, and I had to keep the conversation going. (Hate eating in silence -- animal sounds of mastication, bubbling stomachs.) Deborah joked about cats being her surrogate children. All seven of them hanging around my legs, rubbing against ankles. My nose began running and my eyes itched. Goddamned allergy. Must remember to start treatments this fall, when I get to Trenton. Deborah sympathetic, Sarr merely watching; she told me my eyes were bloodshot, offered antihistamine. Told them I was glad they at least believe in modern medicine -- I'd been afraid she'd offer herbs or mud or something. Sarr said some of the locals still use "snake oil." Asked him how snakes were killed, quoting line from Vathek: "The oil of the serpents I have pinched to death will be a pretty present. . . ." We discussed wisdom of pinching snakes. Apparently there's a copperhead out back, near the brook. . . .

The meal was good -- lamb and noodles. Not bad for fifteen dollars a week, since I detest cooking. Spice cake for dessert, home-made, of course. Deborah is a good cook. Handsome woman, too.

Still light when I left their kitchen. Fireflies already on the lawn -- I've never seen so many. Knelt and watched them a while, listening to the crickets. Think I'll like it here.

Took nearly an hour to arrange my books the way I wanted them. Alphabetical order by authors? No, chronological. . . . But anthologies mess that system up, so back to authors. Why am I so neurotic about my books?

Anyway, they look nice there on the shelves.

Sat up tonight finishing The Mysteries of Udolpho. Figure it's best to get the long ones out of the way first. Radcliffe's unfortunate penchant for explaining away all her ghosts and apparitions really a mistake and a bore. All in all, not exactly the most fascinating reading, though a good study in Romanticism. Montoni the typical Byronic hero/villain. But can't demand students read Udolpho -- too long. In fact, had to keep reminding myself to slow down, have patience with the book. Tried to put myself in frame of mind of 1794 reader with plenty of time on his hands. It works, too -- I do have plenty of time out here, and already I can feel myself beginning to unwind. What New York does to people. . . .

It's almost two A.M. now, and I'm about ready to turn in. Too bad there's no bathroom in this building -- I hate pissing outside at night. God knows what's crawling up your ankles. . . . But it's hardly worth stumbling through the darkness to the farmhouse, and maybe waking up Sarr and Deborah. The nights out here are really pitch-black. . . .

. . . Felt vulnerable, standing there against the night. But what made me even uneasier was the view I got of this building. The lamp on the desk casts the only light for miles, and as I stood outside looking into this room I could see dozens of flying shapes making right for the screens. When you're inside here it's as if you're in a display case -- the whole night can see you, but all you can see is darkness. I wish this room didn't have windows on three of the walls -- though that does let in the breeze. And I wish the woods weren't so close to my windows by the bed. I suppose privacy is what I wanted -- but feel a little unprotected out here.

Those moths are still batting themselves against the screens, but as far as I can see the only things that have gotten in are a few gnats flying around this lamp. The crickets sound good -- you sure don't hear them in the city. Frogs are croaking in the brook.

My nose is only now beginning to clear up. Those goddamned cats. Must remember to buy some Contac. Even though the cats are all outside during the day, that farmhouse is full of their scent. But I don't expect to be spending that much time inside the house anyway; this allergy will keep me away from the TV and out here with the books.

Just saw an unpleasantly large spider scurry across the floor near the foot of my bed. Vanished behind the footlocker. Must remember to buy some insect spray tomorrow.

- June 11

Hot today, but at night comes a chill. The dampness of this place seems to magnify temperature. Sat outside most of the day finishing the Maturin book, Melmoth the Wanderer, and feeling vaguely guilty each time I heard Sarr or Deborah working out there in the field. Well, I've paid for my reading time, so I guess I'm entitled to enjoy it. Though some of these old Gothics are a bit hard to enjoy. The trouble with Melmoth is that it wants you to hate. You're especially supposed to hate the Catholics. No doubt its picture of the Inquisition is accurate, but all a book like this can do is put you in an unconstructive rage. Those vicious characters have been dead for centuries, and there's no way to punish them. Still, it's a nice, cynical book for those who like atrocity scenes -- starving prisoners forced to eat their girlfriends, delightful things like that. And narratives within narratives within narratives within narratives. I may assign some sections to my class. . . .

Just before dinner, in need of a break, read a story by Arthur Machen. Welsh writer, turn of century, though think the story's set somewhere in England: old house in the hills, dark woods with secret paths and hidden streams. God, what an experience! I was a little confused by the framing device and all its high-flown talk of "cosmic evil," but the sections from the young girl's notebook were . . . staggering. That air of paganism, the malevolent little faces peeping from the shadows, and those rites she can't dare talk about. . . . It's called "The White People," and it must be the most persuasive horror tale ever written.

Afterward, strolling toward the house, I was moved to climb the old tree in the side yard -- the Poroths had already gone in to get dinner ready -- and stood upright on a great heavy branch near the middle, making strange gestures and faces that no one could see. Can't say exactly what it was I did, or why. It was getting dark -- fireflies below me and a mist rising off the field. I must have looked like a madman's shadow as I made signs to the woods and the moon.

Lamb tonight, and damned good. I may find myself getting fat. Offered, again, to wash the dishes, but apparently Deborah feels that's her role, and I don't care to dissuade her. So talked a while with Sarr about his cats -- the usual subject of conversation, especially because, now that summer's coming, they're bringing in dead things every night. Fieldmice, moles, shrews, birds, even a little garter snake. They don't eat them, just lay them out on the porch for the Poroths to see -- sort of an offering, I guess. Sarr tosses the bodies in the garbage can, which, as a result, smells indescribably foul. Deborah wants to put bells around their necks; she hates mice but feels sorry for the birds. When she finished the dishes, she and Sarr sat down to watch one of their godawful TV programs, so I came out here to read.

Spent the usual ten minutes going over this room, spray can in hand, looking for spiders to kill. Found a couple of little ones, then spent some time spraying bugs that were hanging on the screens hoping to get in.

Watched a lot of daddy longlegs curl up and die. . . . Tended not to kill the moths, unless they were making too much of a racket banging against the screen; I can tolerate them okay, but it's only fireflies I really like. I always feel a little sorry when I kill one by mistake and see it hold that cold glow too long. (That's how you know they're dead: the dead ones don't wink. They just keep their light on till it fades away.)

The insecticide I'm using is made right here in New Jersey, by the Ortho Chemical Company. The label on the can says, "WARNING: For Outdoor Use Only." That's why I bought it -- figured it's the most powerful brand available.

Sat in bed reading Algernon Blackwood's witch/cat story, "Ancient Sorceries" (nowhere near as good as Machen, or as his own tale "The Willows"), and it made me think of those seven cats. The Poroths have around a dozen names for each one of them, which seems a little ridiculous since the creatures barely respond to even one name. Sasha, for example, the orange one, is also known as Butch, which comes from Bouche, mouth. And that's short for Eddie La Bouche, so he's also called Ed or Eddie -- which in turn comes from some friend's mispronunciation of the cat's original name, Itty, short for Itty Bitty Kitty, which, apparently, he once was. And Zoë, the cutest of the kittens, is also called Bozo and Bisbo. Let's see, how many others can I remember? (I'm just learning to tell some of them apart). . . . Felix, or "Flixie," was originally called Paleface, and Phaedra, his mother, is sometimes known as Phuddy, short for Phuddy Duddy.

Come to think of it, the only cat that hasn't got multiple names is Bwada, Sarr's cat. (All the others were acquired after he married Deborah, but Bwada was his pet years before.) She's the oldest of the cats, and the meanest. Fat and sleek, with fine grey fur, darker than silver grey, lighter than charcoal. She's the only cat that's ever bitten anyone -- Deborah, as well as friends of the Poroths -- and after seeing the way she snarls at the other cats when they get in her way, I decided to keep my distance. Fortunately she's scared of me and retreats whenever I approach. I think being spayed is what's messed her up and given her an evil disposition.

Sounds are drifting from the farmhouse. I can vaguely make out a psalm of some kind. It's late, past eleven, and I guess the Poroths have turned off the TV and are singing their evening devotions. . . .

And now all is silence. They've gone to bed. I'm not very tired yet, so I guess I'll stay up a while and read some --

Something odd just happened. I've never heard anything like it. While writing for the past half hour I've been aware, if half-consciously, of the crickets. Their regular chirping can be pretty soothing, like the sound of a well-tuned machine. But just a few seconds ago they seemed to miss a beat! They'd been singing along steadily, ever since the moon came up, and all of a sudden they just stopped for a beat -- and then they began again, only they were out of rhythm for a moment or two, as if a hand had jarred the record, or there'd been some kind of momentary break in the natural flow. . . .

They sound normal enough now, though. Think I'll go back to Otranto and let that put me to sleep. It may be the foundation of the English Gothics, but I can't imagine anyone actually reading it for pleasure. I wonder how many pages I'll be able to get through before I drop off. . . .

- June 12

Slept late this morning, and then, disinclined to read Walpole on such a sunny day, took a walk. Followed the little brook that runs past my building. There's still a lot of that greenish scum clogging one part of it, and if we don't have some rain soon I expect it will get worse. But the water clears up considerably when it runs past the cornfield and through the woods.

Passed Sarr out in the field -- he yelled to watch out for the copperhead, which put a pall on my enthusiasm for exploration. . . . But as it happened I never ran into any snakes, and have a fair idea I'd survive even if bitten. Walked around half a mile into the woods, branches snapping in my face. Made an effort to avoid walking into the little yellow caterpillars that hang from every tree. At one point I had to get my feet wet because the trail that runs alongside the brook disappeared and the undergrowth was thick. Ducked under a low arch made by decaying branches and vines, my sneakers sloshing in the water. Found that as the brook runs west it forms a small circular pool with banks of wet sand, surrounded by tall oaks, their roots thrust into the water. Lots of animal tracks in the sand -- deer, I believe, and what may be a fox or perhaps some farmer's dog. Obviously a watering place. Waded into the center of the pool -- it only came up a little past my ankles -- but didn't stand there long because it started looking like rain.

The weather remained nasty all day, but no rain has come yet. Cloudy now, though; can't see any stars.

Finished Otranto, began The Monk. So far so good -- rather dirty, really. Not for today, of course, but I can imagine the sensation it must have caused back at the end of the eighteenth century.

Had a good time at dinner tonight, since Sarr had walked into town and brought back some wine. (Medical note: I seem to be less allergic to cats when mildly intoxicated.) We sat around the kitchen afterward playing poker for matchsticks -- very sinful indulgence, I understand; Sarr and Deborah told me, quite seriously, that they'd have to say some extra prayers tonight by way of apology to the Lord.

Theological considerations aside, though, we all had a good time and Deborah managed to clean us both out. Women's intuition, she says. I'm sure she must have it -- she's the type. Enjoy being around her, and not always so happy to trek back outside, through the high grass, the night dew, the things in the soil. . . . I've got to remember, though, that they're a couple, I'm the single one, and I mustn't intrude too long. So left them tonight at eleven -- or actually a little after that, since their clock is slightly out of kilter. They have this huge grandfather-type clock, a wedding present from Sarr's parents, that has supposedly been keeping perfect time for a century or more. You can hear its ticking all over the house when everything else is still. Deborah said that last night, just as they were going to bed, the clock seemed to slow down a little, then gave a couple of faster beats and started in as before. Sarr, who's pretty good with mechanical things, examined it, but said he saw nothing wrong. Well, I guess everything's got to wear out a bit, after years and years.

Back to The Monk. May Brother Ambrosio bring me pleasant dreams.

- June 13

Read a little in the morning, loafed during the afternoon. At 4:30 watched The Thief of Bagdad -- ruined on TV and portions omitted, but still a great film. Deborah puttered around the kitchen and Sarr spent most of the day outside. Before dinner I went out back with a scissors and cut away a lot of ivy that has tried to grow through the windows of my building. The little shoots fasten onto the screens and really cling.

Beef with rice tonight, and apple pie for dessert. Great. I stayed inside the house after dinner to watch the late news with the Poroths. The announcer mentioned that today was Friday the thirteenth, and I nearly gasped. I'd known, on some dim automatic level, that it was the thirteenth, if only from keeping this journal; but I hadn't had the faintest idea it was Friday. That's how much I've lost track of time out here; day drifts into day, and every one but Sunday seems completely interchangeable. Not a bad feeling, really, though at certain moments this isolation makes me feel somewhat adrift. I'd been so used to living by the clock and the calendar. .

We tried to figure out if anything unlucky happened to any of us today. About the only incident we could come up with was Sarr's getting bitten by some animal a cat had left on the porch. The cats had been sitting by the front door waiting to be let in for their dinner, and when Sarr came in from the field he was greeted with the usual assortment of dead mice and moles. As he always did, he began gingerly picking the bodies up by the tails and tossing them into the garbage can, meanwhile scolding the cats for being such natural-born killers. There was one body, he told us, that looked different from the others he'd seen: rather like a large shrew, only the mouth was somehow askew, almost as if it were vertical instead of horizontal, with a row of little yellow teeth exposed. He figured that, whatever it was, the cats had pretty well mauled it, which probably accounted for its unusual appearance; it was quite tattered and bloody by this time.

In any case, he'd bent down to pick it up, and the thing had bitten him on the thumb. Apparently it had just been feigning death, like an opossum, because as soon as he yelled and dropped it the thing ran off into the grass, with Bwada and the rest in hot pursuit. Deborah had been afraid of rabies -- always a real danger around here, rare though it is -- but apparently the bite hadn't even pierced the skin. Just a nip, really. Hardly a Friday-the-thirteenth tragedy.

Lying in bed now, listening to sounds in the woods. The trees come really close to my windows on one side and there's always some kind of sound coming from the underbrush in addition to the tapping at the screens. A million creatures out there, after all -- most of them insects and spiders, a colony of frogs in the swampy part of the woods, and perhaps even skunks and raccoons. Depending on your mood, you can either ignore the sounds and just go to sleep or -- as I'm doing now -- remain awake listening to them. When I lie here thinking about what's out there, I feel more protected with the light off. So I guess I'll put away this writing. . . .

- June 15

Something really weird happened today. I still keep trying to figure it out.

Sarr and Deborah were gone almost all day; Sunday worship is, I guess, the center of their religious activity. They walked into Gilead early in the morning and didn't return till after four. They'd left, in fact, before I woke up. Last night they'd asked me if I'd like to come along, but I got the impression they'd invited me mainly to be polite, so I declined. I wouldn't want to make them uncomfortable during services, but perhaps someday I'll accompany them anyway, since I'm curious to see a fundamentalist church in action.

In any case, I was left to share the farm with the Poroths' seven cats and the four hens they'd bought last week. From my window I could see Bwada and Phaedra chasing after something near the barn; lately they'd taken to stalking grasshoppers. As I do every morning, I went into the farmhouse kitchen and made myself some breakfast, leafing through one of the Poroths' religious magazines, and then returned to my rooms out back for some serious reading. I picked up Dracula again, which I'd started yesterday, but the soppy Victorian sentimentality began to annoy me; the book had begun so well, on such a frightening note -- Jonathan Harker trapped in that Carpathian castle, inevitably the prey of its terrible owner -- that when Stoker switched the locale to England and his main characters to women he simply couldn't sustain that initial tension.

With the Poroths gone I felt a little lonely and bored, something I hadn't felt out here yet. Though I'd brought shelves of books to entertain me, I felt restless and wished I owned a car; I'd have gone for a drive, perhaps visited friends at Princeton. As things stood, though, I had nothing to do except watch television or take a walk.

I followed the stream again into the woods and eventually came to the circular pool. There were some new animal tracks in the wet sand and, ringed by oaks, the place was very beautiful, but still I felt bored. Again I waded into the center of the water and looked up at the sky through the trees. Feeling myself alone, I began to make some of the odd signs with face and hands that I had that evening in the tree -- but I felt that these movements had been unaccountably robbed of their power. Standing there up to my ankles in water, I felt foolish.

Worse than that, upon leaving it I found a red-brown leech clinging to my right ankle. It wasn't large and I was able to scrape it off with a stone, but it left me with a little round bite that oozed blood, and a feeling of -- how shall I put it? -- physical helplessness. I felt that the woods had somehow become hostile to me and, more important, would forever remain hostile. Something had passed.

I followed the stream back to the farm, and there I found Bwada, lying on her side near some rocks along its bank. Her legs were stretched out as if she were running, and her eyes were wide and astonished-looking. Flies were crawling over them.

She couldn't have been dead for long, since I'd seen her only a few hours before, but she was already stiff. There was foam around her jaws. I couldn't tell what had happened to her until I turned her over with a stick and saw, on the side that had lain against the ground, a gaping red hole that opened like some new orifice. The skin around it was folded back in little triangular flaps, exposing the pink flesh beneath. I backed off in disgust, but I could see even from several feet away that the hole had been made from the inside.

I can't say that I was very upset at Bwada's death, because I'd always hated her. What did upset me, though, was the manner of it -- I can't figure out what could have done that to her. I vaguely remember reading about a kind of slug that, when eaten by a bird, will bore its way out through the bird's stomach. . . . But I'd never heard of something like this happening with a cat. And far stranger than that, how could. . . .

Well, anyway, I saw the body and thought, Good riddance. But I didn't know what to do with it. Looking back, of course, I wish I'd buried it right there. . . . But I didn't want to go near it again. I considered walking into town and trying to find the Poroths, because I knew their cats were like children to them, even Bwada, and that they'd want to know right away. But

I really didn't feel like running around Gilead asking strange people where the Poroths were -- or, worse yet, stumbling into their forbidding-looking church in the middle of a ceremony. . . .

Finally I made up my mind to simply leave the body there and pretend I'd never seen it. Let Sarr discover it himself. I didn't want to have to tell him when he got home that his pet had been killed; I prefer to avoid unpleasantness. Besides, I felt strangely guilty, the way one often does after someone else's misfortune.

So I spent the rest of the afternoon reading in my room, slogging through the Stoker. I wasn't in the best mood to concentrate. Sarr and Deborah got back after four -- they shouted hello and went into the house. When Deborah called me for dinner, they still hadn't come outside.

All the cats except Bwada were inside having their evening meal when I entered the kitchen, and Sarr asked me if I'd seen her during the day. I lied and said I hadn't. Deborah suggested that occasionally Bwada ignored the supper call because, unlike the other cats, she sometimes ate what she killed and might simply be full. That rattled me a bit, but I had to stick to my lie.

Sarr seemed more concerned than Deborah, and when he told her he intended to search for the cat after dinner (it would still be light), I readily offered my help. I figured I could lead him to the spot where the body lay.

And then, in the middle of our dinner, came that scratching at the door. Sarr got up and opened it. Bwada walked in.

Now I know she was dead. She was stiff dead. That wound in her side had been huge, and now it was only . . . a reddish swelling. Hairless. Luckily the Poroths didn't notice my shock; they were busy fussing over her, seeing what was wrong. "Look, she's hurt herself," said Deborah. "She's bumped into something." The animal didn't walk well, and there was a clumsiness in the way she held herself. When Sarr put her down after examining the swelling, she slipped when she tried to walk away.

The Poroths concluded that she had run into a rock or some other object and had badly bruised herself; and now they believe her lack of coordination is due to the shock, or perhaps to a pinching of the nerves. That sounds logical enough. Sarr told me before I came out here for the night that if she's worse tomorrow he'll take her to the local vet, even though he'll have trouble paying for treatment. I immediately offered to lend him money, or even pay for the visit myself, because I desperately want to hear a doctor's opinion.

My own conclusion is really not that different from Sarr's. I tend to think now that maybe, just maybe, I was wrong in thinking the cat dead. Maybe what I mistook for rigor mortis was some kind of fit -- after all, I know almost nothing about medicine. Maybe she really did run into something sharp, and then went into some kind of shock . . . . whose effect hasn't yet worn off. Is this possible?

But I could swear that hole came from inside her.

I couldn't continue dinner and told the Poroths my stomach hurt, which was partly true. We all watched Bwada stumble around the kitchen floor, ignoring the food Deborah put before her as if it weren't there. Her movements were stiff, tentative, like a newborn animal still unsure how to move its muscles. I guess that's the result of her fit.

When I left the house tonight, a little while ago, she was huddled in the corner staring at me. Deborah was crooning over her, but the cat was staring at me.

Killed a monster of a spider behind my suitcase tonight. That Ortho spray really does a job. When Sarr was in here a few days ago he said the room smelled of spray, but I guess my allergy's too bad for me to smell it.

I enjoy watching the zoo outside my screens. Put my face close and stare the bugs eye to eye. Zap the ones whose faces I don't like with my spray can.

Tried to read more of the Stoker -- but one thing keeps bothering me. The way that cat stared at me. Deborah was brushing its back, Sarr fiddling with his pipe, and that cat just stared at me and never blinked. I stared back, said, "Hey, Sarr? Look at Bwada. That damned cat's not blinking." And just as he looked up, it blinked. Heavily.

Hope we can go to the vet tomorrow, because I want to ask him whether cats can impale themselves on a rock or a stick, and if such an accident might cause a fit of some kind that would make them rigid.

Cold night. Sheets are damp and the blanket itches. Wind from the woods -- ought to feel good in the summer, but it doesn't feel like summer.

That damned cat didn't blink till I mentioned it.

Almost as if it understood me.

- June 17

. . . Swelling on her side's all healed now. Hair growing back over it. She walks fine, has a great appetite, shows affection to the Poroths. Sarr says her recovery demonstrates how the Lord watches over animals -- affirms his faith. Says if he'd taken her to a vet he'd just have been throwing away money.

Read some LeFanu. "Green Tea," about the phantom monkey with eyes that glow, and "The Familiar," about the little staring man who drives the hero mad. Not the smartest choices right now, the way I feel, because for all the time that fat grey cat purrs over the Poroths, it just stares at me. And snarls. I suppose the accident may have addled its brain a bit. I mean, if spaying can change a cat's personality, certainly a goring on a rock might.

Spent a lot of time in the sun today. The flies made it pretty hard to concentrate on the stories, but figured I'd get a suntan. I probably have a good tan now (hard to tell because the mirror in here is small and the light dim), but suddenly it occurs to me that I'm not going to be seeing anyone for a long time anyway, except the Poroths, so what the hell do I care how I look?

Can hear them singing their nightly prayers now. A rather comforting sound, I must admit, even if I can't share the sentiments.

Petting Felix today -- my favorite of the cats, real charm -- came away with a tick on my arm which I didn't discover till taking a shower before dinner. As a result, I can still feel imaginary ticks crawling up and down my back. Damned cat.

- June 21

. . . Coming along well with the Victorian stuff. Zipped through "The Uninhabited House" and "Monsieur Maurice," both very literate, sophisticated. Deep into the terrible suffering of "The Amber Witch," poor priest and daughter near starvation, when Deborah called me in for dinner. Roast beef, with salad made from garden lettuce. Quite good. And Deborah was wearing one of the few sleeveless dresses I've seen on her. So she has a body after all. . . .

A rainy night. Hung around the house for a while reading in their living room while Sarr whittled and Deborah crocheted. Rain sounded better from in there than it does out here where it's not so cozy. . . .

At eleven we turned on the news, cats purring around us, Sarr with Zoë on his lap, Deborah petting Phaedra, me sniffling. . . . Halfway through the wrapup I pointed to Bwada, curled up at my feet, and said, "Look at her. You'd think she was watching the news with us." Deborah laughed and leaned over to scratch Bwada behind the ears. As she did so, Bwada turned to look at me.

The rain is letting up slightly. I can still hear the dripping from the trees, leaf to leaf to the dead leaves lining the forest floor. It will probably continue on and off all night. Occasionally I think I hear thrashings in one of the oaks near the barn, but then the sound turns into the falling of the rain.

Mildew higher on the walls of this place. Glad my books are on shelves off the ground. So damp in here my envelopes are ruined -- glue moistened, sealing them all shut. Stamps that had been in my wallet are stuck to the dollar bills. At night my sheets are clammy and cold, but each morning I wake up sweating.

Finished "The Amber Witch," really fine. Would that all lives had such happy endings.

- June 22

. . . When Poroths returned from church, helped them prepare strips of molding for the upstairs study. Worked out in the tool shed, one of the old wooden outbuildings. I measured, Sarr sawed, Deborah sanded. All in all, hardly felt useful, but what the hell?

While they were busy I sat staring out the window. There's a narrow cement walk running from the shed to the main house, and, as was their habit, Minnie and Felix, two of the kittens, were crouched in the middle of it taking in the late afternoon sun. Suddenly Bwada appeared on the house's front porch and began slinking along the cement path in our direction, tail swishing from side to side. When she neared the kittens she gave a snarl -- I could see her mouth working -- and they leaped to their feet, bristling, and ran off into the grass.

Called this to Poroths' attention. They said, in effect, Yes, we know, she's always been nasty to the kittens, probably because she never had any of her own. And besides, she's getting older.

When I turned back to the window, Bwada was gone. Asked the Poroths if they didn't think she'd gotten worse lately. Realized that, in speaking, I'd unconsciously dropped my voice, as if someone might be listening through the chinks in the floorboards.

Deborah conceded that, yes, the cat is behaving worse these days toward the others. And not just toward the kittens, as before. Butch, the adult orange male, seems particularly afraid of her. . . .

Am a little angry at the Poroths. Will have to tell them when I see them tomorrow morning. They claim they never come into these rooms, respect privacy of a tenant, etc. etc., but one of them must have been in here because I've just noticed my can of insect spray is missing. I don't mind their borrowing it, but I like to have it by my bed on nights like this. Went over room looking for spiders, just in case; had a fat copy of American Scholar in my hand to crush them (only thing it's good for). But found nothing.

Tried to read some Walden as a break from all the horror stuff, but found my eyes too irritated, watery. Keep scratching them as I write this. Nose pretty clogged, too -- the damned allergy's worse tonight. Probably because of the dampness. Expect I'll have trouble getting to sleep.

- June 24

Slept very late this morning because the noise from the woods kept me up late last night. (Come to think of it, the Poroths' praying was unusually loud as well, but that wasn't what bothered me.) I'd been in the middle of writing in this journal -- some thoughts on A. E. Coppard -- when it came. I immediately stopped writing and shut off the light.

At first it sounded like something in the woods near my room -- an animal? a child? I couldn't tell, but smaller than a man -- shuffling through the dead leaves, kicking them around as if it didn't care who heard it. There was a snapping of branches and, every so often, a silence and then a bump, as if it were hopping over fallen logs. I stood in the dark listening to it, then crept to the window and looked out. Thought I noticed some bushes moving, back there in the undergrowth, but it may have been the wind.

The sound grew farther away. Whatever it was must have been walking directly out into the deepest part of the woods, where the ground gets swampy and treacherous, because, very faintly, I could hear the sucking sounds of feet slogging through the mud.

I stood by the window for almost an hour, occasionally hearing what I thought were movements off there in the swamp, but finally all was quiet except for the crickets and the frogs. I had no intention of going out there with my flashlight in search of the intruder -- that's for guys in stories, I'm much too chicken -- and I wondered if I should call Sarr. But by this time the noise had stopped and whatever it was had obviously moved on. Besides, I tend to think he'd have been angry if I'd awakened him and Deborah just because some stray dog had wandered near the farm. I recalled how annoyed he'd been earlier that day when -- maybe not all that tactfully -- I'd asked him what he'd done with my bug spray. (Must remember to walk into town tomorrow and pick up a can. Still can't figure out where I misplaced mine.)

I went over to the windows on the other side and watched the moonlight on the barn for a while; my nose probably looked crosshatched from pressing against the screen. In contrast to the woods, the grass looked peaceful under the full moon. Then I lay in bed, but had a hard time falling asleep. Just as I was getting relaxed the sounds started again. High-pitched wails and caterwauls, from deep within the woods. Even after thinking about it all today, I still don't know whether the noise was human or animal. There were no actual words, of that I'm certain, but nevertheless there was the impression of singing. In a crazy, tuneless kind of way the sound seemed to carry the same solemn rhythm as the Poroths' prayers earlier that night.

The noise only lasted a minute or two, but I lay awake till the sky began to get lighter. Probably should have read a little more Coppard, but was reluctant to turn on the lamp.

. . . Slept all morning and, in the afternoon, followed the road the opposite direction from Gilead, seeking anything of interest. But the road just gets muddier and muddier till it disappears altogether by the ruins of an old homestead -- rocks and cement covered with moss - - and it looked so much like poison ivy around there that I didn't want to risk tramping through.

At dinner (pork chops, home-grown stringbeans, and pudding -- quite good), mentioned the noise of last night. Sarr acted very concerned and went to his room to look up something in one of his books; Deborah and I discussed the matter at some length and concluded that the shuffling sounds weren't necessarily related to the wailing. The former were almost definitely those of a dog -- dozens in the area, and they love to prowl around at night, exploring, hunting coons -- and as for the wailing . . . well, it's hard to say. She thinks it may have been an owl or whippoorwill, while I suspect it may have been that same stray dog. I've heard the howl of wolves and I've heard hounds baying at the moon, and both have the same element of, I suppose, worship in them that these did.

Sarr came back downstairs and said he couldn't find what he'd been looking for. Said that when he moved into this farm he'd had "a fit of piety" and had burned a lot of old books he'd found in the attic; now he wishes he hadn't.

Looked up something on my own after leaving the Poroths. Field Guide to Mammals lists both red and grey foxes and, believe it or not, coyotes as surviving here in New Jersey. No wolves left, though -- but the guide might be wrong.

Then, on a silly impulse, opened another reference book, Barbara Byfield's Glass Harmonica. Sure enough, my hunch was right: looked up June twenty-third and it said, "St. John's Eve. Sabbats likely."

I'll stick to the natural explanation. Still, I'm glad Mrs. Byfield lists nothing for tonight; I'd like to get some sleep. There is, of course, a beautiful full moon -- werewolf weather, as Maria Ouspenskaya might have said. But then, there are no wolves left in New Jersey. . . .

(Which reminds me, really must read some Marryat and Endore. But only after Northanger Abbey; my course always comes first.)

- June 25

. . . After returning from town, the farm looked very lonely. Wish they had a library in Gilead with more than religious tracts. Or a stand that sold the Times. (Though it's strange how, after a week or two, you no longer miss it.)

Overheated from walk -- am I getting out of shape? Or is it just the hot weather? Took a cold shower. When I opened the bathroom door I accidentally let Bwada out -- I'd wondered why the chair was propped against it. She raced into the kitchen, pushed open the screen door by herself, and I had no chance to catch her. (Wouldn't have attempted to anyway; her claws are wicked.) I apologized later when Deborah came in from the fields.

She said Bwada had become vicious toward the other cats and that Sarr had confined her to the bathroom as punishment. The first time he'd shut her in there, Deborah said, the cat had gotten out; apparently she's smart enough to turn the doorknob by swatting at it a few times. Hence the chair.

Sarr came in carrying Bwada, both obviously out of temper. He'd seen a streak of orange running through the field toward him, followed by a grey blur. Butch had stopped at his feet and Bwada had pounced on him, but before she could do any damage Sarr had grabbed her around the neck and carried her back here. He'd been bitten once and scratched a lot on his hands, but not badly; maybe the cat still likes him best. He threw her back in the bathroom and shoved the chair against the door, then sat down and asked Deborah to join him in some silent prayer. I thumbed uneasily through a religious magazine till they were done, and we sat down to dinner.

I apologized again, but he said he wasn't mad at me, that the Devil had gotten into his cat. It was obvious he meant that quite literally. During dinner (omelet -- the hens have been laying well) we heard a grating sound from the bathroom, and Sarr ran in to find her almost out the window; somehow she must have been strong enough to slide it up partway. She seemed so placid, though, when Sarr pulled her down from the sill -- he'd been expecting another fight -- that he let her out into the kitchen. At this she simply curled up near the stove and went to sleep; I guess she'd worked off her rage for the day. The other cats gave her a wide berth, though.

Watched a couple of hours of television with the Poroths. They may have gone to college, but the shows they find interesting . . . God! I'm ashamed of myself for sitting there like a cretin in front of that box. I won't even mention what we watched, lest history record the true abysmality of my tastes.

And yet I find that the TV draws us closer together, as if we were having an adventure together. Shared experience, really. Like knowing the same people or going to the same school.

But there's a lot of duplicity in those Poroths -- and I don't mean just religious hypocrisy, either. Came out here after watching the news, and though I hate to accuse anyone of spying on me, there's no doubt that Sarr or Deborah has been inside this room today. I began tonight's entry with great irritation because I found my desk in disarray; this journal wasn't even put back in the right drawer. I keep all my pens on one side, all my pencils on another, ink and erasers in the middle, etc., and when I sat down tonight I saw that everything was out of place. Thank God I haven't included anything too personal in here. . . . What I assume happened was that Deborah came in to wash the mildew off the walls -- she's mentioned doing so several times, and she knew I'd be in town part of the day -- and got sidetracked into reading this, thinking it must be some kind of secret diary.

(I'm sure she was disappointed to find that it's merely a literary journal, with nothing about her in it.)

What bugs me is the difficulty of broaching the subject. I can't just walk in and charge Deborah with being a sneak -- Sarr is moody enough as it is -- and even if I hint at "someone messing up my desk," they'll know what I mean and perhaps get angry. Whenever possible I prefer to avoid unpleasantness. I guess the best thing to do is simply hide this book under my mattress from now on and say nothing. If it happens again, though, I'll definitely move out of here.

. . . I've been reading some Northanger Abbey. Really quite witty, as all her stuff is, but it's obvious the mock-Gothic bit isn't central to the story. I'd thought it was going to be a real parody. . . . Love stories always tend to bore me, and normally I'd be asleep right now, but my damned nose is so clogged tonight that it's hard to breathe when I lie back. Usually being out here clears it up. I've used this goddamned inhaler a dozen times in the past hour, but within a few minutes I sneeze and have to use it again. Wish Deborah'd gotten around to cleaning off the mildew instead of wasting her time looking in here for True Confessions and deep dark secrets. . . .

Think I hear something moving outside. Best to shut off my light.

- June 30

Slept late. Read some Shirley Jackson stories over breakfast, but got so turned off at her view of humanity that I switched to old Aleister Crowley, who at least keeps a sunny disposition. For her, people in the country are callous and vicious, those in the city are callous and vicious, husbands are (of course) callous and vicious, and children are merely sadistic. The only ones with feelings are her put-upon middle-aged heroines, with whom she obviously identifies. I guess if she didn't write so well the stories wouldn't sting so.

Inspired by Crowley, walked back to the pool in the woods. Had visions of climbing a tree, swinging on vines, anything to commemorate his exploits. . . . Saw something dead floating in the center of the pool and ran back to the farm. Copperhead? Caterpillar? It had somehow opened up. .

Joined Sarr chopping stakes for tomatoes. Could hear his ax all over the farm. He told me Bwada hadn't come home last night, and no sign of her this morning. Good riddance, as far as I'm concerned. Helped him chop some stakes, while he was busy peeling off bark. That ax can get heavy fast! My arm hurt after three lousy stakes, and Sarr had already chopped fifteen or sixteen. Must start exercising. But I'll wait till my arm's less tired. . .

- July 2

Unpleasant day. Two A.M. now and still can't relax.

Sarr woke me up this morning -- stood at my window calling "Jeremy . . . Jeremy . . ." over and over very quietly. He had something in his hand which, through the screen, I first took for a farm implement; then I saw it was a rifle. He said he wanted me to help him. With what? I asked.

"A burial."

Last night, after he and Deborah had gone to bed, they'd heard the kitchen door open and someone enter the house. They both assumed it was me, come to use the bathroom -- but then they heard the cats screaming. Sarr ran down and switched on the light in time to see Bwada on top of Butch, claws in his side, fangs buried in his neck. From the way he described it, sounds almost sexual in reverse. Butch had stopped struggling, and Minnie, the orange kitten, was already dead. The door was partly open, and when Bwada saw Sarr, she ran out.

Sarr and Deborah hadn't followed her; they'd spent the night praying over the bodies of Minnie and Butch. I thought I'd heard their voices late last night, but that's all I heard, probably because I'd been playing my radio. (Something I rarely do -- you can't hear noises from the woods with it on.)

Poroths took deaths the way they'd take the death of a child. Regular little funeral service over by the unused pasture. (Hard to say if Sarr and Deborah were dressed in mourning, since that's the way they always dress.) Must admit I didn't feel particularly involved -- my allergy's never permitted me to take much interest in the cats, though I'm fond of Felix -- but I tried to act concerned: when Sarr asked, appropriately, "Is there no balm in Gilead? Is there no physician there?" (Jeremiah VIII:22), I nodded gravely. Read passages out of Deborah's Bible (Sarr seemed to know them all by heart), said amen when they did, knelt when they knelt, and tried to comfort Deborah when she cried. Asked her if cats could go to heaven, received a tearful "Of course." But Sarr added that Bwada would burn in hell.

What concerned me, apparently a lot more than it did either of them, was how the damned thing could get into the house. Sarr gave me this stupid, earnest answer: "She was always a smart cat." Like an outlaw's mother, still proud of her baby. . . .

Yet he and I looked all over the land for her so he could kill her. Barns, tool shed, old stables, garbage dump, etc. He called her and pleaded with her, swore to me she hadn't always been like this.

We could hardly check every tree on the farm -- unfortunately -- and the woods are a perfect hiding place, even for animals larger than a cat. So naturally we found no trace of her. We did try, though; we even walked up the road as far as the ruined homestead.

But for all that, we could have stayed much closer to home. . . .

We returned for dinner, and I stopped at my room to change clothes. My door was open. Nothing inside was ruined, everything was in its place, everything as it should be -- except the bed. The sheets were in tatters right down to the mattress, and the pillow had been ripped to shreds. Feathers were all over the floor. There were even claw marks on my blanket.

At dinner the Poroths demanded they be allowed to pay for the damage -- nonsense, I said, they have enough to worry about -- and Sarr suggested I sleep downstairs in their living room. "No need for that," I told him, "I've got lots more sheets." But he said no, he didn't mean that: he meant for my own protection. He believes the thing is particularly inimical, for some reason, toward me.

It seemed so absurd at the time. . . . I mean, nothing but a big fat grey cat. But now, sitting out here, a few feathers still scattered on the floor around my bed, I wish I were back inside the house. I did give in to Sarr when he insisted I take his ax with me. . . . But what I'd rather have is simply a room without windows.

I don't think I want to go to sleep tonight, which is one reason I'm continuing to write this. Just sit up all night on my new bedsheets, my back against the Poroths' pillow, leaning against the wall behind me, the ax beside me on the bed, this journal on my lap. . . . The thing is, I'm rather tired out from all the walking I did today. Not used to that much exercise.

I'm pathetically aware of every sound. At least once every five minutes some snapping of a branch or rustling of leaves makes me jump.

"Thou art my hope in the day of evil." At least that's what the man said. . . .

- July 3

Woke up this morning with the journal and the ax cradled in my arms. What awakened me was the trouble I had breathing -- nose all clogged, gasping for breath. Down the center of one of my screens, facing the woods, was a huge slash. . . .

- July 15

Pleasant day, St. Swithin's Day -- and yet, my birthday. Thirty years old, lordy lordy lordy. Today I am a man. First dull thoughts on waking: "Damnation. Thirty today." But another voice inside me, smaller but more sensible, spat contemptuously at such an artificial way of charting time. "Ah, don't give it another thought," it said. "You've still got plenty of time to fool around." Advice I took to heart.

Weather today? Actually, somewhat nasty. And thus the weather for the next forty days, since "If rain on St. Swithin's Day, forsooth, no summer drouthe," or something like that. My birthday predicts the weather. It's even mentioned in The Glass Harmonica.

As one must, took a critical self-assessment. First area for improvement: flabby body. Second? Less bookish, perhaps? Nonsense -- I'm satisfied with the progress I've made. "And seekest thou great things for thyself? Seek them not." (Jeremiah XLV:5) So I simply did what I remembered from the RCAF exercise series and got good and winded. Flexed my stringy muscles in the shower, certain I'll be a Human Dynamo by the end of the summer. Simply a matter of willpower.

Was so ambitious I trimmed the ivy around my windows again. It's begun to block the light, and someday I may not be able to get out the door.

Read Ruthven Todd's Lost Traveller. Merely the narrative of a dream turned to nightmare, and illogical as hell. Wish, too, that there'd been more than merely a few hints of sex. On the whole, rather unpleasant; that gruesome ending is so inevitable. . . . Took me much of the afternoon. Then came upon an incredible essay by Lafcadio Hearn, something entitled "Gaki," detailing the curious Japanese belief that insects are really demons, or the ghosts of evil men. Uncomfortably convincing!

Dinner late because Deborah, bless her, was baking me a cake. Had time to walk into town and phone parents. Happy birthday, happy birthday. Both voiced first worry -- mustn't I be getting bored out here? Assured them I still had plenty of books and did not grow tired of reading.

"But it's so . . . secluded out there," Mom said. "Don't you get lonely?"

Ah, she hadn't reckoned on the inner resources of a man of thirty. How can I get lonely, I asked, when there's still so much to read? Besides, there are the Poroths to talk to.

Then the kicker: Dad wanted to know about the cat. Last time I'd spoken to them it had sounded like a very real danger. "Are you still sleeping inside the farmhouse, I hope?"

No, I told him, really, I only had to do that for a few days, while it was prowling around at night. Yes, it had killed some chickens -- a hen every night, in fact. But there were only four of them, and then it stopped. We haven't had a sign of it in more than a week. (I didn't tell him that it had left the hens uneaten, dead in the nest. No need to upset him further.)

"But what it did to your sheets . . . " he went on. "If you'd been sleeping . . . Such savagery."

Yes, that was unfortunate, but there's been no trouble since. Honest. It was only an animal, after all, just a housecat gone a little wild. It posed the same kind of threat as a . . . (I was going to say, logically, wildcat; but for Mom said) nasty little dog. Like Mrs. Miller's bull terrier. Besides, it's probably miles and miles away by now. Or dead.

They offered to drive out with packages of food, magazines, a portable TV, but I made it clear I needed nothing. Getting too fat, actually.

Still light when I got back. Deborah had finished the cake, Sarr brought up some wine from the cellar, and we had a nice little celebration. The two of them being over thirty, they were happy to welcome me to the fold.

It's nice out here. The wine has relaxed me and I keep yawning. It was good to talk to Mom and Dad again. Just as long as I don't dream of The Lost Traveller, I'll be content. And happier still if I don't dream at all. . .

- July 30

Well, Bwada is dead -- this time for sure. We'll bury her tomorrow. Deborah was hurt, just how badly I can't say, but she managed to fight Bwada off. Tough woman, though she seems a little shaken. And with good reason.

It happened this way: Sarr and I were in the tool shed after dinner, building more shelves for the upstairs study. Though the fireflies were out, there was still a little daylight left. Deborah had gone up to bed after doing the dishes; she's been tired a lot lately, falls asleep early every night while watching TV with Sarr. He thinks it may be something in the well water.

It had begun to get dark, but we were still working. Sarr dropped a box of nails, and while we were picking them up, he thought he heard a scream. Since I hadn't heard anything, he shrugged and was about to start sawing again when -- fortunately -- he changed his mind and ran off to the house. I followed him as far as the porch, not sure whether to go upstairs, until I heard him pounding on their bedroom door and calling Deborah's name. As I ran up the stairs I heard her say, "Wait a minute. Don't come in. I'll unlock the door . . . soon." Her voice was extremely hoarse, practically a croaking. We heard her rummaging in the closet -- finding her bathrobe, I suppose -- and then she opened the door.

She looked absolutely white. Her long hair was in tangles and her robe buttoned incorrectly. Around her neck she had wrapped a towel, but we could see patches of blood soaking through it. Sarr helped her over to the bed, shouting at me to bring up some bandages from the bathroom.

When I returned Deborah was lying in bed, still pressing the towel to her throat. I asked Sarr what had happened; it almost looked as if the woman had tried suicide.

He didn't say anything, just pointed to the floor on the other side of the bed. I stepped around for a look. A crumpled grey shaped was lying there, half covered by the bedclothes. It was Bwada, a wicked-looking wound in her side. On the floor next to her lay an umbrella -- the thing that Deborah had used to kill her.

She told us she'd been asleep when she felt something crawl heavily over her face. It had been like a bad dream. She'd tried to sit up, and suddenly Bwada was at her throat, digging in. Luckily she'd had the strength to tear the animal off and dash to the closet, where the first weapon at hand was the umbrella. Just as the cat sprang at her again, Deborah said, she'd raised the weapon and lunged. Amazing. . . . How many women, I wonder, would have had such presence of mind? The rest sounds incredible to me, but it's probably the sort of crazy thing that happens in moments like this: somehow the cat had impaled itself on the umbrella.

Her voice, as she spoke, was barely more than a whisper. Sarr had to persuade her to remove the towel from her throat; she kept protesting that she wasn't hurt that badly, that the towel had stopped the bleeding. Sure enough, when Sarr finally lifted the cloth from her neck, the wounds proved relatively small, the slash marks already clotting. Thank God that thing didn't really get its teeth in. . . .

My guess -- only a guess -- is that it had been weakened from days of living in the woods. (It was obviously incapable of feeding itself adequately, as I think was proved by its failure to eat the hens it had killed.) While Sarr dressed Deborah's wounds, I pulled back the bedclothes and took a closer look at the animal's body. The fur was matted and patchy. Odd that an umbrella could make a puncture like that, ringed by flaps of skin, as if the flesh had been pushed outward . . . though I suspect it has a simple explanation: it was Deborah's extraordinary good luck to have jabbed the animal precisely in its old wound, which had reopened. Naturally I didn't mention this to Sarr.

He made dinner for us tonight -- soup, actually, because he thought that was best for Deborah. Her voice sounded so bad he told her not to strain it any more by talking, at which she nodded and smiled. We both had to help her downstairs, as she was clearly weak from shock.

In the morning Sarr will have the doctor out. He'll have to examine the cat, too, to check for rabies, so we put the body in the freezer to preserve it as well as possible. Afterward we'll bury it.

Deborah seemed okay when I left. Sarr was reading through some medical books, and she was just lying on the living room couch gazing at her husband with a look of purest gratitude -- not moving, not saying anything, not even blinking.

I feel quite relieved. God knows how many nights I've lain here thinking every sound I heard was Bwada. I'll feel more relieved, of course, when that demon's safely underground; but I think I can say, at the risk of being melodramatic, that the reign of terror is over.

Hmm, I'm still a little hungry -- used to more than soup for dinner. These daily push-ups burn up energy. I'll probably dream of hamburgers and chocolate layer cakes.

- July 31

. . . The doctor collected scrapings from Bwada's teeth and scolded us for doing a poor job of preserving the body. Said storing it in the freezer was a sensible idea, but that we should have done so sooner, since it was already decomposing. The dampness, I imagine, must act fast on dead flesh.

He pronounced Deborah in excellent condition -- the marks on her throat are, remarkably, almost healed -- but he said her reflexes were a little off. Sarr invited him to stay for the burial, but he declined -- and quite emphatically, at that. He's not a member of their order, doesn't live in the area, and apparently doesn't get along that well with the people of Gilead, most of whom mistrust modern science. (Not that the old geezer sounded very representative of modern science. When I asked him for some good exercises, he recommended "chopping wood and running down deer.")

Standing under the heavy clouds, Sarr looked like a revivalist minister. His sermon was from Jeremiah XXII:19, "He shall be buried with the burial of an ass." The burial took place far from the graves of Bwada's two victims, and closer to the woods. We sang one song, Deborah just mouthing the words (still mustn't strain throat muscles). Sarr solemnly asked the Lord to look mercifully upon all His creatures, and I muttered an "amen." Then we walked back to the house, Deborah leaning on Sarr's arm; she's still a little stiff.

It was grey the rest of the day, and I sat in my room reading The King in Yellow -- or rather, Chambers' collection of the same name. One look at the real book, so Chambers would claim, and I might not live to see the morrow, at least through the eyes of a sane man. (That single gimmick -- masterful, I admit -- seems to be his sole inspiration.)

I was disappointed that dinner was again made by Sarr; Deborah was upstairs resting, he said. He sounded concerned, felt there were things wrong with her the doctor had overlooked. We ate our meal in silence, and I came back here immediately after washing the dishes. Feel very drowsy and, for some reason, also rather depressed. It may be the gloomy weather -- we are, after all, just animals, more affected by the sun and the seasons than we like to admit. More likely it was the absence of Deborah tonight. Hope she feels better.

Note: The freezer still smells of the cat's body; opened it tonight and got a strong whiff of decay.

- August 1

Writing this, breaking habit, in early morning. Went to bed last night just after finishing the entry above, but was awakened around two by sounds coming from the woods. Wailing, deeper than before, followed by a low, guttural monologue. No words, at least that I could distinguish. If frogs could talk . . . For some reason I fell asleep before the sounds ended, so I don't know what followed.

Could very well have been an owl of some kind, and later a large bullfrog. But I quote, without comment, from The Glass Harmonica: "July 31: Lammas Eve. Sabbats likely."

- August 4

Little energy to write tonight, and even less to write about. (Come to think of it, I slept most of the day: woke up at eleven, later took an afternoon nap. Alas, senile at thirty!) Too tired to shave, and haven't had the energy to clean this place, either; thinking about work is easier than doing it. The ivy's beginning to cover the windows again, and the mildew's been climbing steadily up the walls. It's like a dark green band that keeps widening. Soon it will reach my books. . . .

Speaking of which, note: opened M. R. James at lunch today -- Ghost Stories of an Antiquary -- and a silverfish slithered out. Omen?

Played a little game with myself this evening --

I just had one hell of a shock. While writing the above I heard a soft tapping, like nervous fingers drumming on a table, and discovered an enormous spider, biggest of the summer, crawling only a few inches from my ankle. It must have been living behind this desk. . . .

When you can hear a spider walk across the floor, you know it's time to keep your socks on. Thank God for insecticide.

Oh, yeah, that game -- the What If game. I probably play it too often. (Vain attempt to enlarge realm of the possible? Heighten my own sensitivity? Or merely work myself into an icy sweat?) I pose unpleasant questions for myself and consider the consequences, e.g., what if this glorified chicken coop is sinking into quicksand? (Wouldn't be at all surprised.) What if the Poroths are tired of me? What if I woke up inside my own coffin?

What if I never see New York again?

What if some horror stories aren't really fiction? If Machen sometimes told the truth? If there are White People, malevolent little faces peering out of the moonlight? Whispers in the grass? Poisonous things in the woods? Perfect hate and evil in the world?

Enough of this foolishness. Time for bed.

- August 9

. . . Read some Hawthorne in the morning and, over lunch, reread this week's Hunterdon County Democrat for the dozenth time. Sarr and Deborah were working somewhere in the fields, and I felt I ought to get some physical activity myself; but the thought of starting my exercises again after more than a week's laziness just seemed too unpleasant. . . . I took a walk down the road a little way, but only as far as a smashed-up cement culvert half buried in the woods. I was bored, but Gilead just seemed too far away.

Was going to cut the ivy away from my windows when I got back, but decided the place looks more artistic covered in vines. Rationalization?

Chatted with Poroths about politics, The World Situation, a little cosmology, blah blah blah. Dinner wasn't very good, probably because I'd been looking forward to it all day. The lamb was underdone and the beans were cold. Still, I'm always the gentleman, and was almost pleased when Deborah agreed to my offer to do the dishes. I've been doing them a lot lately.

I didn't have much interest in reading tonight and would have been up for some television, but Sarr's recently gotten into one of his religious kicks and began mumbling prayers to himself immediately after dinner. (Deborah, more human, wanted to watch the TV news. She seems to have an insatiable curiosity about world events, yet she claims the isolation here appeals to her.) Absorbed in his chanting, Sarr made me uncomfortable -- I didn't like his face -- and so after doing the dishes, I left.

I've been listening to the radio for the last hour or so. . . . I recall days when I'd have gotten uptight at having wasted an hour -- but out here I've lost all track of time. Feel adrift -- a little disconcerting, but healthy, I'm sure.

. . . Shut the radio off a moment ago, and now realize my room is filled with crickets. Up close their sound is hardly pleasant -- cross between a radiator and a tea-kettle, very shrill. They'd been sounding off all night, but I'd thought it was interference on the radio.

Now I notice them; they're all over the room. A couple of dozen, I should think. Hate to kill them, really -- they're one of the few insects I can stand, along with ladybugs and fireflies. But they make such a racket!

Wonder how they got in. . . .

- August 14

Played with Felix all morning -- mainly watching him chase insects, climb trees, doze in the sun. Spectator sport. After lunch went back to my room to look up something in Lovecraft, and discovered my books were out of order. (Saki, for example, was filed under "S," whereas -- whether out of fastidiousness or pedantry -- I've always preferred to file him as "H. H. Munro.") This is definitely one of the Poroths' doing. I'm pissed they didn't mention coming in here, but also a little surprised they'd have any interest in this stuff.

Arranged them correctly again, then sat down to reread Lovecraft's essay on "Supernatural Horror in Literature." It upset me to see how little I've actually read, how far I still have to go. So many obscure authors, so many books I've never come across. . . . Left me feeling depressed and tired, so I took a nap for the rest of the afternoon.

Over dinner -- vegetable omelet, rather tasteless -- Deborah continued to question us on current events. It's getting to be like junior high school, with daily newspaper quizzes. . . . Don't know how she got started on this, or why the sudden interest, but it obviously annoys the hell out of Sarr.

Sarr used to be a sucker for her little-girl pleadings -- I remember how he used to carry her upstairs, becoming pathetically tender, the moment she'd say, "Oh, honey, I'm so tired" -- but now he just becomes angry. Often he goes off morose and alone to pray, and the only time he laughs is when he watches television.

Tonight, thank God, he was in a mood to forego the prayers, and so after dinner we all watched a lot of offensively ignorant programs. I was disturbed to find myself laughing along with the canned laughter, but I have to admit the TV helps us get along better together. Came back here after the news.

Not very tired, having slept so much of the afternoon, so began to read John Christopher's The Possessors; but good though it was, my mind began to wander to all the books I haven't yet read, and I got so depressed I turned on the radio. Find it takes my mind off things.

- August 19

Slept long into the morning, then walked down to the brook, scratching groggily. Deborah was kneeling by the water, lost, it seemed, in daydream, and I was embarrassed because I'd come upon her talking to herself. We exchanged a few insincere words and she went back toward the house.

Sat by some rocks, throwing blades of grass into the water. The sun on my head felt almost painful, as if my brain were growing too large for my skull. I turned and looked at the farmhouse. In the distance it looked like a picture at the other end of a large room, the grass for a carpet, the ceiling the sky. Deborah was stroking a cat, then seemed to grow angry when it struggled from her arms; I could hear the screen door slam as she went into the kitchen, but the sound reached me so long after the visual image that the whole scene struck me as, somehow, fake. I gazed up at the maples behind me and they seemed trees out of a cheap postcard, the kind in which thinly colored paint is dabbed over a black-and-white photograph; if you look closely you can see that the green in the trees is not merely in the leaves, but rather floats as a vapor over leaves, branches, parts of the sky. . . . The trees behind me seemed the productions of a poor painter, the color and shape not quite meshing. Parts of the sky were green, and pieces of the green seemed to float away from my vision. No matter how hard I tried I couldn't follow them.

Far down the stream I could see something small and kicking, a black beetle, legs in the air, borne swiftly along in the current. Then it was gone.

Thumbed through the Bible while I ate my lunch -- mostly cookies. By late afternoon I was playing word games while I lay on the grass near my room. The shrill twitter of the birds, I would say, the birds singing in the sun. . . . And inexorably I'd continue with the sun dying in the moonlight, the moonlight falling on the floor, the floor sagging to the cellar, the cellar filling with water, the water seeping into the ground, the ground twisting into smoke, the smoke staining the sky, the sky burning in the sun, the sun dying in the moonlight, the moonlight falling on the floor. . . . Thus the melancholy progressions that held my mind like a whirlpool.

Sarr woke me for dinner; I had dozed off, and my clothes were damp from the grass. As we walked up to the house together he whispered that, earlier in the day, he'd come upon his wife bending over me, peering into my sleeping face. "Her eyes were wide," he said. "Like Bwada's." I said I didn't understand why he was telling me this.

"Because," he recited in a whisper, gripping my arm, "the heart is deceitful above all things, and desperately wicked: who can know it?"

I recognized that. Jeremiah XVII:9.

Dinner was especially uncomfortable; the two of them sat picking at their food, occasionally raising their eyes to one another like children in a staring contest. I longed for the conversations of our early days, inconsequential though they must have been, and wondered where things had first gone wrong.

The meal was dry and unappetizing, but the dessert looked delicious -- chocolate mousse, made from an old family recipe. Deborah had served it earlier in the summer and knew both Sarr and I loved it. This time, however, she gave none to herself, explaining that she had to watch her weight.

"Then we'll not eat any!" Sarr shouted, and with that he snatched my dish from in front of me, grabbed his own, and hurled them both against the wall, where they splattered like mudballs.

Deborah was very still; she said nothing, just sat there watching us. She didn't look particularly afraid of this madman, I was happy to see -- but I was. He may have read my thoughts, because as I got up from my seat he said much more gently, in the soft voice normal to him, "Sorry, Jeremy. I know you hate scenes. We'll pray for each other, all right?"

"Are you okay?" I asked Deborah. "I'm going out now, but I'll stay if you think you'll need me for anything." She stared at me with a slight smile and shook her head. I raised my eyebrows and nodded toward her husband, and she shrugged.

"Things will work out," she said. I could hear Sarr laughing as I shut the door.

When I snapped on the light out here I took off my shirt and stood in front of the little mirror. It had been nearly a week since I'd showered, and I'd become used to the smell of my body. My hair had wound itself into greasy brown curls, my beard was at least two weeks old, and my eyes . . . well, the eyes that stared back at me looked like those of an old man. The whites were turning yellow, like old teeth. I looked at my chest and arms, flabby at thirty, and I thought of the frightening alterations in my friend Sarr, and I knew I'd have to get out of here.

Just glanced at my watch. It's now quite late: two-thirty. I've been packing my things.

- August 20

I woke about an hour ago and continued packing. Lots of books to put away, but I'm just about done. It's not even nine A.M. yet, much earlier than I normally get up; but I guess the thought of leaving here fills me with energy.

The first thing I saw on rising was a garden spider whose body was as big as some of the mice the cats have killed. It was sitting on the ivy that grows over my window sill -- fortunately, on the other side of the screen. Apparently it had had good hunting all summer, preying on the insects that live in the leaves. Concluding that nothing so big and fearsome has a right to live, I held the spray can against the screen and doused the creature with poison. It struggled halfway up the screen, then stopped, arched its legs, and dropped backwards into the ivy.

I plan to walk into town this morning and telephone the office in Flemington where I rented my car. If they can have one ready today I'll hitch there to pick it up; otherwise I'll spend tonight here and pick it up tomorrow. I'll be leaving a little early in the season, but the Poroths already have my month's rent, so they shouldn't be too offended.

And anyway, how could I be expected to stick around here with all that nonsense going on, never knowing when my room might be ransacked, having to put up with Sarr's insane suspicions and Deborah's moodiness?

Before I go into town, though, I really must shave and shower for the good people of Gilead. I've been sitting inside here waiting for some sign the Poroths are up, but as yet -- it's almost nine -- I've heard nothing. I wouldn't care to barge in on them while they're still having breakfast or, worse, just getting up. . . . So I'll just wait here by the window till I see them.

. . . Ten o'clock now, and they still haven't come out. Perhaps they're having a talk. . . . I'll give them half an hour more, then I'm going in.

Here my journal ends. Until today, almost a week later, I have not cared to set down any of the events that followed. But here in the temporary safety of this hotel room, protected by a heavy brass travel-lock I had sent up from the hardware store down the street, watched over by the good people of Flemington -- and perhaps by something not good -- I can continue my narrative.

The first thing I noticed as I approached the house was that the shades were drawn, even in the kitchen. Had they decided to sleep late this morning? I wondered. Throughout my thirty years I have come to associate drawn shades with a foul smell, the smell of a sickroom, of shamefaced poverty and food gone bad, of people lying too long beneath blankets; but I was not ready for the stench of decay that met me when I opened the kitchen door and stepped into the darkness. Something had died in that room -- and not recently.

At the moment the smell first hit, four little shapes scrambled across the linoleum toward me and out into the daylight. The Poroths' cats.

By the other wall a lump of shadow moved; a pale face caught light penetrating the shades. Sarr's voice, its habitual softness exaggerated to a whisper: "Jeremy. I thought you were still asleep."

"Can I -- "

"No. Don't turn on the light." He got to his feet, a black form towering against the window. Fiddling nervously with the kitchen door -- the tin doorknob, the rubber bands stored around it, the fringe at the bottom of the drawn window shade -- I opened it wider and let in more sunlight. It fell on the dark thing at his feet, over which he had been crouching: Deborah, the flesh at her throat torn and wrinkled like the skin of an old apple.

Her clothing lay in a heap beside her. She appeared long dead. The eyes were shriveled, sunken into sockets black as a skull's.

I think I may have staggered at that moment, because he came toward me. His steady, unblinking gaze looked so sincere -- but why was he smiling? "I'll make you understand," he was saying, or something like that; even now I feel my face twisting into horror as I try to write of him. "I had to kill her. . . ."

"You -- "

"She tried to kill me," he went on, silencing all questions. "The same thing that possessed Bwada . . . possessed her."

My hand played behind my back with the bottom of the window shade. "But her throat -- "

"That happened a long time ago. Bwada did it. I had nothing to do with . . . that part." Suddenly his voice rose. "Don't you understand? She tried to stab me with the bread knife." He turned, stooped over and, clumsy in the darkness, began feeling about him on the floor. "Where is that thing?" he was mumbling. "I'll show you. . . ." As he crossed a beam of sunlight, something gleamed like a silver handle on the back of his shirt.

Thinking, perhaps, to help him search, I pulled gently on the window shade, then released it; it snapped upward like a gunshot, flooding the room with light. From deep within the center of his back protruded the dull wooden haft of the bread knife, buried almost completely but for an inch or two of gleaming steel.

He must have heard my intake of breath -- that sight chills me even today, the grisly absurdity of the thing -- he must have heard me, because immediately he stood, his back to me, and reached up behind himself toward the knife, his arm stretching in vain, his fingers curling around nothing. The blade had been planted in a spot he couldn't reach.

He turned towards me and shrugged in embarrassment, a child caught in a foolish error. "Oh, yeah," he said, grinning at his own weakness, "I forgot it was there."

Suddenly he thrust his face into mine, fixing me in a gaze that never wavered, his eyes wide with candor. "It's easy for us to forget things," he explained -- and then, still smiling, still watching, volunteered that last trivial piece of information, that final message whose words released me from inaction and left me free to dash from the room, to sprint in panic down the road to town, pursued by what had once been the farmer Sarr Poroth.

It serves no purpose here to dwell on my flight down that twisting dirt road, breathing in such deep gasps that I was soon moaning with every breath; how, with my enemy racing behind me, not even winded, his steps never flagging, I veered into the woods; how I finally lost him, perhaps from the inexperience of whatever thing now controlled his body, and was able to make my way back to the road, only to come upon him again as he rounded a bend; his laughter as he followed me, and how it continued long after I had evaded him a second time; and how, after hiding until nightfall in the old cement culvert, I ran the rest of the way in pitch-darkness, stumbling in the ruts, torn by vines, nearly blinding myself when I ran into a low branch, until

I arrived in Gilead filthy, exhausted, and nearly incoherent.

Suffice it to say that my escape was largely a matter of luck, a physical wreck fleeing something oblivious to pain or fatigue; but that, beyond mere luck, I had been impelled by an almost ecstatic sense of dread produced by his last words to me, that last communication from an alien face smiling inches from my own, and which I chose to take as his final warning:

"Sometimes we forget to blink."

You can read the rest in the newspapers. The Hunterdon County Democrat covered most of the story, though its man wrote it up as merely another lunatic wife-slaying, the result of loneliness, religious mania, and a mysteriously tainted well. (Traces of insecticide were found, among other things, in the water.) The Somerset Reporter took a different slant, implying that I had been the third member of an erotic triangle and that Sarr had murdered his wife in a fit of jealousy.

Needless to say, I was by this time past caring what was written about me. I was too haunted by visions of that lonely, abandoned farmhouse, the wails of its hungry cats, and by the sight of Deborah's corpse, discovered by the police, protruding from that hastily dug grave beyond the cornfield.

Accompanied by state troopers, I returned to my ivy-covered outbuilding. A bread knife had been plunged deep into its door, splintering the wood on the other side. The blood on it was Sarr's.

My journal had been hidden under my mattress, and so was untouched, but (I look at them now, piled in cardboard boxes beside my suitcase) my precious books had been hurled about the room, their bindings slashed. My summer is over, and now I sit inside here all day listening to the radio, waiting for the next report. Sarr -- or his corpse -- has not been found.

I should think the evidence was clear enough to corroborate my story, but I suppose I should have expected the reception it received from the police. They didn't laugh at my theory of "possession" -- not to my face, anyway -- but they ignored it in obvious embarrassment. Some see a nice young bookworm gone slightly deranged after contact with a murderer; others believe my story to be the desperate fabrication of an adulterer trying to avoid the blame for Deborah's death.

I can understand their reluctance to accept my explanation of the events, for it's one that goes a little beyond the "natural," a little beyond the scientific considerations of motive, modus operandi, and fingerprints. But I find it quite unnerving that at least one official -- an assistant district attorney, I think, though I'm afraid I'm rather ignorant of these matters -- believes I am guilty of murder.

There has, of course, been no arrest. Still, I've been given the time-honored instructions against leaving town.

The theory proposing my own complicity in the events is, I must admit, rather ingenious -- and so carefully worked out that it will surely gain more adherents than my own. This police official is going to try to prove that I killed poor Deborah in a fit of passion and, immediately afterward, disposed of Sarr. He points out that their marriage had been an observably happy one until I arrived, a disturbing influence from the city. My motive, he says, was simple lust -- unrequited, to be sure -- aggravated by boredom. The heat, the insects, and, most of all, the oppressive loneliness -- all constituted an environment alien to any I'd been accustomed to, and all worked to unhinge my reason.

I have no cause for fear, however, because this affidavit will certainly establish my innocence. Surely no one can ignore the evidence of my journal (though I can imagine an antagonistic few maintaining that I wrote the journal not at the farm but here in the Union Hotel, this very week).

What galls me is not the suspicions of a few detectives, but the predicament their suspicions place me in. Quite simply, I cannot run away. I am compelled to remain locked up in this room, potential prey to whatever the thing that was Sarr Poroth has now become -- the thing that was once a cat, and once a woman, and once . . . what? A large white moth? A serpent? A shrewlike thing with wicked teeth?

A police chief? A president? A boy with eyes of blood that sits beneath my window?

Lord, who will believe me?

It was that night that started it all, I'm convinced of it now. The night I made those strange signs in the tree. The night the crickets missed a beat.

I'm not a philosopher, and I can supply no ready explanation for why this new evil has been released into the world. I'm only a poor scholar, a bookworm, and I must content myself with mumbling a few phrases that keep running through my mind, phrases out of books read long ago when such abstractions meant, at most, a pleasant shudder. I am haunted by scraps from the myth of Pandora, and by a semantic discussion I once read comparing "unnatural" and "supernatural."

And something about "a tiny rent in the fabric of the universe. . . ."

Just large enough to let something in. Something not of nature, and hard to kill. Something with its own obscure purpose.

Ironically, the police may be right. Perhaps it was my visit to Gilead that brought about the deaths. Perhaps I had a hand in letting loose the force that, to date, has snuffed out the lives of four hens, three cats, and at least two people -- but will hardly be content to stop there.

I've just checked. He hasn't moved from the steps of the courthouse; and even when I look out my window, the rose spectacles never waver. Who knows where the eyes beneath them point? Who knows if they remember to blink?

Lord, this heat is sweltering. My shirt is sticking to my skin, and droplets of sweat are rolling down my face and dripping onto this page, making the ink run.

My hand is tired from writing, and I think it's time to end this affidavit.

If, as I now believe possible, I inadvertently called down evil from the sky and began the events at Poroth Farm, my death will only be fitting. And after my death, many more. We are all, I'm afraid, in danger. Please, then, forgive this prophet of doom, old at thirty, his last jeremiad: "The harvest is past, the summer is ended, and we are not saved."

The Last Feast of Harlequin

By Thomas Ligotti

1.

My interest in the town of Mirocaw was first aroused when I heard that an annual festival was held there which promised to include, to some extent, the participation of clowns among its other elements of pageantry. A former colleague of mine, who is now attached to the anthropology department of a distant university, had read one of my recent artides ("The Clown Figure in American Media," Journal of Popular Culture), and wrote to me that he vaguely remembered reading or being told of a town somewhere in the state that held a kind of "Fool's Feast" every year, thinking that this might be pertinent to my peculiar line of study. It was, of course, more pertinent than he had reason to think, both to my academic aims in this area and to my personal pursuits.

Aside from my teaching, I had for some years been engaged in various anthropological projects with the primary ambition of articulating the significance of the clown figure in diverse cultural contexts. Every year for the past twenty years I have attended the pre-Lenten festivals that are held in various places throughout the southern United States. Every year I learned something more concerning the esoterics of celebration. In these studies I was an eager participant--along with playing my part as an anthropologist, I also took a place behind the clownish mask myself. And I cherished this role as I did nothing else in my life. To me the title of Clown has always carried connotations of a noble sort. I was an adroit jester, strangely enough, and had always taken pride in the skills I worked so diligently to develop.

I wrote to the State Department of Recreation, indicating what information I desired and exposing an enthusiastic urgency which came naturally to me on this topic. Many weeks later I received a tan envelope imprinted with a government logo. Inside was a pamphlet that catalogued all of the various seasonal festivities of which the state was officially aware, and I noted in passing that there were as many in late autumn and winter as in the warmer seasons. A letter inserted within the pamphlet explained to me that, according to their voluminous records, no festivals held in the town of

Mirocaw had been officially registered. Their files, nonetheless, could be placed at my disposal if I should wish to research this or similar matters in connection with some definite project. At the time this offer was made I was already laboring under so many professional and personal burdens that, with a weary hand, I simply deposited the envelope and its contents in a drawer, never to be consulted again.

Some months later, however, I made an impulsive digression from my responsibilities and, rather haphazardly, took up the Mirocaw project. This happened as I was driving north one afternoon in late summer with the intention of examining some journals in the holdings of a library at another university. Once out of the city limits the scenery changed to sunny fields and farms, diverting my thoughts from the signs that I passed along the highway. Nevertheless, the subconscious scholar in me must have been regarding these with studious care. The name of a town loomed into my vision. Instantly the scholar retrieved certain records from some deep mental drawer, and I was faced with making a few hasty calculations as to whether there was enough time and motivation for an investigative side trip. But the exit sign was even hastier in making its appearance, and I soon found myself leaving the highway, recalling the roadsign's promise that the town was no more than seven miles east.

These seven miles included several confusing turns, the forced taking of a temporarily alternate route, and a destination not even visible until a steep rise had been fully ascended. On the descent another helpful sign informed me that I was within the city limits of Mirocaw. Some scattered houses on the outskirts of the town were the first structures I encountered. Beyond them the numerical highway became Townshend Street, the main avenue of Mirocaw.

The town impressed me as being much larger once I was within its limits than it had appeared from the prominence just outside. I saw that the general hilliness of the surrounding countryside was also an internal feature of Mirocaw. Here, though, the effect was different. The parts of the town did not look as if they adhered very well to one another. This condition might be blamed on the irregular topography of the town. Behind some of the old stores in the business district, steeply roofed houses had been erected on a sudden incline, their peaks appearing at an extraordinary elevation above the lower buildings. And because the foundations of these houses could not be glimpsed, they conveyed the illusion of being either precariously suspended in air, threatening to topple down, or else constructed with an unnatural loftiness in relation to their width and mass. This situation also created a weird distortion of perspective. The two levels of structures overlapped each other without giving a sense of depth, so that the houses, because of their higher elevation and nearness to the foreground buildings, did not appear diminished in size as background objects should. Consequently, a look of flatness, as in a photograph, predominated in this area. Indeed, Mirocaw could be compared to an album of old snapshots, particularly ones in which the camera had been upset in the process of photography, causing the pictures to develop on an angle: a cone-roofed turret, like a pointed hat jauntily askew, peeked over the houses on a neighboring street; a billboard displaying a group of grinning vegetables tipped its contents slightly westward; cars parked along steep curbs seemed to be flying skyward in the glare-distorted windows of a five-and-ten; people leaned lethargically as they trod up and down sidewalks; and on that sunny day the clock tower, which at first I mistook for a church steeple, cast a long shadow that seemed to extend an impossible distance and wander into unlikely places in its progress across the town. I should say that perhaps the disharmonies of Mirocaw are more acutely affecting my imagination in retrospect than they were on that first day, when I was primarily concerned with locating the city hall or some other center of information.

I pulled around a corner and parked. Sliding over to the other side of the seat, I rolled down the window and called to a passerby: "Excuse me, sir," I said. The man, who was shabbily dressed and very old, paused for a moment without approaching the car. Though he had apparently responded to my call, his vacant expression did not betray the least awareness of my presence, and for a moment I thought it just a coincidence that he halted on the sidewalk at the same time I addressed him. His eyes were focused somewhere beyond me with a weary and imbecilic gaze. After a few moments he continued on his way and I said nothing to call him back, even though at the last second his face began to appear dimly familiar. Someone else finally came along who was able to direct me to the Mirocaw City Hall and Community Center.

The city hall turned out to be the building with the clock tower. Inside I stood at a counter behind which some people were working at desks and walking up and down a back hallway. On one wall was a poster for the state lottery: a jack-in-the-box with both hands grasping green bills. After a few moments, a tall, middle-aged woman came over to the counter.

"Can I help you?" she asked in a neutral, bureaucratic voice.

I explained that I had heard about the festival--saying nothing about being a nosy academic-and asked if she could provide me with further information or direct me to someone who could.

"Do you mean the one held in the winter?" she asked.

"How many of them are there?"

"Just that one."

"I suppose, then, that that's the one I mean." I smiled as if sharing a joke with her.

Without another word, she walked off into the back hallway. While she was absent I exchanged glances with several of the people behind the counter who periodically looked up from their work.

"There you are," she said when she returned, handing me a piece of paper that looked like the product of a cheap copy machine. Please Come to the Fun, it said in large letters. Parades, it went on, Street Masquerade, Bands, The Winter Raffle, and The Coronation of the Winter Queen. The page continued with the mention of a number of miscellaneous festivities. I read the words again. There was something about that imploring little "please" at the top of the announcement that made the whole affair seem like a charity function.

"When is it held? It doesn't say when the festival takes place."

"Most people already know that." She abruptly snatched the page from my hands and wrote something at the bottom. When she gave it back to me, I saw "Dec. 19-21" written in blue-green ink. I was immediately struck by an odd sense of scheduling on the part of the festival committee. There was, of course, solid anthropological and historical precedent for holding festivities around the winter solstice, but the timing of this particular event did not seem entirely practical.

"If you don't mind my asking, don't these days somewhat conflict with the regular holiday season? I mean, most people have enough going on at that time."

"It's just tradition," she said, as if invoking some venerable ancestry behind her words.

"That's very interesting," I said as much to myself as to her.

"Is there anything else?" she asked.

"Yes. Could you tell me if this festival has anything to do with clowns? I see there's something about a masquerade."

"Yes, of course there are some people in . . . costumes. I've never been in that position myself . . . that is, yes, there are clowns of a sort."

At that point my interest was definitely aroused, but I was not sure how much further I wanted to pursue it. I thanked the woman for her help and asked the best means of access to the highway, not anxious to retrace the labyrinthine route by which I had entered the town. I walked back to my car with a whole flurry of half-formed questions, and as many vague and conflicting answers, cluttering my mind.

The directions the woman gave me necessitated passing through the south end of Mirocaw. There were not many people moving about in this section of town. Those that I did see, shuffling lethargically down a block of battered storefronts, exhibited the same sort of forlorn expression and manner as the old man from whom I had asked directions earlier. I must have been traversing a central artery of this area, for on either side stretched street after street of poorly tended yards and houses bowed with age and indifference. When I came to a stop at a streetcorner, one of the citizens of this slum passed in front of my car. This lean, morose, and epicene person turned my way, and sneered outrageously with a taut little mouth, yet seemed to be looking at no one in particular. After progressing a few streets farther, I came to a road that led back to the highway. I felt detectably more comfortable as soon as I found myself traveling once again through the expanses of sun-drenched farmlands.

I reached the library with more than enough time for my research, and so I decided to make a scholarly detour to see what material I could find that might illuminate the winter festival held in Mirocaw. The library, one of the oldest in the state, included in its holdings the entire run of the Mirocaw Courier. I thought this would be an excellent place to start. I soon found, however, that there was no handy way to research information from this newspaper, and I did not want to engage in a blind search for articles concerning a specific subject.

I next turned to the more organized resources of the newspapers for the larger cities located in the same county, which incidentally shares its name with Mirocaw. I uncovered very little about the town, and almost nothing concerning its festival, except in one general article on annual events in the area that erroneously attributed to Mirocaw a "large Middle-Eastern community" which every spring hosted a kind of ethnic jamboree. From what I had already observed, and from what I subsequently learned, the citizens of Mirocaw were solidly midwestern-American, the probable descendants in a direct line from some enterprising pack of New Englanders of the last century. There was one brief item devoted to a Mirocavian event, but this merely turned out to be an obituary notice for an old woman who had quietly taken her life around Christmastime. Thus, I returned home that day all but empty-handed on the subject of Mirocaw.

However, it was not long afterward that I received another letter from the former colleague of mine who had first led me to seek out Mirocaw and its festival. As it happened, he rediscovered the article that caused him to stir my interest in a local "Fool's Feast." This article had its sole appearance in an obscure festschrift of anthropology studies published in Amsterdam twenty years ago. Most of these papers were in Dutch, a few in German, and only one was in English: "The Last Feast of Harlequin: Preliminary Notes on a Local Festival." It was exciting, of course, finally to be able to read this study, but even more exciting was the name of its author: Dr. Raymond Thoss.

2.

Before proceeding any further, I should mention something about Thoss, and inevitably about myself. Over two decades ago, at my alma mater in Cambridge, Mass., Thoss was a professor of mine. Long before playing a role in the events I am about to describe, he was already one of the most important figures in my life. A striking personality, he inevitably influenced everyone who came in contact with him. I remember his lectures on social anthropology, how he turned that dim room into a brilliant and profound circus of learning. He moved in an uncannily brisk manner. When he swept his arm around to indicate some common term on the blackboard behind him, one felt he was presenting nothing less than an item of fantastic qualities and secret value. When he replaced his hand in the pocket of his old jacket this fleeting magic was once again stored away in its well-worn pouch, to be retrieved at the sorcerer's discretion. We sensed he was teaching us more than we could possibly learn, and that he himself was in possession of greater and deeper knowledge than he could possibly impart. On one occasion I summoned up the audacity to offer an interpretation--which was somewhat opposed to his own--regarding the tribal clowns of the Hopi Indians. I implied that personal experience as an amateur clown and special devotion to this study provided me with an insight possibly more valuable than his own. It was then he disclosed, casually and very obiter dicta, that he had actually acted in the role of one of these masked tribal fools and had celebrated with them the dance of the kachinas. In revealing these facts, however, he somehow managed not to add to the humiliation I had already inflicted upon myself. And for this I was grateful to him.

Thoss's activities were such that he sometimes became the object of gossip or romanticized speculation. He was a fieldworker par excellence, and his ability to insinuate himself into exotic cultures and situations, thereby gaining insights where other anthropologists merely collected data, was renowned. At various times in his career there had been rumors of his having "gone native" a la the Frank Hamilton Cushing legend. There were hints, which were not always irresponsible or cheaply glamorized, that he was involved in projects of a freakish sort, many of which focused on New England. It is a fact that he spent six months posing as a mental patient at an institution in western Massachusetts, gathering information on the "culture" of the psychically disturbed. When his book Winter Solstice: The Longest Night of a Society was published, the general opinion was that it was disappointingly subjective and impressionistic, and that, aside from a few moving but "poetically obscure" observations, there was nothing at all to give it value. Those who defended Thoss claimed he was a kind of super-anthropologist: while much of his work emphasized his own mind and feelings, his experience had in fact penetrated to a rich core of hard data which he had yet to disclose in objective discourse. As a student of Thoss, I tended to support this latter estimation of him. For a variety of tenable and untenable reasons, I believed Thoss capable of unearthing hitherto inaccessible strata of human existence. So it was gratifying at first that this article entitled "The Last Feast of Harlequin" seemed to uphold the Thoss mystique, and in an area I personally found captivating.

Much of the content of the article I did not immediately comprehend, given its author's characteristic and often strategic obscurities. On first reading, the most interesting aspect of this brief study--the "notes" encompassed only twenty pages--was the general mood of the piece. Thoss's eccentricities were definitely present in these pages, but only as a struggling inner force which was definitely contained--incarcerated, I might say--by the somber rhythmic movements of his prose and by some gloomy references he occasionally called upon. Two references in particular shared a common theme. One was a quotation from Poe's "The Conqueror Worm," which Thoss employed as a rather sensational epigraph. The point of the epigraph, however, was nowhere echoed in the text of the article save in another passing reference. Thoss brought up the well-known genesis of the modern Christmas celebration, which of course descends from the Roman Saturnalia. Then, making it clear he had not yet observed the Mirocaw festival and had only gathered its nature from various informants, he established that it too contained many, even more overt, elements of the Saturnalia. Next he made what seemed to me a trivial and purely linguistic observation, one that had less to do with his main course of argument than it did with the equally peripheral Poe epigraph. He briefly mentioned that an early sect of the Syrian Gnostics called themselves "Saturnians" and believed, among other religious heresies, that mankind was created by angels who were in turn created by the Supreme Unknown. The angels, however, did not possess the power to make their creation an erect being and for a time he crawled upon the earth like a worm. Eventually, the Creator remedied this grotesque state of affairs. At the time I supposed that the symbolic correspondences of mankind's origins and ultimate condition being associated with worms, combined with a year-end festival recognizing the winter death of the earth, was the gist of this Thossian "insight," a poetic but scientifically valueless observation.

Other observations he made on the Mirocaw festival were also strictly etic; in other words, they were based on second-hand sources, hearsay testimony. Even at that juncture, however, I felt Thoss knew more than he disclosed; and, as I later discovered, he had indeed included information on certain aspects of Mirocaw suggesting he was already in possession of several keys which for the moment he was keeping securely in his own pocket. By then I myself possessed a most revealing morsel of knowledge. A note to the "Harlequin" article apprised the reader that the piece was only a fragment in rude form of a more wide-ranging work in preparation. This work was never seen by the world. My former professor had not published anything since his withdrawal from academic circulation some twenty years ago. Now I suspected where he had gone.

For the man I had stopped on the streets of Mirocaw and from whom I tried to obtain directions, the man with the disconcertingly lethargic gaze, had very much resembled a superannuated version of Dr. Raymond Thoss.

3.

And now I have a confession to make. Despite my reasons for being enthusiastic about Mirocaw and its mysteries, especially its relationship to both Thoss and my own deepest concerns as a scholar--I contemplated the days ahead of me with no more than a feeling of frigid numbness and often with a sense of profound depression. Yet I had no reason to be surprised at this emotional state, which had little relevance to the outward events in my life but was determined by inward conditions that worked according to their own, quite enigmatic, seasons and cycles. For many years, at least since my university days, I have suffered from this dark malady, this recurrent despondency in which I would become buried when it came time for the earth to grow cold and bare and the skies heavy with shadows. Nevertheless, I pursued my plans, though somewhat mechanically, to visit Mirocaw during its festival days, for I superstitiously hoped that this activity might diminish the weight of my seasonal despair. In Mirocaw would be parades and parties and the opportunity to play the clown once again.

For weeks in advance I practiced my art, even perfecting a new feat of juggling magic, which was my special forte in foolery. I had my costumes cleaned, purchased fresh makeup, and was ready. I received permission from the university to cancel some of my classes prior to the holiday, explaining the nature of my project and the necessity of arriving in the town a few days before the festival began, in order to do some preliminary research, establish informants, and so on. Actually, my plan was to postpone any formal inquiry until after the festival and to involve myself beforehand as much as possible in its activities. I would, of course, keep a journal during this time.

There was one resource I did want to consult, however. Specifically, I returned to that outstate library to examine those issues of the Mirocaw Courier dating from December two decades ago. One story in particular confirmed a point Thoss made in the "Harlequin" article, though the event it chronicled must have taken place after Thoss had written his study.

The Courier story appeared two weeks after the festival had ended for that year and was concerned with the disappearance of a woman named Elizabeth Beadle, the wife of Samuel Beadle, a hotel owner in Mirocaw. The county authorities speculated that this was another instance of the "holiday suicides" which seemed to occur with inordinate seasonal regularity in the Mirocaw region. Thoss documented this phenomenon in his "Harlequin" article, though I suspect that today these deaths would be neatly categorized under the heading "seasonal affective disorder". In any case, the authorities searched a half-frozen lake near the outskirts of Mirocaw where they had found many successful suicides in years past. This year, however, no body was discovered. Alongside the article was a picture of Elizabeth Beadle. Even in the grainy microfilm reproduction one could detect a certain vibrancy and vitality in Mrs. Beadle's face. That an hypothesis of "holiday suicide" should be so readily posited to explain her disappearance seemed strange and in some way unjust.

Thoss, in his brief article, wrote that every year there occurred changes of a moral or spiritual cast which seemed to affect Mirocaw along with the usual winter metamorphosis. He was not precise about its origin or nature but stated, in typically mystifying fashion, that the effect of this "subseason" on the town was conspicuously negative. In addition to the number of suicides actually accomplished during this time, there was also a rise in treatment of "hypochondriacal" conditions, which was how the medical men of twenty years past characterized these cases in discussions with Thoss. This state of affairs would gradually worsen and finally reach a climax during the days scheduled for the Mirocaw festival. Thoss speculated that given the secretive nature of small towns, the situation was probably even more intensely pronounced than casual investigation could reveal.

The connection between the festival and this insidious subseasonal climate in Mirocaw was a point on which Thoss did not come to any rigid conclusions. He did write, nevertheless, that these two "climatic aspects" had had a parallel existence in the town's history as far back as available records could document A late nineteenth-century history of Mirocaw County speaks of the town by its original name of New Colstead, and castigates the townspeople for holding a "ribald and soulless feast" to the exclusion of normal Christmas observances. (Thoss comments that the historian had mistakenly fused two distinct aspects of the season, their actual relationship being essentially antagonistic.) The "Harlequin" article did not trace the festival to its earliest appearance (this may not have been possible), though Thoss emphasized the New England origins of Mirocaw's founders. The festival, therefore, was one imported from this region and could reasonably be extended at least a century; that is, if it had not been brought over from the Old World, in which case its roots would become indefinite until further research could be done. Surely Thoss's allusion to the Syrian Gnostics suggested the latter possibility could not entirely be ruled out.

But it seemed to be the festival's link to New England that nourished Thoss's speculations. He wrote of this patch of geography as if it were an acceptable place to end the search. For him, the very words "New England" seemed to be stripped of all traditional connotations and had come to imply nothing less than a gateway to all lands, both known and suspected, and even to ages beyond the civilized history of the region. Having been educated partly in New England, I could somewhat understand this sentimental exaggeration, for indeed there are places that seem archaic beyond chronological measure, appearing to transcend relative standards of time and achieving a kind of absolute antiquity which cannot be logically fathomed. But how this vague suggestion related to a small town in the Midwest I could not imagine. Thoss himself observed that the residents of Mirocaw did not betray any mysteriously primitive consciousness. On the contrary, they appeared superficially unaware of the genesis of their winter merrymaking. That such a tradition had endured through the years, however, even eclipsing the conventional Christmas holiday, revealed a profound awareness of the festival's meaning and function.

I cannot deny that what I had learned about the Mirocaw festival did inspire a trite sense of fate, especially given the involvement of such an important figure from my past as Thoss. It was the first time in my academic career that I knew myself to be better suited than anyone else to discern the true meaning of scattered data, even if I could only attribute this special authority to chance circumstances.

Nevertheless, as I sat in that library on a morning in mid December I doubted for a moment the wisdom of setting out for Mirocaw rather than returning home, where the more familiar rite de passage of winter depression awaited me. My original scheme was to avoid the cyclical blues the season held for me, but it seemed this was also a part of the history of Mirocaw, only on a much larger scale. My emotional instability, however, was exactly what qualified me most for the particular fieldwork ahead, though I did not take pride or consolation in the fact. And to retreat would have been to deny myself an opportunity that might never offer itself again. In retrospect, there seems to have been no fortuitous resolution to the decision I had to make. As it happened, I went ahead to the town.

4.

Just past noon, on December 18, I started driving toward Mirocaw. A blur of dull, earthen-colored scenery extended in every direction. The snowfalls of late autumn had been sparse, and only a few white patches appeared in the harvested fields along the highway. The clouds were gray and abundant. Passing by a stretch of forest, I noticed the black, ragged clumps of abandoned nests clinging to the twisted mesh of bare branches. I thought I saw black birds skittering over the road ahead, but they were only dead leaves and they flew into the air as I drove by.

I approached Mirocaw from the south, entering the town from the direction I had left it on my visit the previous summer. This took me once again through that part of town which seemed to exist on the wrong side of some great invisible barrier dividing the desirable sections of Mirocaw from the undesirable. As lurid as this district had appeared to me under the summer sun, in the thin light of that winter afternoon it degenerated into a pale phantom of itself. The frail stores and starved-looking houses suggested a borderline region between the material and nonmaterial worlds, with one sardonically wearing the mask of the other. I saw a few gaunt pedestrians who turned as I passed by, though seemingly not because I passed by, making my way up to the main street of Mirocaw.

Driving up the steep rise of Townshend Street, I found the sights there comparatively welcoming. The rolling avenues of the town were in readiness for the festival. Streetlights had their poles raveled with evergreen, the fresh boughs proudly conspicuous in a barren season. On the doors of many of the businesses on Townshend were holly wreaths, equally green but observably plastic. However, although there was nothing unusual in this traditional greenery of the season, it soon became apparent to me that Mirocaw had quite abandoned itself to this particular symbol of Yuletide. It was garishly in evidence everywhere. The windows of stores and houses were framed in green lights, green streamers hung down from storefront awnings, and the beacons of the Red Rooster Bar were peacock green floodlights. I supposed the residents of Mirocaw desired these decorations, but the effect was one of excess. An eerie emerald haze permeated the town, and faces looked slightly reptilian.

At the time I assumed that the prodigious evergreen, holly wreaths, and colored lights (if only of a single color) demonstrated an emphasis on the vegetable symbols of the Nordic Yuletide, which would inevitably be muddled into the winter festival of any northern country just as they had been adopted for the Christmas season. In his "Harlequin" article Thoss wrote of the pagan aspect of Mirocaw's festival, likening it to the ritual of a fertility cult, with probable connections to chthonic divinities at some time in the past. But Thoss had mistaken, as I had, what was only part of the festival's significance for the whole.

The hotel at which I had made reservations was located on Townshend. It was an old building of brown brick, with an arched doorway and a pathetic coping intended to convey an impression of neoclassicism. I found a parking space in front and left my suitcases in the car.

When I first entered the hotel lobby it was empty. I thought perhaps the Mirocaw festival would have attracted enough visitors to at least bolster the business of its only hotel, but it seemed I was mistaken. Tapping a little bell, I leaned on the desk and turned to look at a small, traditionally decorated Christmas tree on a table near the entranceway. It was complete with shiny, egg-fragile bulbs; miniature candy canes; flat, laughing Santas with arms wide; a star on top nodding awkwardly against the delicate shoulder of an upper branch; and colored lights that bloomed out of flower-shaped sockets. For some reason this seemed to me a sorry little piece.

"May I help you?" said a young woman arriving from a room adjacent to the lobby.

I must have been staring rather intently at her, for she looked away and seemed quite uneasy. I could hardly imagine what to say to her or how to explain what I was thinking. In person she immediately radiated a chilling brilliance of manner and expression. But if this woman had not committed suicide twenty years before, as the newspaper article had suggested, neither had she aged in that time.

"Sarah," called a masculine voice from the invisible heights of a stairway. A tall, middle-aged man came down the steps. "I thought you were in your room," said the man, whom I took to be Samuel Beadle. Sarah, not Elizabeth, Beadle glanced sideways in my direction to indicate to her father that she was conducting the business of the hotel. Beadle apologized to me, and then excused the two of them for a moment while they went off to one side to continue their exchange.

I smiled and pretended everything was normal, while trying to remain within earshot of their conversation. They spoke in tones that suggested their conflict was a familiar one: Beadle's overprotective concern with his daughter's whereabouts and Sarah's frustrated understanding of certain restrictions placed upon her. The conversation ended, and Sarah ascended the stairs, turning for a moment to give me a facial pantomime of apology for the unprofessional scene that had just taken place.

"Now, sir, what can I do for you?" Beadle asked, almost demanded.

"Yes, I have a reservation. Actually, I'm a day early, if that doesn't present a problem." I gave the hotel the benefit of the doubt that its business might have been secretly flourishing.

"No problem at all, sir," he said, presenting me with the registration form, and then a brass-colored key dangling from a plastic disc bearing the number 44.

"Luggage?"

"Yes, it's in my car."

"I'll give you a hand with that."

While Beadle was settling me in my fourth-floor room it seemed an opportune moment to broach the subject of the festival, the holiday suicides, and perhaps, depending upon his reaction, the fate of his wife. I needed a respondent who had lived in the town for a good many years and who could enlighten me about the attitude of Mirocavians toward their season of sea-green lights.

"This is just fine," I said about the clean but somber room. "Nice view. I can see the bright green lights of Mirocaw just fine from up here. Is the town usually all decked out like this? For the festival, I mean."

"Yes, sir, for the festival," he replied mechanically.

"I imagine you'll probably be getting quite a few of us out-of-towners in the next couple days."

"Could be. Is there anything else?"

"Yes, there is. I wonder if you could tell me something about the festivities."

"Such as . . ."

"Well, you know, the clowns and so forth."

"Only clowns here are the ones that're . . . well, picked out, I suppose you would say."

"I don't understand."

"Excuse me, sir. I'm very busy right now. Is there anything else?"

I could think of nothing at the moment to perpetuate our conversation. Beadle wished me a good stay and left.

I unpacked my suitcases. In addition to regular clothing I had also brought along some of the items from my clown's wardrobe. Beadle's comment that the clowns of Mirocaw were "picked out" left me wondering exactly what purpose these street masqueraders served in the festival. The clown figure has had so many meanings in different times and cultures. The jolly, well-loved joker familiar to most people is actually but one aspect of this protean creature. Madmen, hunchbacks, amputees, and other abnormals were once considered natural clowns; they were elected to fulfil a comic role which could allow others to see them as ludicrous rather than as terrible reminders of the forces of disorder in the world. But sometimes a cheerless jester was required to draw attention to this same disorder, as in the case of King Lear's morbid and honest fool, who of course was eventually hanged, and so much for his clownish wisdom. Clowns have often had ambiguous and sometimes contradictory roles to play. Thus, I knew enough not to brashly jump into costume and cry out, "Here I am again!"

That first day in Mirocaw I did not stray far from the hotel. I read and rested for a few hours and then ate at a nearby diner. Through the window beside my table I watched the winter night turn the soft green glow of the town into a harsh and almost totally new color as it contrasted with the darkness. The streets of Mirocaw seemed to me unusually busy for a small town at evening. Yet it was not the kind of activity one normally sees before an approaching Christmas holiday. This was not a crowd of bustling shoppers loaded with bright bags of presents. Their arms were empty, their hands shoved deep in their pockets against the cold, which nevertheless had not driven them to the solitude of their presumably warm houses. I watched them enter and exit store after store without buying; many merchants remained open late, and even the places that were closed had left their neons illuminated. The faces that passed the window of the diner were possibly just stiffened by the cold, I thought; frozen into deep frowns and nothing else. In the same window I saw the reflection of my own face. It was not the face of an adept clown; it was slack and flabby and at that moment seemed the face of someone less than alive. Outside was the town of Mirocaw, its streets dipping and rising with a lunatic severity, its citizens packing the sidewalks, its heart bathed in green: as promising a field of professional and personal challenge as I had ever encountered--and I was bored to the point of dread. I hurried back to my hotel room.

"Mirocaw has another coldness within its cold," I wrote in my journal that night. "Another set of buildings and streets that exists behind the visible town's facade like a world of disgraceful back alleys." I went on like this for about a page, across which I finally engraved a big "X". Then I went to bed.

In the morning I left my car at the hotel and walked toward the main business district a few blocks away. Mingling with the good people of Mirocaw seemed like the proper thing to do at that point in my scientific sojourn. But as I began laboriously walking up Townshend (the sidewalks were cramped with wandering pedestrians), a glimpse of someone suddenly replaced my haphazard plan with a more specific and immediate one. Through the crowd and about fifteen paces ahead was my goal.

"Dr. Thoss," I called.

His head almost seemed to turn and look back in response to my shout, but I could not be certain. I pushed past several warmly wrapped bodies and green-scarved necks, only to find that the object of my pursuit appeared to be maintaining the same distance from me, though I did not know if this was being done deliberately or not. At the next corner, the dark-coated Thoss abruptly turned right onto a steep street which led downward directly toward the dilapidated south end of Mirocaw. When I reached the corner I looked down the sidewalk and could see him very clearly from above. I also saw how he managed to stay so far ahead of me in a mob that had impeded my own progress. For some reason the people on the sidewalk made room so that he could move past them easily, without the usual jostling of bodies. It was not a dramatic physical avoidance, thought it seemed nonetheless intentional. Fighting the tight fabric of the throng, I continued to follow Thoss, losing and regaining sight of him.

By the time I reached the bottom of the sloping street the crowd had thinned out considerably, and after walking a block or so farther I found myself practically a lone pedestrian pacing behind a distant figure that I hoped was still Thoss. He was now walking quite swiftly and in a way that seemed to acknowledge my pursuit of him, though really it felt as if he were leading me as much as I was chasing him. I called his name a few more times at a volume he could not have failed to hear, assuming that deafness was not one of the changes to have come over him; he was, after all, not a young man, nor even a middle-aged one any longer.

Thoss suddenly crossed in the middle of the street. He walked a few more steps and entered a signless brick building between a liquor store and a repair shop of some kind. In the "Harlequin" article Thoss had mentioned that the people living in this section of Mirocaw maintained their own businesses, and that these were patronized almost exclusively by residents of the area. I could well believe this statement when I looked at these little sheds of commerce, for they had the same badly weathered appearance as their clientele. The formidable shoddiness of these buildings notwithstanding, I followed Thoss into the plain brick shell of what had been, or possibly still was, a diner.

Inside it was unusually dark. Even before my eyes made the adjustment I sensed that this was not a thriving restaurant cozily cluttered with chairs and tables--as was the establishment where I had eaten the night before--but a place with only a few disarranged furnishings, and very cold. It seemed colder, in fact, than the winter streets outside.

"Dr. Thoss?" I called toward a lone table near the center of the long room. Perhaps four or five were sitting around the table, with some others blending into the dimness behind them. Scattered across the top of the table were some books and loose papers. Seated there was an old man indicating something in the pages before him, but it was not Thoss. Beside him were two youths whose wholesome features distinguished them from the grim weariness of the others. I approached the table and they all looked up at me. None of them showed a glimmer of emotion except the two boys, who exchanged worried and guilt-ridden glances with each other, as if they had just been discovered in some shameful act. They both suddenly burst from the table and ran into the dark background, where a light appeared briefly as they exited by a back door.

"I'm sorry," I said diffidently. "I thought I saw someone I knew come in here."

They said nothing. Out of a back room others began to emerge, no doubt interested in the source of the commotion. In a few moments the room was crowded with these tramp-like figures, all of them gazing emptily in the dimness. I was not at this point frightened of them; at least I was not afraid they would do me any physical harm. Actually, I felt as if it was quite within my power to pummel them easily into submission, their mousy faces almost inviting a succession of firm blows. But there were so many of them.

They slid slowly toward me in a worm-like mass. Their eyes seemed empty and unfocused, and I wondered a moment if they were even aware of my presence. Nevertheless, I was the center upon which their lethargic shuffling converged, their shoes scuffing softly along the bare floor. I began to deliver a number of hasty inanities as they continued to press toward me, their weak and unexpectedly odorless bodies nudging against mine. (I understood now why the people along the sidewalks seemed to instinctively avoid Thoss.) Unseen legs became entangled with my own; I staggered and then regained my balance. This sudden movement aroused me from a kind of mesmeric daze into which I must have fallen without being aware of it. I had intended to leave that dreary place long before events had reached such a juncture, but for some reason I could not focus my intentions strongly enough to cause myself to act. My mind had been drifting farther away as these slavish things approached. In a sudden surge of panic I pushed through their soft ranks and was outside.

The open air revived me to my former alertness, and I immediately started pacing swiftly up the hill. I was no longer sure that I had not simply imagined what had seemed, and at the same time did not seem, like a perilous moment. Had their movements been directed toward a harmful assault, or were they trying merely to intimidate me? As I reached the green-glazed main street of Mirocaw I really could not determine what had just happened.

The sidewalks were still jammed with a multitude of pedestrians, who now seemed more lively than they had been only a short time before. There was a kind of vitality that could only be attributed to the imminent festivities. A group of young men had begun celebrating prematurely and strode noisily across the street at midpoint, obviously intoxicated. From the laughter and joking among the still sober citizens I gathered that, mardi-gras style, public drunkenness was within the traditions of this winter festival. I looked for anything to indicate the beginnings of the Street Masquerade, but saw nothing: no brightly garbed harlequins or snow-white pierrots. Were the ceremonies even now in preparation for the coronation of the Winter Queen? "The Winter Queen," I wrote in my journal. "Figure of fertility invested with symbolic powers of revival and prosperity. Elected in the manner of a high school prom queen. Check for possible consort figure in the form of a representative from the underworld."

In the pre-darkness hours of December 19 I sat in my hotel room and wrote and thought and organized. I did not feel too badly, all things considered. The holiday excitement which was steadily rising in the streets below my window was definitely infecting me. I forced myself to take a short nap in anticipation of a long night. When I awoke, Mirocaw's annual feast had begun.

5.

Shouting, commotion, carousing. Sleepily I went to the window and looked out over the town. It seemed all the lights of Mirocaw were shining, save in that section down the hill which became part of the black void of winter. And now the town's greenish tinge was even more pronounced, spreading everywhere like a great green rainbow that had melted from the sky and endured, phosphorescent, into the night. In the streets was the brightness of an artificial spring. The byways of Mirocaw vibrated with activity: on a nearby corner a brass band blared; marauding cars blew their horns and were sometimes mounted by laughing pedestrians; a man emerged from the Red Rooster Bar, threw up his arms, and crowed. I looked closely at the individual celebrants, searching for the vestments of clowns. Soon, delightedly, I saw them. The costume was red and white, with matching cap, and the face painted a noble alabaster. It almost seemed to be a clownish incarnation of that white-bearded and black-booted Christmas fool.

This particular fool, however, was not receiving the affection and respect usually accorded to a Santa Claus. My poor fellow-clown was in the middle of a circle of revelers who were pushing him back and forth from one to the other. The object of this abuse seemed to accept it somewhat willingly, but this little game nevertheless appeared to have humiliation as its purpose. "Only clowns here are the one's that're picked out," echoed Beadle's voice in my memory. "Picked on" seemed closer to the truth.

Packing myself in some heavy clothes, I went out into the green gleaming streets. Not far from the hotel I was stumbled into by a character with a wide blue and red grin and bright baggy clothes. Actually he had been shoved into me by some youths outside a drugstore.

"See the freak," said an obese and drunken fellow. "See the freak fall."

My first response was anger, and then fear as I saw two others flanking the fat drunk. They walked toward me and I tensed myself for a confrontation.

"This is a disgrace," one said, the neck of a wine bottle held loosely in his left hand.

But it was not to me they were speaking; it was to the clown, who had been pushed to the sidewalk. His three persecutors helped him up with a sudden jerk and then splashed wine in his face. They ignored me altogether.

"Let him loose," the fat one said. "Crawl away, freak. Oh, he flies!"

The clown trotted off, becoming lost in the throng.

"Wait a minute," I said to the rowdy trio, who had started lumbering away. I quickly decided that it would probably be futile to ask them to explain what I had just witnessed, especially amid the noise and confusion of the festivities. In my best jovial fashion I proposed we all go someplace where I could buy them each a drink. They had no objection and in a short while we were all squeezed around a table in the Red Rooster.

Over several drinks I explained to them that I was from out of town, which pleased them no end for some reason. I told them there were things I did not understand about their festival.

"I don't think there's anything to understand," the fat one said. "It's just what you see."

I asked him about the people dressed as clowns.

"Them? They're the freaks. It's their turn this year. Everyone takes their turn. Next year it might be mine. Or yours," he said, pointing at one of his friends across the table. "And when we find out which one you are-- "

"You're not smart enough," said the defiant potential freak.

This was an important point: the fact that individuals who played the clowns remain, or at least attempted to remain, anonymous. This arrangement would help remove inhibitions a resident of Mirocaw might have about abusing his own neighbor or even a family relation. From what I later observed, the extent of this abuse did not go beyond a kind of playful roughhousing. And even so, it was only the occasional group of rowdies who actually took advantage of this aspect of the festival, the majority of the citizens very much content to stay on the sidelines.

As far as being able to illuminate the meaning of this custom, my three young friends were quite useless. To them it was just amusement, as I imagine it was to the majority of Mirocavians. This was understandable. I suppose the average person would not be able to explain exactly how the profoundly familiar Christmas holiday came to be celebrated in its present form.

I left the bar alone and not unaffected by the drinks I had consumed there. Outside, the general merrymaking continued. Loud music emanated from several quarters. Mirocaw had fully transformed itself from a sedate small town to an enclave of Saturnalia within the dark immensity of a winter night. But Saturn is also the planetary symbol of melancholy and sterility, a clash of opposites contained within that single word. And as I wandered half-drunkenly down the street, I discovered that there was a conflict within the winter festival itself. This discovery indeed appeared to be that secret key which Thoss withheld in his study of the town. Oddly enough, it was through my unfamiliarity with the outward nature of the festival that I came to know its true nature.

I was mingling with the crowd on the street, warmly enjoying the confusion around me, when I saw a strangely designed creature lingering on the corner up ahead. It was one of the Mirocaw clowns. Its clothes were shabby and nondescript, almost in the style of a tramp-type down, but not humorously exaggerated enough. The face, though, made up for the lackluster costume. I had never seen such a strange conception for a clown's countenance. The figure stood beneath a dim streetlight, and when it turned its head my way I realized why it seemed familiar. The thin, smooth, and pale head; the wide eyes; the oval-shaped features resembling nothing so much as the skull-faced, screaming creature in that famous painting (memory fails me). This clownish imitation rivaled the original in suggesting stricken realms of abject horror and despair: an inhuman likeness more proper to something under the earth than upon it.

From the first moment I saw this creature, I thought of those inhabitants of the ghetto down the hill. There was the same nauseating passivity and languor in its bearing. Perhaps if I had not been drinking earlier I would not have been bold enough to take the action I did. I decided to join in one of the upstanding traditions of the winter festival, for it annoyed me to see this morbid impostor of a clown standing up. When I reached the corner I laughingly pushed myself into the creature--"Whoops!"--who stumbled backward and ended up on the sidewalk. I laughed again and looked around for approval from the festivalers in the vicinity. No one, however, seemed to appreciate or even acknowledge what I had done. They did not laugh with me or point with amusement, but only passed by, perhaps walking a little faster until they were some distance from this streetcorner incident. I realized instantly I had violated some tacit rule of behavior, though I had thought my action well within the common practice. The idea occurred to me that I might even be apprehended and prosecuted for what in any other circumstances was certainly a criminal act. I turned around to help the clown back to his feet, hoping to somehow redeem my offense, but the creature was gone. Solemnly I walked away from the scene of my inadvertent crime and sought other streets away from its witnesses.

Along the various back avenues of Mirocaw I wandered, pausing exhaustedly at one point to sit at the counter of a small sandwich shop that was packed with customers. I ordered a cup of coffee to revive my overly alcoholed system. Warming my hands around the cup and sipping slowly from it, I watched the people outside as they passed the front window. It was well after midnight but the thick flow of passersby gave no indication that anyone was going home early. A carnival of profiles filed past the window and I was content simply to sit back and observe, until finally one of these faces made me start. It was that frightful little clown I had roughed up earlier. But although its face was familiar in its ghastly aspect, there was something different about it. And I wondered that there should be two such hideous freaks.

Quickly paying the man at the counter, I dashed out to get a second glimpse of the clown, who was now nowhere in sight. The dense crowd kept me from pursuing this figure with any speed, and I wondered how the clown could have made its way so easily ahead of me. Unless the crowd had instinctively allowed this creature to pass unhindered through its massive ranks, as it did for Thoss. In the process of searching for this particular freak, I discovered that interspersed among the celebrating populous of Mirocaw, which included the sanctioned festival clowns, there was not one or two, but a considerable number of these pale, wraith-like creatures. And they all drifted along the streets unmolested by even the rowdiest of revelers. I now understood one of the taboos of the festival. These other clowns were not to be disturbed and should even be avoided, much as were the residents of the slum at the edge of town. Nevertheless, I felt instinctively that the two groups of clowns were somehow identified with each other, even if the ghetto clowns were not welcome at Mirocaw's winter festival. Indeed, they were not simply part of the community and celebrating the season in their own way. To all appearances, this group of melancholy mummers constituted nothing less than an entirely independent festival--a festival within a festival.

Returning to my room. I entered my suppositions into the journal I was keeping for this venture. The following are excerpts:

There is a superstitiousness displayed by the residents of Mirocaw with regard to these people from the slum section, particularly as they lately appear in those dreadful faces signifying their own festival. What is the relationship between these simultaneous celebrations? Did one precede the other? If so, which? My opinion at this point--and I claim no conclusiveness for it--is that Mirocaw's winter festival is the later manifestation, that it appeared after the festival of those depressingly pallid clowns, in order to cover it up or mitigate its effect. The holiday suicides come to mind, and the subclimate Thoss wrote about, the disappearance of Elizabeth Beadle twenty years ago, and my own experience with this pariah clan existing outside yet within the community. Of my own experience with this emotionally deleterious subseason I would rather not speak at this time. Still not able to say whether or not my usual winter melancholy is the cause. On the general subject of mental health, I must consider Thoss's book about his stay in a psychiatric hospital (in western Mass., almost sure of that. Check on this book & Mirocaw's New England roots). The winter solstice is tomorrow, albeit sometime past midnight (how blurry these days and nights are becoming!). It is, of course, the day of the year in which night hours surpass daylight hours by the greatest margin. Note what this has to do with the suicides and a rise in psychic disorder. Recalling Thoss's list of documented suicides in his article, there seemed to be a recurrence of specific family names, as there very likely might be for any kind of data collected in a small town. Among these names was a Beadle or two. Perhaps, then, there is a genealogical basis for the suicides which has nothing to do with Thoss's mystical subclimate, which is a colorful idea to be sure and one that seems fitting for this town of various outward and inward aspects, but is not a conception that can be substantiated.

One thing that seems certain, however, is the division of Mirocaw into two very distinct types of citizenry, resulting in two festivals and the appearance of similar clowns--a term now used in an extremely loose sense. But there is a connection, and I believe I have some idea of what it is. I said before that the normal residents of the town regard those from the ghetto, and especially their clown figures, with superstition. Yet it's more than that: there is fear, perhaps a kind of hatred--the particular kind of hatred resulting from some powerful and irrational memory. What threatens Mirocaw I think I can very well understand. I recall the incident earlier today in that vacant diner.

"Vacant" is the appropriate word here, despite its contradiction of fact. The congregation of that half-lit room formed less a presence than an absence, even considering the oppressive number of them. Those eyes that did not or could not focus on anything, the pining lassitude of their faces, the lazy march of their feet. I was spiritually drained when I ran out of there. I then understood why these people and their activities are avoided.

I cannot question the wisdom of those ancestral Mirocavians who began the tradition of the winter festival and gave the town a pretext for celebration and social intercourse at a time when the consequences of brooding isolation are most severe, those longest and darkest days of the solstice. A mood of Christmas joviality obviously would not be sufficient to counter the menace of this season. But even so, there are still the suicides of individuals who are somehow cut off, I imagine, from the vitalizing activities of the festival.

It is the nature of this insidious subseason that seems to determine the outward forms of Mirocaw's winter festival: the optimistic greenery in a period of gray dormancy; the fertile promise of the Winter Queen; and, most interesting to my mind, the clowns. The bright clowns of Mirocaw who are treated so badly; they appear to serve as substitute figures for those dark-eyed mummers of the slums. Since the latter are feared for some power or influence they possess, they may still be symbolically confronted and conquered through their counterparts, who are elected for precisely this function. If I am right about this, I wonder to what extent there is a conscious awareness among the town's populace of this indirect show of aggression. Those three young men I spoke with tonight did not seem to possess much insight beyond seeing that there was a certain amount of robust fun in the festival's tradition. For that matter, how much awareness is there on the other side of these two antagonistic festivals? Too horrible to think of such a thing, but I must wonder if, for all their apparent aimlessness, those inhabitants of the ghetto are not the only ones who know what they are about. No denying that behind those inhumanly limp expressions there seems to lie a kind of obnoxious intelligence.

Now I realize the confusion of my present state, but as I wobbled from street to street tonight, watching those oval-mouthed clowns, I could not help feeling that all the merrymaking in Mirocaw was somehow allowed only by their sufferance. This I hope is no more than a fanciful Thossian intuition, the sort of idea that is curious and thought-provoking without ever seeming to gain the benefit of proof. I know my mind is not entirely lucid, but I feel that it may be possible to penetrate Mirocaw's many complexities and illuminate the hidden side of the festival season. In particular I must look for the significance of the other festival. Is it also some kind of fertility celebration? From what I have seen, the tenor of this "celebrating" sub-group is one of anti-fertility, if anything. How have they managed to keep from dying out completely over the years? How do they maintain their numbers?

But I was too tired to formulate any more of my sodden speculations. Falling onto my bed, I soon became lost in dreams of streets and faces.

6.

I was, of course, slightly hung over when I woke up late the next morning. The festival was still going strong, and blaring music outside roused me from a nightmare. It was a parade. A number of floats proceeded down Townshend, a familiar color predominating. There were theme floats of pilgrims and Indians, cowboys and Indians, and clowns of an orthodox type. In the middle of it all was the Winter Queen herself, freezing atop an icy throne. She waved in all directions. I even imagined she waved up at my dark window.

In the first few groggy moments of wakefulness I had no sympathy with my excitation of the previous night. But I discovered that my former enthusiasm had merely lain dormant, and soon returned with an even greater intensity. Never before had my mind and senses been so active during this usually inert time of year. At home I would have been playing lugubrious old records and looking out the window quite a bit. I was terribly grateful in a completely abstract way for my commitment to a meaningful mania. And I was eager to get to work after I had had some breakfast at the coffee shop.

When I got back to my room I discovered the door was unlocked. And there was something written on the dresser mirror. The writing was red and greasy, as if done with a clown's make-up pencil--my own, I realized. I read the legend, or rather I should say riddle, several times: "What buries itself before it is dead?" I looked at it for quite a while, very shaken at how vulnerable my holiday fortifications were. Was this supposed to be a warning of some kind? A threat to the effect that if I persisted in a certain course I would end up prematurely interred? I would have to be careful, I told myself. My resolution was to let nothing deter me from the inspired strategy I had conceived for myself. I wiped the mirror clean, for it was now needed for other purposes.

I spent the rest of the day devising a very special costume and the appropriate face to go with it. I easily shabbied up my overcoat with a torn pocket or two and a complete set of stains. Combined with blue jeans and a pair of rather scuffed-up shoes, I had a passable costume for a derelict. The face, however, was more difficult, for I had to experiment from memory. Conjuring a mental image of the screaming pierrot in that painting (The Scream, I now recall), helped me quite a bit. At nightfall I exited the hotel by the back stairway.

It was strange to walk down the crowded street in this gruesome disguise. Though I thought I would feel conspicuous, the actual experience was very close, I imagined, to one of complete invisibility. No one looked at me as I strolled by, or as they strolled by, or as we strolled by each other. I was a phantom--perhaps the ghost of festivals past, or those yet to come.

I had no clear idea where my disguise would take me that night, only vague expectations of gaining the confidence of my fellow specters and possibly in some way coming to know their secrets. For a while I would simply wander around in that lackadaisical manner I had learned from them, following their lead in any way they might indicate. And for the most part this meant doing almost nothing and doing it silently. If I passed one of my kind on the sidewalk there was no speaking, no exchange of knowing looks, no recognition at all that I was aware of. We were there on the streets of Mirocaw to create a presence and nothing more. At least this is how I came to feel about it. As I drifted along with my bodiless invisibility, I felt myself more and more becoming an empty, floating shape, seeing without being seen and walking without the interference of those grosser creatures who shared my world. It was not an experience completely without interest or even pleasure. The clown's shibboleth of "here we are again" took on a new meaning for me as I felt myself a novitiate of a more rarified order of harlequinry. And very soon the opportunity to make further progress along this path presented itself.

Going the opposite direction, down the street, a pickup truck slowly passed, gently parting a sea of zigging and zagging celebrants. The cargo in the back of this truck was curious, for it was made up entirely of my fellow sectarians. At the end of the block the truck stopped and another of them boarded it over the back gate. One block down I saw still another get on. Then the truck made a U-turn at an intersection and headed in my direction.

I stood at the curb as I had seen the others do. I was not sure the truck would pick me up, thinking that somehow they knew I was an imposter. The truck did, however, slow down, almost coming to a stop when it reached me. The others were crowded on the floor of the truck bed. Most of them were just staring into nothingness with the usual indifference I had come to expect from their kind. But a few actually glanced at me with some anticipation. For a second I hesitated, not sure I wanted to pursue this ruse any further. At the last moment, some impulse sent me climbing up the back of the truck and squeezing myself in among the others.

There were only a few more to pick up before the truck headed for the outskirts of Mirocaw and beyond. At first I tried to maintain a clear orientation with respect to the town. But as we took turn after turn through the darkness of narrow country roads, I found myself unable to preserve any sense of direction. The majority of the others in the back of the truck exhibited no apparent awareness of their fellow passengers. Guardedly, I looked from face to ghostly face. A few of them spoke in short whispered phrases to others close by. I could not make out what they were saying but the tone of their voices was one of innocent normalcy, as if they were not of the hardened slum-herd of Mirocaw. Perhaps, I thought, these were thrill-seekers who had disguised themselves as I had done, or, more likely, initiates of some kind. Possibly they had received prior instructions at such meetings as I had stumbled onto the day before. It was also likely that among this crew were those very boys I had frightened into a precipitate exit from that old diner.

The truck was now speeding along a fairly open stretch of country, heading toward those higher hills that surrounded the now distant town of Mirocaw. The icy wind whipped around us, and I could not keep myself from trembling with cold. This definitely betrayed me as one of the newcomers among the group, for the two bodies that pressed against mine were rigidly still and even seemed to be radiating a frigidity of their own. I glanced ahead at the darkness into which we were rapidly progressing.

We had left all open country behind us now, and the road was enclosed by thick woods. The mass of bodies in the truck leaned into one another as we began traveling up a steep incline. Above us, at the top of the hill, were lights shining somewhere within the woods. When the road leveled off, the truck made an abrupt turn, steering into what looked like a great ditch. There was an unpaved path, however, upon which the truck proceeded toward the glowing in the near distance.

This glowing became brighter and sharper as we approached it, flickering upon the trees and revealing stark detail where there had formerly been only smooth darkness. As the truck pulled into a clearing and came to a stop, I saw a loose assembly of figures, many of which held lanterns that beamed with a dazzling and frosty light. I stood up in the back of the truck to unboard as the others were doing. Glancing around from that height I saw approximately thirty more of those cadaverous clowns milling about. One of my fellow passengers spied me lingering in the truck and in a strangely high-pitched whisper told me to hurry, explaining something about the "apex of darkness". I thought again about this solstice night; it was technically the longest period of darkness of the year, even if not by a very significant margin from many other winter nights. Its true significance, though, was related to considerations having little to do with either statistics or the calendar.

I went over to the place where the others were forming into a tighter crowd, which betrayed a sense of expectancy in the subtle gestures and expressions of its individual members. Glances were now exchanged, the hand of one lightly touched the shoulder of another, and a pair of circled eyes gazed over to where two figures were setting their lanterns on the ground about six feet apart. The illumination of these lanterns revealed an opening in the earth. Eventually the awareness of everyone was focused on this roundish pit, and as if by prearranged signal we all began huddling around it. The only sounds were those of the wind and our own movements as we crushed frozen leaves and sticks underfoot.

Finally, when we had all surrounded this gaping hole, the first one jumped in, leaving our sight for a moment but then reappearing to take hold of a lantern which another handed him from above. The miniature abyss filled with light, and I could see it was no more than six feet deep. One of its walls opened into the mouth of a tunnel. The figure holding the lantern stooped a little and disappeared into the passage.

Each of us, in turn, dropped into the darkness of this pit, and every fifth one took a lantern. I kept to the back of the group, for whatever subterranean activities were going to take place, I was sure I wanted to be on their periphery. When only about ten of us remained on the ground above, I maneuvered to let four of them precede me so that as the fifth I might receive a lantern. This was exactly how it worked out, for after I had leaped to the bottom of the hole a light was ritually handed down to me. Turning about-face, I quickly entered the passageway. At that point I shook so with cold that I was neither curious nor afraid, but only grateful for the shelter.

I entered a long, gently sloping tunnel, just high enough for me to stand upright. It was considerably warmer down there than outside in the cold darkness of the woods. After a few moments I had sufficiently thawed out so that my concerns shifted from those of physical comfort to a sudden and justified preoccupation with my survival. As I walked I held my lantern close to the sides of the tunnel. They were relatively smooth as if the passage had not been made by manual digging but had been burrowed by something which left behind a clue to its dimensions in the tunnel's size and shape. This delirious idea came to me when I recalled the message that had been left on my hotel room mirror: "What buries itself before it is dead?"

I had to hurry along to keep up with those uncanny spelunkers who preceded me. The lanterns ahead bobbed with every step of their bearers, the lumbering procession seeming less and less real the farther we marched into that snug little tunnel. At some point I noticed the line ahead of me growing shorter. The processioners were emptying out into a cavernous chamber where I, too, soon arrived. This area was about thirty feet in height, its other dimensions approximating those of a large ballroom. Gazing into the distance above made me uncomfortably aware of how far we had descended into the earth. Unlike the smooth sides of the tunnel, the walls of this cavern looked jagged and irregular, as though they had been gnawed at. The earth had been removed, I assumed, either through the tunnel from which we had emerged, or else by way of one of the many other black openings that I saw around the edges of the chamber, for possibly they too led back to the surface.

But the structure of this chamber occupied my mind a great deal less than did its occupants. There to meet us on the floor of the great cavern was what must have been the entire slum population of Mirocaw, and more, all with the same eerily wide-eyed and oval-mouthed faces. They formed a circle around an altar-like object which had some kind of dark, leathery covering draped over it. Upon the altar, another covering of the same material concealed a lumpy form beneath.

And behind this form, looking down upon the altar, was the only figure whose face was not greased with makeup.

He wore a long snowy robe that was the same color as the wispy hair berimming his head. His arms were calmly at his sides. He made no movement. The man I once believed would penetrate great secrets stood before us with the same professorial bearing that had impressed me so many years ago, yet now I felt nothing but dread at the thought of what revelations lay pocketed within the abysmal folds of his magisterial attire. Had I really come here to challenge such a formidable figure? The name by which I knew him seemed itself insufficient to designate one of his stature. Rather I should name him by his other incarnations: god of all wisdom, scribe of all sacred books, father of all magicians, thrice great and more--rather I should call him Thoth.

He raised his cupped hands to his congregation and the ceremony was underway.

It was all very simple. The entire assembly, which had remained speechless until this moment, broke into the most horrendous high-pitched singing that can be imagined. It was a choir of sorrow, of shrieking delirium, and of shame. The cavern rang shrilly with the dissonant, whining chorus. My voice, too, was added to the congregation's, trying to blend with their maimed music. But my singing could not imitate theirs, having a huskiness unlike their cacophonous keening wail. To keep from exposing myself as an intruder I continued to mouth their words without sound. These words were a revelation of the moody malignancy which until then I had no more than sensed whenever in the presence of these figures. They were singing to the "unborn in paradise," to the "pure unlived lives." They sang a dirge for existence, for all its vital forms and seasons. Their ideals were those of darkness, chaos, and a melancholy half-existence consecrated to all the many shapes of death. A sea of thin, bloodless faces trembled and screamed with perverted hopes. And the robed, guiding figure at the heart of all this--elevated over the course of twenty years to the status of high priest--was the man from whom I had taken so many of my own life's principles. It would be useless to describe what I felt at that moment and a waste of the time I need to describe the events which followed.

The singing abruptly stopped and the towering white haired figure began to speak. He was welcoming those of the new generation--twenty winters had passed since the "Pure Ones" had expanded their ranks. The word "pure" in this setting was a violence to what sense and composure I still retained, for nothing could have been more foul than what was to come. Thoss--and I employ this defunct identity only as a convenience--closed his sermon and drew closer to the dark-skinned altar. Then, with all the flourish of his former life, he drew back the topmost covering. Beneath it was a limp-limbed effigy, a collapsed puppet sprawled upon the slab. I was standing toward the rear of the congregation and attempted to keep as dose to the exit passage as I could. Thus, I did not see everything as clearly as I might have.

Thoss looked down upon the crooked, doll-like form and then out at the gathering. I even imagined that he made knowing eye-contact with myself. He spread his arms and a stream of continuous and unintelligible words flowed from his moaning mouth. The congregation began to stir, not greatly but perceptibly. Until that moment there was a limit to what I believed was the evil of these people. They were, after all, only that. They were merely morbid, self-tortured souls with strange beliefs. If there was anything I had learned in all my years as an anthropologist it was that the world is infinitely rich in strange ideas, even to the point where the concept of strangeness itself had little meaning for me. But with the scene I then witnessed, my conscience bounded into a realm from which it will never return.

For now was the transformation scene, the culmination of every harlequinade.

It began slowly. There was increasing movement among those on the far side of the chamber from where I stood. Someone had fallen to the floor and the others in the area backed away. The voice at the altar continued its chanting. I tried to gain a better view but there were too many of them around me. Through the mass of obstructing bodies I caught only glimpses of what was taking place.

The one who had swooned to the floor of the chamber seemed to be losing all former shape and proportion. I thought it was a clown's trick. They were clowns, were they not? I myself could make four white balls transform into four black balls as I juggled them. And this was not my most astonishing feat of clownish magic. And is there not always a sleight-of-hand inherent in all ceremonies, often dependent on the transported delusions of the celebrants? This was a good show, I thought, and giggled to myself. The transformation scene of Harlequin throwing off his fool's facade. O God, Harlequin, do not move like that! Harlequin, where are your arms? And your legs have melted together and begun squirming upon the floor. What horrible, mouthing umbilicus is that where your face should be? What is it that buries itself before it is dead? The almighty serpent of wisdom--the Conqueror Worm.

It now started happening all around the chamber. Individual members of the congregation would gaze emptily caught for a moment in a frozen trance--and then collapse to the floor to begin the sickening metamorphosis. This happened with ever-increasing frequency the louder and more frantic Thoss chanted his insane prayer or curse. Then there began a writhing movement toward the altar, and Thoss welcomed the things as they curled their way to the altar-top. I knew now what lax figure lay upon it.

This was Kora and Persephone, the daughter of Ceres and the Winter Queen: the child abducted into the underworld of death. Except this child had no supernatural mother to save her, no living mother at all. For the sacrifice I witnessed was an echo of one that had occurred twenty years before, the carnival feast of the preceding generation--O carne vale! Now both mother and daughter had become victims of this subterranean sabbath. I finally realized this truth when the figure stirred upon the altar, lifted its head of icy beauty, and screamed at the sight of mute mouths closing around her.

I ran from the chamber into the tunnel. (There was nothing else that could be done, I have obsessively told myself.) Some of the others who had not yet changed began to pursue me. They would have caught up to me, I have no doubt, for I fell only a few yards into the passage. And for a moment I imagined that I too was about to undergo a transformation, but I had not been prepared as the others had been. When I heard the approaching footsteps of my pursuers I was sure there was an even worse fate facing me upon the altar. But the footsteps ceased and retreated. They had received an order in the voice of their high priest. I too heard the order, though I wish I had not, for until then I had imagined that Thoss did not remember who I was. It was that voice which taught me otherwise.

For the moment I was free to leave. I struggled to my feet and, having broken my lantern in the fall, retraced my way back through cloacal blackness.

Everything seemed to happen very quickly once I emerged from the tunnel and climbed up from the pit. I wiped the reeking greasepaint from my face as I ran through the woods and back to the road. A passing car stopped, though I gave it no other choice except to run me down.

"Thank you for stopping."

"What the hell are you doing out here?" the driver asked.

I caught my breath. "It was a joke. The festival. Friends thought it would be funny.... Please drive on."

My ride let me off about a mile out of town, and from there I could find my way. It was the same way I had come into Mirocaw on my first visit the summer before. I stood for a while at the summit of that high hill just outside the city limits, looking down upon the busy little hamlet. The intensity of the festival had not abated, and would not until morning. I walked down toward the welcoming glow of green, slipped through the festivities unnoticed, and returned to the hotel. No one saw me go up to my room. Indeed, there was an atmosphere of absence and abandonment throughout that building, and the desk in the lobby was unattended.

I locked the door to my room and collapsed upon the bed.

7.

When I awoke the next morning I saw from my window that the town and surrounding countryside had been visited during the night by a snowstorm, one which was entirely unpredicted. The snow was still falling on the now deserted streets of Mirocaw. The festival was over. Everyone had gone home.

And this was exactly my own intention. Any action on my part concerning what I had seen the night before would have to wait until I was away from the town. I am still not sure it will do the slightest good to speak up like this. Any accusations I could make against the slum populace of Mirocaw would be resisted, as well they should be, as unbelievable. Perhaps in a very short while none of this will be my concern.

With packed suitcases in both hands I walked up to the front desk to check out. The man behind the desk was not Samuel Beadle, and he had to fumble around to find my bill.

"Here we are. Everything all right?"

"Fine," I answered in a dead voice. "Is Mr. Beadle around?"

"No, I'm afraid he's not back yet. Been out all night looking for his daughter. She's a very popular girl, being the Winter Queen and all that nonsense. Probably find she was at a party somewhere."

A little noise came out of my throat.

I threw my suitcases in the back seat of my car and got behind the wheel. On that morning nothing I could recall seemed real to me. The snow was falling and I watched it through my windshield, slow and silent and entrancing. I started up my car, routinely glancing in my rear view mirror. What I saw there is now vividly framed in my mind, as it was framed in the back window of my car when I turned to verify its reality.

In the middle of the street behind me, standing ankle-deep in snow, was Thoss and another figure. When I looked closely at the other I recognized him as one of the boys whom I surprised in that diner. But he had now taken on a corrupt and listless resemblance to his new family. Both he and Thoss stared at me, making no attempt to forestall my departure. Thoss knew that this was unnecessary.

I had to carry the image of those two dark figures in my mind as I drove back home. But only now has the full weight of my experience descended upon me. So far I have claimed illness in order to avoid my teaching schedule. To face the normal flow of life as I had formerly known it would be impossible. I am now very much under the influence of a season and a climate far colder and more barren than all the winters in human memory. And mentally retracing past events does not seem to have helped; I can feel myself sinking deeper into a velvety white abyss.

At certain times I could almost dissolve entirely into this inner realm of awful purity and emptiness. I remember those invisible moments when in disguise I drifted through the streets of Mirocaw, untouched by the drunken, noisy forms around me: untouchable. But instantly I recoil at this grotesque nostalgia, for I realize what is happening and what I do not want to be true, though Thoss proclaimed it was. I recall his command to those others as I lay helplessly prone in the tunnel. They could have apprehended me, but Thoss, my old master, called them back. His voice echoed throughout that cavern, and it now reverberates within my own psychic chambers of memory.

"He is one of us," it said. "He has always been one of us."

It is this voice which now fills my dreams and my days and my long winter nights. I have seen you, Dr. Thoss, through the snow outside my window. Soon I will celebrate, alone, that last feast which will kill your words, only to prove how well I have learned their truth.

To the memory of H. P. Lovecraft

Strange Manuscript Found in the Vermont Woods

By Lin Carter

NOTE: In the early spring of 1936 the following manuscript was found buried in the snowbanks in the woods south of the village of Townshend in Windham County, Vermont, by a local farmer, one Seth Adkins. When Mr. Adkins reported the discovery of the manuscript, which he turned over to Constable Homer T. Whitlaw, he said it was found in a leather briefcase which was curiously charred as if from exposure to intense heat, and seared here and there as if from the action of some virulent acid, and was also stained with a black slime-like substance which stank horribly. He also added that the briefcase and its contents were not only buried deep under a heavy snowdrift, but were partially impacted in the still-frozen soil, as if it had fallen from an incredible height. The spring thaw, it seems, had exposed one corner of the leather case to view, attracting the farmer's attention.

Upon examining the contents of the valise, Constable Whitlaw found a sheaf of handwritten manuscript inscribed in a neat hand which eventually deteriorated into a scarcely-readable scrawl, as if the later portions of the document had been scribbled hurriedly, under tension or duress. Furthermore, the edges of the several handwritten pages were crisped as if from exposure to severe temperature, and in places illegible due to leakage from the thawing snow.

The manuscript was written on both sides of sheets of correspondence paper embossed with the name of Winthrop Hoag, with a Boston address. Recalling the mysterious and still unexplained disappearance of a certain Winthrop Hoag from a cabin in the woods north of Arkham, Massachusetts only three months earlier, the Constable forwarded the valise and its contents, together with an account of their discovery, to County Sheriff Wilbur F. Tate in Arkham. At Sheriff Tate's direction, the manuscript was transcribed exactly as it appears below. Certain of the words and entire passages remained illegible, even though studied by handwriting experts.

The mystery remains unsolved to this day.

JOURNAL OF WINTHROP HOAG

I arrived in Arkham in early fall on the Boston train and went at once to the law offices of Mr. Silas Harding, who had been my cousin, Jared Fuller's lawyer until his death or disappearance seven years before, and who was the custodian of his last will and testament, in which, Harding's recent letter had informed me, I was declared sole beneficiary to his estate.

I found Mr. Harding a gaunt, silver-haired man in a dark suit, who spoke affably but with a pronounced Yankee twang. Ushering me to a seat, he explained that since the waiting period allowed by law in the case of missing persons had now expired, my cousin's property was legally mine. Said property consisted of a small cabin on a bit of land in the woods north of town, and its contents, the most valuable of which were probably certain old books which might prove worth a considerable sum in the hands of a rare book specialist.

The lawyer informed me that the cabin had been stoutly padlocked on his instructions, and the windows shuttered and barred. He had, he said, visited the property as recently as last week, and was pleased to report that the roofing was sound, the interior dry, and that the place was perfectly habitable, if lacking in certain of the civilized amenities of life.

"Is there any sort of plumbing?" I inquired. He shook his head.

"Too far out of town for thet, sir! But there's a privy in the back and a decent well has been dug. Walls seem secure; you'll git good heat from the Franklin stove. There's even a goodly supply of well-dried firewood under a tarpaulin in the shed. You'll need thet, come winter."

In my reply to Harding's letter informing me of my small bequest, I had stated my intention to live in the cabin, despite the nearness of winter -- and they can be cruel and bitter winters, north of Arkham! -- for I needed seclusion in which to prepare the notes for my master's thesis. He had written back, rather insistently, arguing against this plan on several points. It amused me that he repeated some of them now.

"You'll be snowed in, you know, for weeks at a time."

"Surely I can lay in supplies of canned goods, coffee, and the like from the nearest grocery," I said gently, humoring him a little.

"There is a general store on the Pike," he admitted grudgingly. "And the bus runs between Dunwich and Arkham pret' regular, cept in case of blizzards. Still have to suggest you just visit the place and take your property, and go back to Boston..."

When I pressed him for his reason, he merely muttered something about those woods "not having the best reputation," but remained close-mouthed on his meaning. When he saw I would not be swerved, he handed over the keys after requiring my signature on a few documents.

"You kin catch the bus to Dunwich at the end of River Street," he said curtly, in answering my request for directions. "Takes the Aylesbury Pike. You git off two, three miles beyond Dean's Corners, they's a mailbox by the road with 'Hoag' painted on it. Painted yer name on it myself, so you'd know. Driver'll know where t' let you off."

I thanked Harding and rose to leave. He laid a restraining hand on my arm.

"Daon't like to talk about sich matters," he said in a low voice. "But the Deep Woods, where you're goin', have an even wust reputation than Billington's Wood just south."

And with that enigmatic warning, he let me leave.

* * *

Driving north and northwest from Arkham, the land grew wild and lonely, thickly overgrown with gnarled and ancient trees with strangely few farmhouses to be seen, at least from the Pike. There were only a few people on the bus, a slatternly middle-aged woman or two, and an old farmer in filthy overalls, so I chose my seat near the driver. He seemed in a chatty mood.

"Daoun't get many young fellers like you up this way," he drawled. "From Boston y' say; but ain't Hoag an old Arkham name?"

"Yes, it is. From back before the Revolution, in the old sea-trading days."

"Heard tell of a Cap'n Abner Hoag onc't," the driver ruminated. "South Seas and Chiny trade, I recollect." I told him that Abner Ezekiel Hoag was my direct ancestor.

"My branch of the family has lived in or around Boston since about 1912," I told him, and he seemed interested in the older Massachusetts genealogies. "Our line descends from Hiram Lapham Hoag who moved to Lowell, near Boston, in that year. He was the younger brother of Zorad Ethan Hoag, who lived in Arkham until recently."

For some reason he became silent and taciturn at that point, and all my conversational gambits were able to elicit from him for the remainder of the trip were a few grunts or shakings of the head.

He dropped me off at my stop, where a narrow dirt road -- well, hardly more than a path -- wound between huge old trees. I trudged along the path and the woods pressed uncomfortably close, as if resenting with some weird sentience the intrusion of man into their ancient domain. The Deep Woods, Silas Harding had called them... odd how, in this oppressive silence, the narrow way walled about by thickly-grown, close-crowding trees, the name had a sinister ring to it...

The cabin my cousin had left me in his will was small enough, but it seemed livable, despite the fact that the clapboard walls could have used a few coats of paint. It stood amidst a small clearing, on a patch of naked earth, and again I could not help noticing (with slight revulsion, even dismay) how disturbingly close the edge of the woods shouldered about the forlorn habitation. These feelings I resolutely dismissed from my mind; I have always been unusually sensitive to the atmosphere of lonely, wooded places...

Once within, the bars removed and shutters opened, I found the interior dry and clean. There was a small Army cot, neatly made, a rickety table with a hoop-back wooden chair drawn up before it, and even a hooked rug before the old iron stove. These, and an empty woodbox, were the sum total of the furnishings: "lacking certain of the civilized amenities of life," even as lawyer Harding had dryly remarked.

Still, I thought I could be comfortable here, even in the depths of winter. There were shelves on the wall with tin plates and cups, sparse tableware, cheap and worn, a coffee pot and two or three pots and a frying pan. I even discovered a dimestore can-opener hung from a hook on the shelf. In a corner of the one-room cabin I found a hurricane lamp in serviceable condition, although the can of kerosene which fueled it proved empty.

Unpacking my clothing and books and papers, which latter took occupation of the table, I went outside and found the well-water fresh and clean, and in the woodshed a good supply of cut and stacked firewood in fine, dry condition, as Harding had promised, together with a rusty axe for cutting more when needed.

That afternoon, I went down the Aylesbury Pike to the little general store I had noticed from the bus. It stood on the outskirts of Dean's Corners, and the proprietor was happy to sell me supplies. As I must be frugal -- my funds being low, and the bequest from my cousin Jared containing no cash worth speaking of -- I settled on canned pork and beans, home-bottled peaches, boxed crackers, ground coffee, ketchup, salt, and a few other things, together with some pipe tobacco.

The storekeeper, an old, withered, wiry backwoodsman named Perkins, proved helpful but very inquisitive as to what I was doing "in this neck o' th' woods." When I told him I was a cousin of Jared Fuller, and had inherited his cabin in the woods a mile or two north, he stared at me incredulously.

"Fuller, y' say? Not in th' Deep Woods?"

"Yes, I 'm afraid so," I smiled. He gave me a strange, almost frightened look.

"Why, daoun't y' know they be even wust than Billington's Woods, south o' here?" he inquired in a whisper, as if fearful of being overheard, although there was no one else in the general store save him and me.

I shook my head. "'Billington's Woods' rings a bell somewhere, but I can't quite place it," I had to admit.

"Ever hear-tell of a feller named Ambrose Dewart? Another one, name of Stephen Bates -- Boston-man, like y'rself, I figger?" he breathed.

A slight chill passed through me. Dewart... Bates... surely, I had read about them in some sensational newspaper items eleven or twelve years ago...

I shook my head reluctantly, not quite able to recall the details. And when I asked what Perkins knew about these two individuals, he became as close-mouthed as the incommunicative bus-driver. All I could get out of him was that my "goods" would be delivered "long abaout sundown-time."

* * *

That afternoon, rather late, it became chill and dank, so I carried some armloads of wood into the cabin and built a fire. While I was loading up my arms with logs and kindling, I noticed a shelf built against the back of the shed and a dilapidated old suitcase of scabbed and peeling leather which stood upon it. I wondered if this might not contain Cousin Jared's "books and papers," to which Silas Harding had alluded. Since I had not found these in the cabin anywhere, this was probably the fact of the matter.

I resolved to look at the contents of the suitcase later.

About sundown I became aware of a persistent honking from the Pike. I went to investigate, and found a battered old Model T Ford parked before the entrance to the path, with a leathery, gaunt driver in worn overalls behind the wheel.

"Name of Hoag?" he grunted. When I replied in the affirmative, he gestured behind him with a calloused thumb.

"Groc'ries in th' rumbleseat," he snapped. Which meant I had to carry them in by myself.

I had expected the inhabitants of these rural backwoods to be a suspicious, unfriendly lot, and thus far my expectations were certainly fulfilled.

Returning to the cabin, where my fire was burning cheerily in the stove, I cleaned and filled the lamp, trimmed the wick and lighted it, for twilight fell quickly this time of year and the darkness was not far behind. I had scrubbed clean the pots and dishes with water from my well, and began heating my meal atop the stove. After dinner I settled down with a mug of hot black coffee and my pipe and began sorting out my notes and references by the yellow light of the hissing lamp. It was a cozy, rustic scene, like something out of Colonial times, almost, and the cabin was warm and comfortable although with darkness, the wind rose and moaned eerily through the stiff black boughs where the last gaudy tatters of foliage clung stubbornly against the autumnal chill.

When my fire collapsed to burning coals, I donned my heavy jacket and went to get more wood from the shed. This time I made another trip to drag forth the old suitcase. I was weary of my work and desired to turn my mind to other matters for awhile; also, I was getting a bit curious to see what "old, rare" books my cousin had bequeathed to me.

Inside the suitcase I found about a dozen volumes, mostly leather-bound, flaking with age, the pages yellowed with the years. They were certainly old enough, but as most of them were in French or German or Latin, I could make little of them, not being proficient in those languages. Anyway, they looked foreboding and not particularly of interest to me, with titles like *Unaussprechlichen Kulten* and *De Vermis Mysteriis* and *Cultes des Goules*.

Two of them, however, proved to be in English. One of these was a slender brochure bound in leatherette, privately published in 1916 by a commercial printer in San Francisco; it contained Professor Harold Hadley Copeland's "disturbing and conjectural" translation of the *Zanthu Tablets* which he had reputedly discovered in the tomb of a "prehistoric" shaman somewhere in the black and secret heart of Asia. I had heard of the *Zanthu Tablets*, for the book had been much notorious in my boyhood and was denounced by press and pulpit and was finally, as I recall, officially suppressed.

Knowing what little I knew about the *Zanthu Tablets*, I assumed (correctly, as it turned out) that the other books were concerned with occultism and demonology -- subjects which have never interested me in the slightest.

Opening the other book in English served but to confirm my supposition, for it was a bound manuscript, written with a quill pen apparently, in a narrow, crabbed hand, and bore the quaint but ominous title, *Of Evill Sorceries Done in New-England of Daemons in no Humane Shape*. It had no date nor the name of its author, and the manuscript had apparently been clumsily bound by the hands of an amateur bookbinder. I leafed through it, finding nothing but the ugly, superstitious village-gossip of a diseased mind -- another Cotton Mather, you might say. Arkham and Salem had a lot of these "God-fearing" (so called) witch-hunters back in the bad old days. I tossed it aside.

At the very bottom of the suitcase I found a dog-eared, scribbled bundle of foolscap, written in my cousin's clear, bold hand. It was entitled *Diary of Jared Fuller: 1929*.

I leafed through the opening pages, and paused to read an entry so intriguing that I copy it here in this Journal.

* * *

From the DIARY OF JARED FULLER

Sept. 4th. At sundown, or shortly thereafter, when the constellation of Perseus rose in the sky, heard again the sound of chanting from the woods in some bestial language that should not come from human lips. Was it from the "dead place" in the Deep Woods, where the Great Stone lies, or further off? Snowfall too light to leave tracks for me to find by morning. Again, strained to make out anything of the howling, grunting, gibbering language but one word or name repeated very frequently: Ossȧdogowah, always followed (as in some liturgical response) by a second uncouth name or whatever: Zvilpoggua. These wooded hills were home of devil-cults and witch-covens long ago God knows, and fiendish Indian secret societies back before the first white settlers came into these parts. No Indians around here now, of course, but the rustics hereabouts are ignorant, superstitious, inbred, degenerate -- and old beliefs die hard, and are long in the dying.

Sept. 8th. Finally heard from young Wilmarth at Miskatonic, supposed to be an enthusiastic amateur folklorist of the region. Says certain Indian tribes in this region, now long gone (the Nansets, Wampanaugs, and esp. Narragansetts) worshiped -- or at least knew how to summon down with spells --. a sky-devil they called Ossadogowah; not a name but a title, it seems: "Son of Sadogowah" -- whoever he was! Will send me photographic copies of (phrase illegible) next week, if possible. Suggests I try rare book-merchants in Salem, Boston, Providence, to obtain copy of something called *Of Evill Sorceries Done in New-England of Daemons in no Humane Shape*, which he read years ago and which bears on Indian devil-worship cults.

Chanting after dark again. This time, hid in the underbrush at the edge of the clearing: bestial gruntings and garglings indeed come from the "dead space" where the Stone lies. Was able to make out something of the words, but they are in no human language I know of. As follows, best as I could make them out over the roaring of the wind:

> Eeeyaah! Eeeyaah nughun nuh-nuh-guy guy eeyaah eeyaah
> nug-hi enyah enyah zhoggoh ffthaghun…

Sept. 17th. Made the trip into Arkham today, but Wilmarth off on a walking-tour somewhere. Ass't Librarian at Miskatonic refused me access to any of the old texts Wilmarth suggested, damn his eyes! Did, however, let me examine back files of the local papers, Ark. *Advertiser* in particular, 1921 thru '22. Ltrs. to editor about chanting heard in the woods to the north; mysterious disappearance of locals named Lew Waterbury and Jason Osborn; Osborn's body turned up later. Autopsy by County Medical Examiner sugg.

corpse had been subjected to "severe changes in temperature," and had "fallen or been dropped from a great height." (Fallen from what? Dropped by... what?)

Conditions of corpse sound dreadfully similar to the body I found in the woods, and buried hastily because of the terrible stench, which was not that of decomposing human flesh. Should have reported disc. to police, I know, but it was torn and mangled and crushed beyond all possibility of identification. Note that "horribly foetid black slime" found on Osborn corpse.

My eyes were getting tired from trying to read by the unsteady light of the lamp, so I put Jared's manuscript aside, carefully marking the last entry I had read, and went to bed.

But not, as it chanced, to sleep for quite some time.

* * *

As I tossed and turned on the hard, narrow cot, it occurred to me that my cousin Jared had lost his reason. This would, of course, explain many of the weirder aspects of what I had read in his diary: chanting from the depths of the Deep Woods, having found and buried a crushed and mangled corpse, his allusions to eldritch lore. However slightly we had known each other, this seemed unlikely, for he had always seemed stable and eminently sane, to my experience...

I gave the problem up and strove to compose myself for sleep. But sleep did not come easily. For one thing, the star Algol shone like a burning green eye through the window, which was closed against the night's cold but which I had left unshuttered. Its unusually brilliant, viridian light seemed to burn through my closed lids like some unearthly searchlight from Beyond...

And when, at length, slumber overtook my weary mind, and I sank through ever-darkening layers of shadow, I still found not the repose I sought. As I hovered between wakefulness and dream, it seemed to me that a dim and distant current of rhythmical sound, like far-heard surf or distant chanting persisted in intruding upon my rest. But this, of course, was absurd, for the woods, as I have already noted, were abnormally silent, and the wind had died. Finally, along towards dawn, I awoke, neither rested nor refreshed.

And it was then that an odd coincidence occurred to me.

Algol is a star in the constellation of Perseus...

* * *

After a meager breakfast, feeling the need for a little fresh air and some exercise before settling down again to the organization of my notes, I decided to take a tramp through the woods. I was particularly interested in finding the barren glade whereof my cousin had written in his diary, and the "Great Stone" that lay amidst it. Donning my winter gear, and finishing off my hot black coffee with a gulp, I left the cabin and entered the woods, striking out at pure random, not knowing in which direction I must travel to find the region my cousin's papers described.

These woods were distinctly unlike any in New England, at least within my personal experience. For one thing, all of the huge, gnarled trees seemed of unnatural, even abnormal age. In such a wood one might expect to find new saplings springing from the fertile mulch, and the skeletal and mouldering remains of fallen treetrunks. Not so, however, here in the Deep Woods: no saplings were to be seen; it was as if some extraordinary source of life and vigor had prolonged the life of these ancient trees immeasurably beyond their natural span.

For another thing, the woods were uncannily, even unhealthily, silent. At this season, I would have expected the underbrush to be filled with rabbits and chipmunks, field mice and squirrels, all scampering through the crisp, dry leaves upon their small tasks and errands. But not so, here in the Deep Woods, where an unwholesome silence and a distinctly odd absence of small life reigned...

I came upon the clearing abruptly, and knew at once that this was the "dead place" Jared had described. For the ground underfoot became abruptly barren of anything but sparse, unhealthy, lank grass which grew in sickly, thin patches as if the soil beneath it was either somehow poisonous or, for one or another reason, hostile to living things.

And there in the very middle of the small open space, ringed about with a thickly-crowded wall of gaunt black trees, lay half-buried in the bare soil a huge, rectangular stone -- surely, the "Great Stone" of which Jared had written. I came closer to examine it: while the trunks of the trees through which I had passed were slimy with mold and moss and lichen, the enormous brick-shaped stone was as bare of life in any visible form as if newly scrubbed clean by industrious hands.

Add one more unnatural thing about the Deep Woods, I thought uneasily to myself.

The block measured some ten feet in length, and about three-and-a-half feet in height and thickness, although it was not possible to measure the height of the stone with much certainty, so deeply was it sunken into the dead earth. As for the composition, it was of the gray granite commonly found in these parts, brought hither aeons before by the glaciers when those vast serpents of age-old Arctic ice came crawling sluggishly down across the continent.

In the exact center of the upper surface I noticed a queer shape seemingly carven therein, like a bas-relief. I had to climb up atop the stone to examine it closely, and some residium of the night's cold, not yet banished by the feeble warmth of daylight, struck bitterly and savagely through my thick gloves and heavy trousers, to sear the flesh with an almost unearthly rigor.

The carving -- for it was unmistakably the work of intelligent hands -- was weathered and very ancient, but so deeply had those primordial chisels gnawed into the recalcitrant granite, that the form it outlined was distinctly visible. It was a grotesque monstrosity, a gross, corpulent, toadlike thing with an obscene, swollen paunch and huge splayed, clawed feet, but without the forelimbs its toadlike shape might be expected to have. The skill of the ancient sculptor was sophisticated enough to suggest webbing between the spread claws of these hindlegs. From a point along the back where the shoulders would have been, sprouted crook-ribbed wings, like those of some monstrous bat or one of the fantastic flying reptiles of the saurian age which preceded the coming of mammalian life. Face it had none, but from the forepart of its sloped, bulging and misshapen head, slithering and snakelike tendrils sprouted, like the serpentine tresses of some hideous Medusa.

I repressed an involuntary shudder of disgust; but, even so, I could not help admiring the sophistication of the nameless sculptor's technique, in bestowing upon this grisly spawn of his unclean imagination such a lifelike air of realism. It was almost as if the sculptor had worked from a living model.

* * *

Returning home from my tramp through the woods, I felt reluctant to take up again the dreary task of organizing my notes, and passed the time before lunch by again perusing the diary of my cousin.

From the DIARY OF JARED FULLER

Sept. 22nd. Rec'd. today photographic copies from Wilmarth of the passages in the *Book of Eibon* he fancied I might find useful. (Or *Liber Ivonis*, I should say, since the pages are from the Latin version made by Phillipus Faber). My Latin being very rusty, it will take me some time to render them into passable English.

In the same mail, haply, came that rare copy of the manuscript titled *Of*

Evill Sorceries et al., for which I paid that skinflint of a dealer in Salem such a high price. Relevant passages too lengthy to quote here in this diary, so I have merely marked them down (here followed page-numbers which doubtless referred to the pagination of the bound manuscript I had already found in my cousin's collection; I decided to look them up later, and read on. -- W. H.), but they proved very informative.

Howled chanting in the woods again last night, clearer than before: the frosty air of this rather early winter obviously permits far sounds to travel more easily. Searched the woods again and found, in the recent-fallen snow, those horribly huge, splayed prints as of some unthinkably prodigious Beast and splatters of stinking black ichor of indescribable foulness.

And my dreams are getting worse...

* * *

With a shiver of distaste I set the manuscript aside and sat there for long moments, listlessly pondering on what I had read and trying to fit together some of the pieces of this weird puzzle. Finally, I dug into the heap of mouldering books and took up the bound manuscript, turning to the parts my cousin had marked. And I read:

. . . gave a very curious and Circumstantial Relation, saying it was sometimes like a great Toad, but sometimes huge and cloudy, with no Shape, though with a Face which had Serpents grown from it. It had ye name Ossadagowah, which signifi'd ye child of Sadogowah (and here my cousin had written in the margin "Tsathoggua?"), *ye which is held to be a Frightful Spirit spoke of by antients as come down from ye Stars and being formerly worshipt in Lands to ye North.*

Ye Wampanaugs and ye Nansets and Nahrrigansets knew how to draw it out of ye Heavens, but never did so because of ye exceeding great Evilness of It. They knew also how to catch and prison It, tho' they cou'd not send It back whence It came. It was declar'd that ye old Tribes of Lamah (here my cousin had scribbled another marginal gloss: "Lomar?"), *who dwelt under the Great Bear and were antiently destroy'd for their Wickedness, knew how to manage It in all Ways.*

Many upstart Men pretended to a Knowledge of such and divers other Outer Secrets, but none in these Parts cou'd give any Proof of truly having ye afore-said Knowledge. It was said by some that Ossadagowah often went back to ye Sky from choice without any sending, but that he cou'd not come back unless Summon'd.

I closed the bound volume and returned to Jared's manuscript, but found nothing I could make sense out of, merely a series of cryptic, and (to me) meaningless jottings:

> 1. Lomar. Quasi-mythical ancient place in extreme north. If worshiped in Lomar, perhaps Zobna and Hyperborea also?
> 2. Child. If of the spawn of Tsath., also known in Hyp.? Tsath. once worshiped there. See *Lib. Ivonis*.
> 3. Elemental. Arctic region suggests air elemental like Ithaqua, Hastur. But Tsath. an earth elemental accord. to *Cultes des G.*
> 4. Must translate passages from Eibon at once.

* * *

That night after another meager meal, I sat up drinking mug after mug of hot black coffee, waiting for Perseus to rise above the horizon, determined to find out whether the bestial howling-like chant I had seemed to hear in my fitful slumbers the night before were actuality or something in my dreams. For some reason, it occurred to me to turn down the wick and blow out the lamp, so that the interior of the cabin would be in darkness.

I had positioned my chair within clear view of the window. Once the familiar stars of the constellation were aloft, I left the window ajar, despite the cold breath of the night air, and listened closely. For a long time I heard nothing at all unusual, merely the wind moaning in the bare black boughs and the comfortable rustling of dying coals in the Franklin stove.

Then suddenly there came to my ears the sound of many distant voices raised in a rhythmic, if uncouth, chanting. I strained to catch the words of that chant, but could not make them out clearly. But they seemed in no language I have ever heard before.

What snatches of the eerie chant I could hear bore a distinct resemblance to some of the weird mouthings Jared had scribbled down in his diary.

I went nearer to the window in order to hear the liturgy better. As I did so, with a thrill of indescribable horror I watched a vast, black shadow drift across the snow-clad clearing before the cabin, vanishing into the Deep Woods. Was it purely my imagination, my nerves wrought by the uncanny things I had read in Jared's diary and in that damnable old book, or did the shadow-shape seem cast by something toadlike, and bloated, and obese, with batlike wings?

* * *

I fell asleep in the wooden chair just before dawn, and woke stiff and groggy and chilled to the bone in very late morning. After heating and devouring the remnants of my supper, and huge draughts of hot coffee, the thought passed through my mind that I would be wise to leave this place at once. Surely, a few dollars would persuade Jenkins to loan me his Model T and the use of his driver, in order to transport my few possessions and Jared's books and the manuscript back to Arkham, where I could arrange to have Silas Harding sell the cabin and grounds.

Why I did not do so, I will never know. Perhaps I feared to see the knowing smirk in the pale eyes of the storekeeper, Jenkins, and to hear his leering chuckle when he learned that I was giving up and running back home to Boston.

Building up the fire a bit later, I found some old newspapers under the stacked kindling in the shed and was about to stuff them into the stove when the headline, HORROR IN BILLINGTON'S WOOD and the names Ambrose Dewart and Stephen Bates leaped from the page to seize my attention. With hands that shook, ever so slightly, I bore the newspapers, brown and withered with age, to the table and read the news item that had caught my eye.

They related, in fragmentary fashion and without any explanation, an account of the mysterious and inexplicable disappearances of Dewart and the young Bostonian, Bates, a visiting relative, from a huge old house in Billington's Wood some miles south of my cabin, and how no trace of the missing men had come to light and the local constabulary was without a single clue. There was nothing in the straightforward newspaper account, written in dry journalese, which hinted at weird horrors from the sky, or the lingering survival into our own time of horribly ancient devil-cults which should have perished or been ruthlessly exterminated generations or even centuries ago . . . nothing which mentioned blasphemous and forbidden old books which any sane man would burn or bury, rather than read . . . but there was a grisly suggestiveness which lurked behind the succinct newspaper items, with their passing reference to a Druidic-like ring of stones deep in the wood, near a crude stone tower of unknown workmanship and uncertain date, which sent a thrill of clammy fear up my spine.

I burned the newspapers in the stove, and resolved to put all of these matters out of my head.

I wish to God I had done so.

* * *

Towards afternoon I donned my winter gear and returned to the woods. I found again the altar-like "Great Stone" amidst the sterile glade, where it squatted like some loathsome altar left behind by a savage and bloodthirsty race when they receded into the dimness of mercifully-forgotten ages. It was not my second sight of that massive block of stone, lying upon the earth like some toppled Druidic menhir, however, that froze me where I stood--

The snow had fallen thickly in the clearing the early evening before, and now it could be seen that the white blanket which covered the dead soil like a burial shroud was marked and trampled under the tread of many feet.

But it was not even this--clear evidence that the cult which worshiped Ossadagowah or "Zvilpoggua" indeed gathered nightly about this stony altar-that chilled me to the bone with fear.

It was the huge marks with which the human footprints were intermingled . . . the marks of splayed, webbed feet, huger than those of any elephant that ever walked the earth, which had broken the crusted snow and left deep tracks sunken in the hard soil as if beneath the tread of ponderous, incredible weight.

* * *

(About one and a half pages which follow are quite illegible.)

(Apparently from the Diary of Jared Fuller):

. . . those passages from the Latin of Phillipus Faber, as follows:

Of the wise Yzduggor, whom the wizards of Commoriom held in the highest repute, it was rumored that he was a devotee of the obsolete and interdicted cults of Zvilpoggua, even he, firstborn of the spawn of Tsathoggua and begotten by the black Thing upon the female entity, Shathak, upon far and frozen Yaksh the seventh world (here my cousin had scribbled another gloss: "7th fr. the Sun? Neptune?"). *Therefore unto his remote, secluded dwelling-place did the fearful Vooth Raluorn forthwith eloign. . .*

\- - -

. . . the eremite at length yielded grudging reply to his entreaties, and erelong did the young Commorian learn from Yzduggor's reluctant lips that presently Zvilpoggua resided upon the dark planet Yrautrom, a world circumambient about the green star Algol, and may be called down to this world during those months of the year when Algol rises above the horizon (here my cousin scribbled: "Algol is in the night sky during the fall") *whereupon it is his grisly wont to feed upon the flesh and to drink of the blood of men, wherefore is he known to sorcerers as the Feaster from the Stars. . .*

At the end of his translations of these fragments, evidently from the *Book of Eibon*, my cousin had scribbled a page-reference to "Nec.," by which he probably meant the *Necronomicon*, which he had several times named in his diary. It would appear that he had entreated the scholar Wilmarth to copy certain parts of this volume for him, and I gather now, from the context, that this was one of the books he had tried in vain to secure permission from the librarian at Miskatonic University to consult. Thereupon fol(lowed? Manuscript illegible here for about three-quarters of a page.)

* * *

. . . which appeared to have been scissored from a letter, doubtless from his correspondence with Wilmarth, as the handwriting is quite different from my cousin Jared's. I read:

From the DIARY OF JARED FULLER

. . . no need to laboriously translate from the Latin of Olaus Wormius for the Miskatonic owns a partial copy of John Dee's English version of the *Necronomicon*, which makes the task easier. The two passages below come from quite different portions of the volume, but as both seem relevant to the matter at hand, I will cite them here.

To Summon-Down the Feaster from the Stars, seek those nights when first Algol riseth above ye Horizon, and, if that ye be Thirteen gather'd in Coven, join hands in ye ring about ye Stone and chaunt in unison as followeth, Ia! Ia! N'ghaa, n'n'ghai-ghai! Ia! Ia! N'ghai, n-yah, n-yah, shoggog, phthaghn! Ia! Ia! Y-hah, y-nyah, y-nyah! N'ghaa, n'n'ghai, waphl phthaghn-Zvilpoggua! Zvilpoggua! N'gui, n'gha'ghaa y'hah, Zvilpoggua! Ai! Ai! Ai! And note well that ye Response to ye Name Zvilpoggua, the which is to be onlie chaunted by ye Coven-Master, is Ghu-Tsathoggua, the which doth signify ye Son of Tsathoggua, and ye above Name onlie may be spake forth in ye common or vulgar Tongue.

I put down the manuscript with trembling hands, then took it up again and leafed back to that earlier passage where Jared had written down what he had heard on the night of September 8, 1929 [see page 7 of the present text]. The two chants were word for word the same, until my cousin's jottings broke off; the only differences between them were that Jared Fuller had set them down phonetically and with little attempt at punctuation.

The pieces of the puzzle were fitting together into a dreadful and horribly meaningful pattern.

I must leave this place soon, very soon. They must know the cabin, situated so fearfully close to their place of worship, is once again inhabited. Surely, it was the Coven-folk, or whatever I should call them, that murdered or carried off my cousin . . . they or the monstrous demon-thing they serve . . . and surely I will be the next victim.

That night I had another of those ghastly dreams that have of late haunted my troubled slumbers [apparently a reference to matter contained in the several passages illegible because of damp]. It seemed I hovered, shivering beneath the bite of ultra-telluric and bone-chilling cold, above a dark and frozen world dimly lit by the spectral light of three pallid moons. Amidst an ice-sheathed plain rose the hoary ruins of a black city of monolithic, windowless walls . . . was it a dream of Yaksh (but Neptune has only one moon, as I recall from my boyhood enthusiasm for astronomy), or of that dark world revolving about Algol, where Zvilpoggua resides?

As I drifted nearer and nearer to the black metropolis, I forced myself awake with a tremendous effort of will, and found myself drenched in cold perspiration and trembling like a frail reed in the wind. And I was screaming...

Most horrible of all, my screams were echoed mockingly by a deep-lunged, howling ululation, but whether from the Wood or from the sky I cannot tell.

* * *

(About three paragraphs totally illegible)

. . . second passage from the *Necronomicon*, either raggedly cut or torn from Wilmarth's letter, and read as follows:

. . . hath the Likeness of a great Toade, black as pitch and glist'ning with foetid slime, bewing'd like ye Bat and with ye nether-limbs of ye Behemothe, splayed and clawed and Webb'd betwixt ye Toes thereof, and Face hath it naught, butte from where ye Face shouldst e'en be sprouteth a Horrid Beard of crawling tentacles. And it feasteth of the Fleshe, and Swilleth of ye Bloode of Men, but at its gluttonous Leisure, for first it is said to bear men aloft into ye Sky, and may bear them thus an hundred Leagues or more ere it will rip and tear and Feede, then dropping them to Earth far from whence it snatch'd them up.

But I can read no more. I will leave the cabin tonight, before Algol rises to peer down at me like the glaring, feral eye of some predatory beast. I will abandon everything, taking only my journal in an old briefcase. But before I leave the cabin, I intend to burn the diary of Jared Fuller . . . would to God I had the time to consign to the wholesome flames those hellish old books which sane men were never meant to read.

(Four sentences illegible)

Too late-Algol almost risen. I must run for it. If I cannot catch the bus to Arkham, I dare not linger so close to the Deep Wood, but must try my luck on the Pike. Perhaps I can make it to Dean's Corners before it is too late.

I wish

(Manuscript breaks off suddenly at this point.)

* * *

NOTE: As of this date (February, 1983), no evidence has ever been found as to the fate or the whereabouts of Winthrop Hoag. The case remains in the "unsolved" files of the County Police.

The editor has no opinion as to the validity of the manuscript, or concerning its authorship. But one or two remarks might be useful at this juncture. It is now fairly certain that the planet Neptune has at least three moons; the existence of two such satellites has been confirmed by visual observation, and, from perturbations in their orbits about their primary, the presence of a third is considered almost certain.

It may be of no particular consequence, but the Islamic peoples, together with certain other cultures of antiquity, held the star Algol in peculiar loathing and abhorrence. The Arabic astrologer of the VII Century, Ibrahim Al-Araq, refers to it, in those of his writings still extant, with an ambivalent phrase which scholars translate either as "the Demon Star" or "the Star from whence the Demon comes."

H.P. Lovecraft
The Unforgotten Source